We've a Story to Tell

125 Years of WMU

We've a Story to Tell

125 Years of WMU

Rosalie H. Hunt

BIRMINGHAM, ALABAMA

Woman's Missionary Union, SBC
P. O. Box 830010
Birmingham, AL 35283-0010

For more information visit our Web site at wmu.com or call 1-800-968-7301.

Dewey Decimal Classification: 266.06

Subject Headings: WOMAN'S MISSIONARY UNION, SBC—HISTORY
BAPTISTS—HISTORY SOUTHERN BAPTIST
CONVENTION—HISTORY

ISBN: 978-1-59669-595-5
W133107 • 0613 • 1.5M

Design by Glynese Northam

Cover by Theresa Barnett

Dedication

To *Alice Wells Hall* (1901-1984), my mother, whose missionary heart exemplified for me all the joy found in ministry through WMU. (1901-1984), my mother, whose missionary heart exemplified for me all the joy found in ministry through WMU.

Table of Contents

Acknowledgements

TWO PEERLESS EDITORS have served as an inspiration in the birth of this new millennium WMU history. Ella Robinson, style editor, has been part of WMU's editorial staff for many years and has proved invaluable in knowledge and encouragement. Cindy McMurtry Johnson, WMU archivist and content editor, was a walking mother-lode of WMU history and expertise. The first reader and leading encourager in the process of research and writing has been my husband Bob. He has a knack for noting an awkward phrase or finding a thought that needs clarification, or simply commenting "Hey, that's a good thought."

Number one acknowledgement must surely extend to those amazing women on our WMU family tree. They served as that cloud of witnesses who lined the way—cheering us on in this new century with its new challenges in sharing the old old story—that we have loved so long.

Preface

TO THE READER:

ONCE UPON A TIME . . . Doesn't everyone love a story that starts with those magic words? Throw in a bit of drama, a spot of color, a trace of suspense, and instantly you are part of the story. We are a part of something way beyond ourselves, for the story of Woman's Missionary Union encompasses the very heart of the Great Commission issued by Christ more than 2,000 years ago. The "missionary story" hasn't changed; the purpose hasn't altered; however, the cast of characters has changed—and we are on the stage. Just how is it that we, as Woman's Missionary Union, relate to the total "mission story" of Baptists?

Without a doubt, writing our complete history is a hazardous business, for the end result has not yet been achieved. That's where we come in—as we become part of the "history" of missions that is still being recorded. Finding that real beginning of WMU is a challenge. It is like a multiple-choice question. Would you pick 1792, when William Carey and a small group of men met in Kettering, England, and concluded that the Great Commission was real and needed to be obeyed? Or, would you choose 1800, when a small paralytic in Boston, Massachusetts, realized that the Commission was her personal directive? Maybe you would go for 1812, when the very first foreign missionaries (as they were called then) were commissioned and sailed for the Far East, not even knowing where they would end up. Or perhaps you might say WMU's history began the day the organization officially organized in 1888.

One thing we are assured of: It is a bit like an iceberg—always much more below the surface than above it. The portion unseen to eyes exploring WMU's saga spans many centuries, from the first century until nearly the end of the eighteenth century. When William Carey lit a fire, the flames could be seen over in the New World—our world—and ultimately brought about Woman's Missionary Union.

Because of our direct link to Polly Webb of Boston, our journey begins with her in 1800 in that key city and continues into this new millennium. It is an undebatable fact that roles for women in the organized church were—and still are—limited. Nonetheless, in the nineteenth century, women were considered the guardians of the Great Commission. Missionary statesmen actually advocated an active involvement by women to ensure the fulfillment of the Great Commission. Is it any surprise that by the early years of the twentieth century, missionary women outnumbered men more than two to one? The prominent issue for the day—women's rights—did not figure into the motivation for the women who were going as missionaries or for those organizing the societies by which missionaries could be trained and supported. A call to serve God was their sole motivation. That was true in 1800; it remains true in the twenty-first century.

Women are considered the glue that holds a family—and a society—together, rather like a mantle passed down from one generation to the next. Just a list of the names of the multitude of heroes of Woman's Missionary Union would fill a book. The historic word pictures drawn of a few of these women of incredible grit and gumption are representative of the thousands of women whose names we will probably never hear. The women whose remarkable courage and dedication we will glimpse in the pages of this book are but a reflection of those dedicated women in "mite societies" and "women's circles" who never sought to be known but merely strove to make a difference. For every story told of an Annie, a Fannie, a Lottie, or a Mallory, a thousand more will remain in obscurity. But because of these women, we stand on a firm foundation today.

Our Woman's Missionary Union story is one of sacrifice, courage, patience, and Divine Intervention in the course of human affairs. Alma Hunt, a name synonymous with Baptist missions, stated in her book, *The History of WMU*, that history, though made day-by-day, needs the seasoning of the years. Stories are the delight of every generation and every age, not just children. Recording documented fact is quite different from fiction, where you can manipulate the character and have her act in whatever way you please. This story of ours is not fiction, nor is it just a simple chronicle of women having meetings. It is a journey into the minds and hearts of our foremothers. This is *our* story—the venture of faith that became the largest missions organization for women in the world.

CHAPTER

There's a Call Comes Ringing

"Dear sisters, let us arise."
—Polly Webb, 1812

MISS POLLY

ONCE UPON A time . . . These words cause memories to come shimmering to the surface. Remember the little nursery rhyme: "Polly, put the kettle on, and we'll all have tea"? Once upon a time, in 1800 in Boston, Massachusetts, little Polly (Mary) Webb put the kettle of missions zeal on the burner and out poured the steam of missions passion. That kettle continues to bubble more than 200 years later. Young Polly could not have imagined what God would do with the gifts she offered Him.

Born in 1779, Mary Webb (lovingly known as Polly) was always full of energy, but at age 5, devastating illness hit and she was paralyzed from the waist down. However, Webb's determination to live fully and happily never wavered. Her little carriage chair became a familiar sight around the streets of Boston. Webb and her older sister, Sally, became regular attendees at Boston's influential Second Baptist where Dr. Thomas Baldwin was pastor. At age 18, Webb accepted Christ, and in 1800, she heard Dr. Baldwin's powerful missions sermon. The idea of women helping share the gospel with those who had never heard it began to germinate in her brilliant mind, and a lifelong passion for missions was born.

Webb revealed uncanny ability to influence others. She began by inviting her friends to meet with her, and by October, 14 women—Baptist and Congregational—met in her home. The world's first woman's missionary society was born—the Boston Female Society for Missionary Purposes. Those women might have used their needles to raise funds, but this was no sewing circle—they were women with a mission. Webb was treasurer, and she wrote thousands of letters going across Massachusetts and then throughout the country.

One of the early beneficiaries of the society was the Cary Baptist mission in India. Soon after, Ann and Adoniram Judson and Luther Rice went as missionaries from America, and the little society was galvanized. By 1812, Polly Webb had prompted some 20 groups to organize. Thanks to Webb and her faithful band, the numbers grew by leaps and bounds, and that germinating seed of missions burst into bloom in 1888 in Richmond, Virginia.

HEPHZIBAH

Meanwhile, a thousand miles from Boston, the dying Hephzibah Jenkins in Charleston, South Carolina, gave birth on March 19, 1780, to tiny Hephzibah, her namesake. The baby miraculously survived. Growing up on Edisto Island, beautiful young Hephzibah married at 15 and converted under the preaching of Richard Furman. From him, she learned of Polly Webb's society and determined to organize one on her little island. Hephzibah's methods of raising funds were ingenious, creative, and successful, as was her skill in influencing others. The new group's first contribution in 1811 was $212.50. The little Edisto and Wadmalaw Islands group goes down as the first women's missionary society in the South. And just a year later, an event occurred in faraway Salem, Massachusetts, that would further rouse women across the nation to missions fervor.

ANN HASSELTINE JUDSON

In 1638, when young Englishman Robert Hasseltine reached the harbor of Salem in Massachusetts Colony, there was no way he could have envisioned that some 200 hundred years later, his ever-so-great granddaughter Ann would become known as "America's woman of the century." The remarkable young 23-year-old Ann Judson who, with her husband, Adoniram Judson, sailed from that very same Salem harbor, indelibly stamped her imprint on missions history. Polly Webb, Hephzibah Jenkins, and thousands of their kindred spirits now had a standard-bearer in Ann Judson. A new era for Baptists in America was begun.

Ann and Adoniram Judson were married February 5, 1812, and the next day, Adoniram, Luther Rice, and three others were ordained as America's first foreign missionaries. On their long 4½ month journey by ship, these young Congregationalists became convinced that baptism meant immersion. The Judsons were baptized in Calcutta in September 1812, and only six weeks later, young Luther Rice did the same. Following Rice's baptism, the group decided that Rice would return to America to urge Baptists to organize so they could support their new missionaries. And Baptists in America were forever changed.

Even before Luther had time to get back to Boston, a letter from William Carey to Baptists in America alerted them to the momentous baptism of the Judsons and Rice. There, in Boston, Dr. Thomas Baldwin immediately invited leading Baptists to his home and began mobilizing those who wanted to provide for the "Judson Mission." Thus Luther Rice entered the stage in America in September 1813 and became a man of destiny for Baptists.

Luther Rice was surely God's man for this vital task. Tall and handsome with a winning personality, Rice was known for his commanding and melodious voice. Immediately upon arriving in Boston, Rice met with the Baptists of Baldwin's missionary society, suggesting that they invite Baptists all across America to participate in support. The group agreed, and thus began Rice's amazing and tireless journeying for missions. Much of his traveling took him to the South where he found rich soil for planting the seeds of missions passion. Right after he left Richmond in October, the Baptist Mission Society of Virginia was organized. Three months later, in Charleston, Rice received the very first contribution from a women's group. Yes, it was Hephzibah and the ladies of the Wadmalaw and Edisto Female Mite Society who gave $44 for the Judson Mission and promised $100 more.

The results of Rice's efforts were soon evident as Baptist leaders gathered for the first time on Wednesday, May 18, 1814, to organize what came to be called The Triennial Convention. There were 16 states in 1814, and 9 had delegates at this organizational meeting. A total of 33 delegates seems few indeed considering there were 2,000 Baptist churches and some 160,000 members. But travel was both strenuous and difficult; there was not even a railroad in the country. The meeting had few in number but was immense in spirit and purpose. The all-men delegates learned that there were already 17 known missionary societies of women, 8 of them in the South.

The convention adopted a constitution and elected officers. Dr. Richard Furman, probably the most renowned Baptist minister in the nation, was elected president, and Polly Webb's pastor, Dr. Thomas Baldwin, became secretary. In addition to Judson being named their missionary, Rice was appointed general missions agent. In so doing, the delegates were inadvertently giving another boost to women's work, for Rice was a true believer in women's missionary societies. Considering the prevailing views of women in leadership, this was foresight indeed.

An early Baptist historian viewed the events leading up to this memorable convention as pivotal: "The bugle call of Judson and Rice was not a foghorn in the night to awaken a slumbering people; it was a bugle at sunrise to notify a people already awakening, of a wider and nobler opportunity, and to hearten them for entering into it."

The official name was the General Convention of the Baptist Denomination in the United States for Foreign Missions. Such a mouthful became The Triennial Convention, since it was to meet once every three years. It functioned effectively this way until 1845. An early Baptist historian declared that "the convention did not count much, but it *weighed* immensely." The news began to spread, and Baptist women from small country churches to large city congregations began to meet, pray, and give. The dream of an organization of women answering Christ's command to go was beginning to bud. Before the century was over, it would blossom.

CHAPTER

There Are Souls to Rescue

"There are souls to save."
—Send the Light

JANE DANIEL, SUSAN WALKER, LUCY THORNTON, AND LUCY COBB

SOMETHING NEW WAS in the air. Mrs. John Bryce and her sister, Jane Daniel, first learned about it from the *Massachusetts Missionary Magazine.* The year was 1813, and Mrs. Bryce's husband, John, was assistant pastor of Richmond's Baptist Church, the city's only Baptist congregation. Mrs. Bryce, her husband, and Jane Daniel were excited to read Polly Webb's appeal for women to organize. One woman after another in the church eagerly looked to be part of such a revolutionary and challenging society. Of course, the naysayers among men of the congregation didn't like the idea of women organizing. They thought that Elder Courtney, their senior pastor, surely would not approve. He wouldn't even countenance having a Sunday School or using hymnbooks. But Courtney surprised them all; his statement was quoted for years to come: "I never heard of praying doing anybody any harm. For my part, the sisters may pray on." And Virginia's first such Baptist society was born in 1813.

Susan Walker and Lucy Thornton lived more than 50 miles away, in Fredericksburg—a considerable distance by horse and buggy. These two Baptist women had never met Mrs. Bryce or her sister, but they heard that there was a Female Missionary Society down the road in Richmond. It was now 1814, and the ladies in Fredericksburg decided to begin a group of their own, even preparing and printing a constitution. Susan was elected "Directress." Recorded for posterity in the minutes of that initial meeting was the attendance of "Brother James" and "Brother Chase," men who approved of what the ladies were beginning, even to the point of being *part* of it.

These Fredericksburg ladies were not the type to keep good news to themselves. Lucy Thornton wrote to her good friend Lucy Cobb who had moved to Athens, Georgia, and even included a copy of the constitution. Her enthusiasm was contagious, and soon Lucy Cobb and friends in Georgia had organized a similar group. And it was that yellowed old copy of the Fredericksburg constitution that survived the years—the oldest existing document of a women's missionary society in the South. The following year, ladies in Bruington, Virginia, formed the Female Hasseltine Missionary Society, named for Ann Hasseltine Judson, their first woman missionary.

MARYLAND

Meanwhile, in Baltimore, Maryland, women heard the call issued by Polly Webb, and in 1813, the Female Missionary Society of the First Baptist Church was organized. These intrepid women discovered ingenious ways to find funds that would make a difference in lives far away. Luther Rice heard of the Baltimore women, and at the organizational meeting of the Triennial Convention, he suggested that the delegates "recognize with pleasure their pious effort, tender their warm thanks and affectionately solicit them to continue their present career of well doing." Here was Rice at his best, recognizing the invaluable role of dedicated women. Only eternity can fully appreciate the contribution of this amazing man to the cause of missions. He evidently was influential as well in establishing the Female Missionary Society in Washington, D.C., in 1818. The city at the center of the US government now had an early women's missionary group.

SOUTH CAROLINA

In South Carolina, word began to spread about the success Hephzibah and her friends were having. This news, along with the clarion call from Polly Webb, prompted women in one church after another to band together to pray and to give. Early records show a list of some the those earliest groups, including Ebenezer Female Missionary Society in 1816, closely followed by Cheraw Hill Female Mite Society the next year. In 1818, Statesburg women organized as well. A year later, Georgetown women joined the growing number of societies in South Carolina.

GEORGIA

About the same time, Georgia was also alive with groups of women wanting to be a part of what God was doing. Ladies on the coast formed the Savannah Baptist Society for Missions. Several other groups cropped up, including the 1817 Sunbury

Female Cent Society for Foreign Missions at Sweet Hill School (what a mouthful!) and the Poweltown Female Praying Society. Georgia Baptist historian B. D. Ragsdale recorded news of the revival of 1827, perhaps the greatest in the history of that state, saying, "I believe the great revival had its origin in a ladies' prayer meeting, which had been faithfully observed by a few members of the Eatonton Church."

KENTUCKY

Kentucky had not been settled as long as most of the eastern states, but Baptists proliferated among the early pioneers to that frontier. The pioneer women quickly gathered to promote missions though little remains of names and actions. One of the earliest documented groups was the Baptist Female Society of Georgetown Baptist Church. There is a surviving copy of their constitution dated 1819, so they organized prior to that year. Most of Kentucky's early groups were named Female Society or Female Missionary Society. As was the tradition, women did not speak out in those early Kentucky Baptist Convention meetings, but records do show several male messengers representing the female societies. Bethel Female Society is listed as organizing in 1822. It was years later before women's names even appeared on membership rolls and usually only by their husbands' names.

NORTH CAROLINA

Catherine Campbell White—"Solitary Female"

Since the earliest years of WMU history, North Carolina has been one of the first states to organize and participate. In this state too, many names of our plucky foremothers are lost to history. However, one for sure is known in North Carolina, due in large part to a letter written by Luther Rice. There were women's organizations prior to 1816, for surviving associational minutes tell of letters sent to the Female Societies near Fayetteville and to the group in Hyco in Caswell County.[11] For a while, Hyco was thought to be the first such society in the South, but no accurate record can be found dating it prior to 1813. And there was Catherine Campbell White's organization, dating to 1822. In his letter, Rice paid her high praise, saying: "A female Society has been formed in Richmond (now Scotland) County, under circumstances that promise usefulness. This was effected by the zeal and piety of a solitary female; and if but one such female could be found in every church, hundreds of similar societies might be originated and an incalculable sum of good accomplished." Young Catherine Campbell was the daughter of wealthy Scotch parents, and when she married Daniel White, she brought with her a generous dowry in gold. Daniel came to North Carolina to preach. Catherine Campbell looked after the farm and raised their children while Daniel traveled and organized churches.

A visit from Luther Rice proved inspiring. Catherine Campbell wasted no time in organizing the Spring Hill Female Mite Society and a Children's Cent Society. The enterprising Campbell served as a volunteer agent for the women and sold for them their butter, eggs, milk, fruit, and garden produce to a hotel in a nearby town. Even the children caught the spirit as they sold walnuts and broom straw, which they gathered. Campbell bought these items from the children and also paid them for jobs around her house and yard. The little ones thus had money for their cent society, and a lifelong love of missions was born in their hearts. Such zeal was infectious, for at the second meeting of the Triennial Convention in Philadelphia in 1817, the report came that there were already 187 missionary societies throughout the states—and 110 of them were women's groups.

ALABAMA

Alabama was another state where early names of pioneer women's leaders are simply not known. There was only one place in Alabama visited by Luther Rice as he traveled to organize churches and societies to support foreign missions—Flint River Association in North Alabama. Even as early as 1822, the association of Baptists there split because of strong anti-missionary sentiment. In spite of that, Rice recorded that "the missions concern was attended to in a satisfactory manner." The state Baptist convention actually organized in the spring of 1823 in Marion, Alabama. There were women's societies already sprinkled across the state, because seven of them had delegates represented at that first meeting. The records show that these women were gratified to find there were sister organizations, for prior to that meeting, they did not even know of one another's existence.

MISSOURI

John Mason Peck

Further west, in Missouri, women were mobilizing as well. A particular factor in the inception of women's societies in pioneer Missouri was a unique man—John Peck. This pioneer "home missionary" of the Triennial Convention strongly felt that mite societies needed to be organized.

Reference to a female mite society appears in a letter to Peck from a Rev. Galusha in January 1816: "Nothing special has occurred since I last saw you, except the establishment of the Shaftsbury-and-Vicinity Missionary Society . . . this Female Mite Society, established by your request, now consists of seventy members." (That's a roaring start!)

ARKANSAS

George Ann Bledsoe

In neighboring Arkansas, George Ann Bledsoe was a beloved citizen of the little town of Tulip. Arkansas was pioneer country, and the great desire of Bledsoe's heart was that Baptists in her new state would organize to promote missions. Her dream was finally realized in 1847, largely due to her interest and unflagging efforts. Bledsoe did not live to see her dream come to fruition, but just before she died, she asked that her most cherished possession, a rare and lovely piano, be sold and the proceeds given to missions. Her heartfelt gesture inspired Baptists of that state, and in 1847, a convention officially organized. Women's groups didn't formally establish as early in Arkansas since traveling was difficult.

TENNESSEE

Here is another pioneer state with plenty of rugged terrain but with frontier women of equally sturdy spirit. Tennessee women began to rally support for missionaries, going to heathen lands to share the gospel. The oldest recorded society was organized in Rural Springs in 1836. Names of early societies come from towns with well-known names and also from some unusual spots. Chattanooga, Jonesboro, and Knoxville had early female societies, as did some places with startling names, like Bells, Sinking Springs, and Dumplin.

MISSISSIPPI

Just to the east of Arkansas, in Mississippi, there were some early female societies, but records are sketchy. The wife of a professor at the University of Mississippi, Mrs. Mary Quinche, writes of the period from 1817 to 1878 in a sweeping stroke and vows that societies were formed beginning as early as 1817—just where, we don't know. Quinche made a bit of an editorial comment when she wrote of the opposition many women encountered, chiefly from their Christian husbands! She quoted one of the early officers who said, "I pray God to enlighten the minds of our benighted husbands and show them their error." The ladies seemed to persevere, organizing in Brandon and Palestine churches as early as 1837.

The ladies in Brandon asked their pastor to take their missions offering and be their delegate to the newly organized state Baptist convention. And, at about the same time, Reverend John Armstrong and his wife, Pamelia, formed one of the strongest churches of that era in Columbus. Almost immediately, they organized a female society that became a vital force in that historic church.

TEXAS

Massie Millard, Annette Lea Bledsoe, and Margaret Lea Houston

In approximately the same time, more and more Americans

with pioneering genes heard the call of the West and headed to Texas territory. Colonization really began on a large scale in about 1821, although the territory was still part of Mexico. Among these hardy pioneers were a number of Baptist families, including some preachers who were willing to brave frontier hardships. Mrs. Massie Millard settled in Nacogdoches in 1832 and promptly made chapels of the deep forest thickets about her home. There she gathered women and children together to pray for protection and guidance. Millard's tender heart hurt for the superstitious Mexican women, and she enlisted her friends in helping to minister to them.

A kindred spirit joined Millard late in the 1830s—Antoinette (Annette) Lea Bledsoe, a 17-year-old bride from Marion, Alabama. She arrived with a passion for missions in her heart and luggage amply supplied with Testaments and leaflets, which she distributed widely. Old North Church was organized, and these women soon had a missionary society. In short order, the missionary society had 65 members ministering to Mexicans, Indians, family, and friends. Young Bledsoe had been a leader at Judson College back in Marion and was the same kind of leader in Texas.

Bledsoe's family history reads a bit like a novel, and the romantic story of her famous sister brings together early Baptist women's work with the forming of the state of Texas. Bledsoe and her sister, Margaret, nearly two years her senior, had been close friends all their lives. When beautiful Margaret was just 19, she met the famous Sam Houston at a garden party near Mobile. He was smitten, but that young woman of deep faith had heard much of the swashbuckling life of the ex-governor of Tennessee, and she hesitated to trust him with her heart.

Less than two years later, however, and over the objection of her mother, Nancy married Sam Houston and went with him to Texas, where he had settled. They lived in Nacogdoches, and Margaret immediately became active in sister Antoinette's church and women's society. Sam had no interest in things religious, but this began to change as his wife's vibrant faith eventually made an eternal difference in his life. Sam Houston professed his faith and was baptized at the Old Rock Church in Independence. He went on to be elected governor of Texas in 1857. Margaret and her sister, as well as their mother, Nancy, were pioneer leaders in Texas Baptist women's work. (Another Baptist distinction of Nancy's was being the only woman to serve as a delegate at the formation of the Alabama Baptist Convention in 1823.)

From 1813 until close to mid-century, Baptist women and youth were rising and meeting the challenge of Christ's command to go. Close to the mid-century, other problems were brewing in the new nation, and differences in regions of the country were leading to even more changes. The Triennial Convention would soon change dramatically. Division would come among Baptists, but the ministry of evangelizing the world would continue, albeit in some different directions. Throughout the changes, Baptist women remained focused.

CHAPTER

To the Ends of the Earth

"How can I not speak, when I know the words of life?"
—Lottie Moon

HENRIETTA HALL SHUCK

THE PETITE, SOFT-SPOKEN Virginia girl could have graced any Southern verandah; instead she helped ignite a passion in the hearts of countless women, women who were rising to the challenge of Christ's command to go into all the world. It was September 8, 1835, and the wedding day of 17-year-old Henrietta Hall to Rev. J. Lewis Shuck, a 23-year-old minister. Two weeks later, the Shucks were on their way to work as missionaries of the Triennial Convention in China, where no Americans had previously served.

Americans were not welcome in China, so Henrietta and Lewis first settled in Macau. Henrietta was incredibly busy as a wife, mother, teacher, evangelist, homemaker, and hostess. She somehow eked out time to write letters—accounts of their missionary work—which inspired women in to South to pray and give. Her letters were honest, confessing that being a missionary isn't "romantic" and adventurous as many might think. "(It is a life of) unostentatious toil and of unending anxiety."

In 1842, the Shucks were finally able to enter China and settle in Hong Kong. Their work prospered: Henrietta immediately began a school, and within a year, the first Chinese church was organized. She gave birth to her fourth child that year as well. With each childbirth, Henrietta became increasingly frail but never lost her sense of purpose or call. In November 1844, her fifth and last child was born. Within a day, Henrietta died, but the impact of that solitary young woman has continued. More than a century and a half later, Henrietta is revered in her beloved adopted country and in the land of her birth. She left a legacy that continues to challenge and inspire Southern Baptist women throughout the nation. News of her death simply motivated women of the South to further zeal.

TRIENNIAL TRIAGE

For 31 years, Baptists in America had been bound together in a common purpose—to support missions. The bond over this purpose had tied together believers from different sections of the country in the Triennial Convention. When the Convention was established in 1814, its goal was to undergird their missionaries and propagate the gospel.

That goal remained firm those 31 years, but then regional tensions stepped in and caused issues to ferment. Abolition had become a divisive question. In the last two sessions of the Triennial Convention, polarization of the question became increasingly apparent. In 1841, the Board of Managers of the Convention stated that no person should be sent as a foreign missionary who owned or "held any interest in human slaves." Some of the strongest supporters of the Convention were slaveholders, and there were even some missionaries who owned slaves. Furthermore, there had been growing concern about the locations of Convention headquarters in New York and Boston when 59 percent of the Baptists in the Triennial Convention lived South of the Mason-Dixon Line. To travel from the South to New England in 1845 meant two or three weeks overland. The Board refused to either rescind or modify the antislavery action, at which point, a division of the convention by region seemed inevitable. The split was not over doctrine; it was over slavery and location.

Doubtless, the links between Southern culture and Southern Baptist denomination consciousness were deep and close to inseparable. Dr. J. B. Jeter of Richmond, Virginia, led out in the call for Baptists across the South to meet in Augusta, Georgia, in May 1845. Eleven states were represented with some 328 messengers on that May 8. They began by passing a resolution: "That for peace and harmony, and in order to accomplish the greatest amount of good, . . . it is proper . . . to organize a Society for the Propagation of the Gospel." They received from the President of the Triennial Convention a letter expressing great appreciation for the Christian spirit by which the division was handled. There was equal division of funds, forces, and fields, and missionaries could choose a board with which to affiliate. Dr. William B. Johnson of South Carolina, known for his leadership skills and deep love for missions, was elected the first president of the newly formed Southern Baptist Convention.

The seeds that had been planted and nurtured by the Triennial Convention did not die; they simply scattered. In the end, the result was positive growth. The new body at the same meeting formed the Foreign Mission Board and the Board of Domestic Missions. And there was something remarkable about the new Convention—it incorporated a dream that came from Luther Rice. Rice had imagined a plan whereby missions work would be a joint project—of the local church, the association, the state conventions, and the Southwide body. Fannie Heck, that future leading light in the early years of the women's national organization, mused that, had Rice known what became of his dream, "the vision would have shortened many a weary mile; his weariness for the time being forgotten, as with new strength he 'thanked God and took courage.'"

However, this new Southern convention did not encourage women to organize. Part of the reluctance on the part of men was related to what was going on in the North during this time. Northern women were organizing, and many were speaking out against slavery. Southern women as a whole were more conservative, often because their culture encouraged meekness and a quiet, non-assertive demeanor.

Nonetheless, if women had waited until a majority of the male population had agreed to their organization and ministry, it would never have happened! At the beginning of the Southern Baptist Convention, there were more than 100 women's societies, but these groups were in only slightly more than 2 percent of the total number of churches.

The split in Baptist conventions somewhat foreshadowed an ominous cloud rising too rapidly over the nation—the Civil War. An entire democracy came close to vanishing, its future precariously hanging in the balance. And its women could only weep, pray, and endure the agonies of civil strife, wondering just what lay ahead.

CHAPTER

Grant Us Wisdom

"Cure Thy children's warring madness; Bend our pride to Thy control"
—God of Grace and God of Glory

CURE THY CHILDREN'S WARRING MADNESS

CAN WE POSSIBLY understand? Just think of actually living through the Civil War. This was brother against brother; this was fighting your own family. The effects of the conflict were disastrous for the South; they threatened every aspect of life. The plantation mentality became a thing of the past. No one and no institution escaped unscathed. Homes were destroyed, children were orphaned, and land was laid waste. The phrase from the Lord's Prayer took on a whole new meaning: "Give us this day our daily bread."

GLOOM, DESPAIR, AND AGONY ON END

Times were perilous. Yet slowly, though painfully, a new lifestyle developed. Much had changed, but some beauty rose from ashes. Churches had not escaped—neither the body of the church—its people—nor the structures themselves. For families and congregations, the bare necessities were hard to come by. During the actual years of fighting, the cause of missions lay nearly fallow. To cite Virginia as an example, the 36 female missionary societies had contributed some $3,000 in 1860, just prior to the war. The following year, offerings were under $1,000, and the next year there was no report. A fair amount was given in 1865, but—it was Confederate money—it had absolutely no value. The Foreign Mission Board had to smuggle money for its missions work abroad through "enemy lines"; many foreign missionaries had to do additional secular work in order to eat, while home missionaries often served as chaplains for the army. The conflict finally came to an end, and a treaty was signed. It took more than mere words, however, to restore the flagging hopes of a region reeling from defeat. One Baptist historian called those postwar years the "period of poverty and peril for the SBC."

The South was a land of beleaguered people. But a spirit of hopelessness did not prevail. The inner courage and depth of people of faith surfaced. Pressure became a privilege for Baptist women in the South. Dire poverty and extreme circumstances afforded women an opportunity to show their mettle. Sheer necessity created teachers, farmers, tradeswomen, and yes, church leaders. Often, times of drastic changes can afford women an unprecedented opportunity to demonstrate leadership skills.

Following the war, there was a desperate need for money to rebuild churches and pay pastors' salaries. Time and again it was the women who sold baked goods, conducted benefits, and provided the necessary funds. A large number of Ladies Aid Societies developed, but focus was a problem. Meeting so many needs at home could distract from the desperate needs of a whole world for the gospel. Some societies had no wish to extend their concerns to encompass needs beyond their own doors.

Slowly but steadily, as poverty abated a bit, women began to lift their eyes beyond local problems and remember the needs of a hopeless world. Mary Gambrell, a leading Baptist woman in Texas, gently chided her sisters for "aiding the pastor to do nothing" for the wider application of the gospel. She advised a pastor who sought help, saying, "No aid society is apt to do much, unless you have the missionary plank in it too, because women centered alone on their own church work grow selfish, and our Lord did not put His churches here just to do work for themselves."

A similar plea came from Mrs. Sarah Ann Chambers of Alabama, who talked about what really mattered. Chambers wondered: "Is this the 'good part' that Mary chose? Our houses will crumble and decay . . . but a single soul saved from death will shine as the stars forever." The good lady went on to talk of making our churches comfortable and beautiful, but she concluded: "We must not wait until every church is lighted with an elegant chandelier before we send the lamp of God's word to the nations that sit in darkness."

No matter how much women did to save their churches from financial ruin, it did not translate into a voice in the decision-making processes of the church body. Defeat in the war, the unraveling of an entire culture's way of life, and the sheer humiliation of Reconstruction made matters even worse in regard to attitudes toward women.

More than ever, Southern men seemed to glory in the "Lost Cause" and maintain that "their women" should be quiet, restrained, ever gentle. It appears to have been yet another attempt to cling to a shattered way of life. Many men regarded women's organizations as a threat to their southern way of life. Periodicals of the era quote many men as stating that "our women" did not want to be public speakers and have organizations or rights.

Lingering poverty, wounded pride, and the echoes of a mourning South slowed the development and reactivation of women's movements. However, mission societies were the first structured groups built by southern women following the war. And from ashes of war, Baptist women with a concern for a lost world reactivated their societies. Slowly but steadily, new groups began to appear.

POST-TRAUMATIC SOCIETY DIFFUSION

Women in the South of the 1800s had never heard the term post-traumatic stress disorder, but they lived to see a real post-traumatic society diffusion as women's societies were resurrected and new ones born. Some skills tempered in the flames of war and honed to a fine edge through struggles were brought into play in forming an organization in which Baptist women believed. And there were new possibilities for women in this century. Factories for textiles and sewing machines actually gave women an opportunity for employment. The development of railroads helped people and news to spread. Southern women also learned of groups of women in various denominations in the North that were organizing mission societies and sending out women missionaries.

Chapter 4

ANN BAKER GRAVES

And here we meet the "Mother of Woman's Missionary Union," Ann Baker Graves of Baltimore, Maryland—one more remarkable lady! Graves was raised a Methodist but became a Baptist in 1868. That same year, she charted a course for Southern Baptist women that grew to be the nation's largest woman's missionary organization. Shy by nature, brilliant of mind, and mother of the first Baptist missionary doctor from America to China, Graves was determined to enlist women in praying and giving. That year, she she conceived the idea of inviting Baptist women to the Southern Baptist Convention to gather in the church balcony for a women's meeting.

Ann's son, Dr. Rosewell Graves, wrote about the importance of Bible women in reaching the women of China. Men could not freely evangelize Chinese women. Supporting Bible women required funds, and Ann Graves was aflame with the desire to involve women in reaching women. She called the women together to consider "a matter of importance." Many women responded. It was just a mother's simple invitation to other women to help answer a real need in China. This, then, was the first general meeting of Southern Baptist women.

The next year, Ann Graves invited a furloughing Methodist missionary to speak to and inspire Baltimore women. The women were so moved that they decided to organize their own Woman's Union Missionary Society, and they did so in 1870. The Baptist pastors of Baltimore were prepared to back the women's group. Graves was named the Society's corresponding secretary. It appeared that the women's societies concept erupted nearly simultaneously in various parts of the South, and one of the reasons was the way Ann Graves and the Baltimore women seemed to enfold the entire region in their outreach. Ann began to issue a circular letter encouraging women to form branches in each state and missions circles in each church.

Ann Graves's first letter encouraged women to raise funds by using a mite box in each home. The Foreign Mission Board (FMB) provided the mite boxes, made of small garnet-colored paper and printed with shining gold letters that said *Woman's Mission to Woman.*

One of the first to respond was a pastor! John Stout, always a supporter of women's work, became pastor at Newberry Church in South Carolina and immediately organized a Woman's Missionary Society. In 1868, at that first women's gathering, Ann Graves's house-guest had been Ellen Hartwell Edwards, whose brother was a missionary in north China. Edwards went home to Society Hill, South Carolina, with a supply of mite boxes. Just two years later, John and Fanny Coker Stout came to pastor Edwards's church. They, along with Ellen and Mattie McIntosh (be listening for this name—you'll hear it again) organized a Woman's Mission to Woman, with Ellen Edwards as president.

Meanwhile, Ann and her pastor and his wife contacted the Foreign Mission Board (FMB) about their plans. Their request: Could women's groups and the Board cooperate, or should the women work independently? James B. Taylor, longtime secretary of the FMB, was willing to accept money from the women, but not anything else. However, very shortly after the women's groups began developing,

Dr. Taylor died. His successor, Dr. Henry Allen Tupper, had different ideas.

HENRY ALLEN TUPPER

What a contrast Henry Tupper was to his predecessor at the Board. He took office in January 1872, and the first order of business was the Baltimore women's proposals for organizing. Charming, wealthy, and brilliant, Tupper was a product of the great First Baptist Church of Charleston.

Tupper's first step was leading the Foreign Mission Board to reverse its anti-woman policy. He skillfully brought about approval for a single woman (Lula Whilden) to accompany her married sister and brother-in-law to China and gained permission for a self-supporting young Edmonia Moon to go as well. Furthermore, Tupper decided that the Board would keep separate accounts for women's contributions and saw to it that the Board would emphasize the evangelization of women. This then gave Ann Graves the confidence to encourage women's groups in each of the states to send their contributions directly to Tupper, rather than to Baltimore. It marked the beginning of a new era in women's missions. Now the Board was requesting Tupper to "do all he can to multiply these societies and to inform the Woman's Missionary Union of Baltimore that the Board heartily approves of its objects."

In a day when the telephone was still on Alexander Graham Bell's drawing board and the Internet was not even a dream, women's societies grew and multiplied by word of mouth, by family, and by friend to friend. Names of families producing several generations of Baptist leadership were emerging. The names Graves, Hartwell, Edwards,

Armstrong, and Moon were among them—names that have lived on into another millennium.

By this pivotal year of 1872, Southern Baptist women had a foreign missions effort just as effective as that of any of the northern denominations, but, as historian Catherine Allen puts it, "with a uniquely Southern Baptist accent." An agricultural analogy pictures what was happening. The earliest women, beginning with Polly Webb, had conceived the vision. Ann Graves and her contemporaries planted the seed, and women across the South worked the soil where the seedlings had landed. The seedlings were independent, yet the work integrated, and the vision grew as the women watered and nurtured it.

The next step didn't sound dramatic—the development of Central Committees. But the concept was ingenious in the way it would allow committed women to organize for the common good. And organize they did!

Grant Us Courage

"that we fail not man nor Thee."
—God of Grace and God of Glory

"THE MOTHER CENTRAL COMMITTEE"
MARYLAND

MARYLAND, THE "MOTHER state" of the Central Committees, never officially had a Central Committee. But Ann Baker Graves and Baltimore's Woman's Mission to Woman had the prototype of the subsequent Committees. Eight women made up the officers of the historic group that formally organized in October 1871 at First Baptist Church in Baltimore. Dr. Tupper, with great admiration, called for Central Committees in each state to organize and expand the ministry of women in missions. There is no way to over-emphasize the importance of Ann Graves's influence on Baptist women. Her passion and unremitting efforts to involve women set the stage for what happened across the South. And it would not be long until the name of Baltimore-born Annie Armstrong became part of missions history.

SOUTH CAROLINA

Mattie, Fannie, and Ellen

What a team they made! Welsh Neck Church in Society Hill, South Carolina, was example A of what God was beginning to do across the South. Three women with distinctive backgrounds came together—Mattie McIntosh, the quiet, capable, descendent of a leading family; Fanny Coker Stout, a pastor's wife who was committed to missions; and Ellen Hartwell Edwards, whose brother served in Tengchow, China, where Lottie Moon had just gone. Fanny's husband, John, had been pastor at Welsh Neck for just a month in 1874 when he called the women together to organize a Woman's Missionary Society. John had corresponded with Ann Graves and had already organized a women's group in Newberry just a couple of years before. In 1872, Ellen Edwards was a guest in Ann Graves's home and came home with mite boxes. The Welsh Neck women were elated to now have an official organization. Such action in the South of that day was really quite bold. For women to organize a society in the 1870s, it was necessary to exercise real courage.

Now enter Central Committees. Dr. Tupper was convinced that a Central Committee in each state was key to promoting mission societies. In 1875, he wisely decided to turn to his home state to try this new plan. Tupper suggested that J. A. Chambliss, the South Carolina foreign missions committee chair, contact the Welsh Neck Church to lead out. Chambliss wrote Mattie McIntosh, saying, "Will it not give your work more form and system if you will suffer our Executive Committee to appoint you at Society Hill the Central Committee (in which case I must beg you to act as chairman) and then with your assistance organize cooperating committees in churches generally?"

Poor Mattie McIntosh was in a quandary. Surely Dr. Chambliss had meant her older sister Louisa?! The outgoing Louisa had been encouraging friends to organize women's groups. Maybe the good doctor had gotten the sisters confused. Mattie, the quiet one, was hesitant to assume such a responsibility, but her pastor and sister were insistent. And it wasn't many years until Mattie discovered just how much God had in mind for her.

As the women began planning, it became evident that a smaller committee would be more practical than the entire society. Mattie McIntosh served as chair, and Fanny Stout was president. There was a wealth of leadership in their group, and in that first year, 42 new societies were organized across the state. (Fantastic growth in any century!) All the ladies became involved in sending circulars, writing letters, and collecting funds. The glowing success of the Central Committee at Welsh Neck was a precursor of women's response in other states. Some states were plagued by local opposition from men, but the majority had women who quietly persevered.

VIRGINIA

Mary Catherine Williams Jennett Dabbs Jeter

That's quite a name, and she was quite a lady. Beautiful Mary Catherine Williams was from a privileged Petersburg, Virginia, family. Her first husband was Christopher Jennett, who became pastor of the historic First Baptist Church of Augusta, Georgia. Tragically, Rev. Jennett died less than two years after their marriage, and Mary returned home.

Five years later, she married Josiah Dabbs, a wealthy Baptist planter. They lived in a beautiful estate just four miles outside of Richmond, but their joy was short-lived. Dabbs died just seven years later, and once again Mary was alone.

With the Civil War raging, Mary sold the estate and stayed in Richmond in the home of dear friends who were living elsewhere. Their pastor, Dr. J. B. Jeter (who had baptized Henrietta Hall Shuck), checked on the house and on the houseguest. He had endured sorrow of his own, having lost three wives in sad succession. Jeter later wrote that he was "bewitched" by the Widow Dabbs, who became Mrs. J. B. Jeter in 1868 and was also a leader both in the church and among women in her state. Mary was at that first women's meeting in Baltimore. According to Virginia Baptist history, Mary Jeter, charming, brilliant, and gifted, became a different person from that hour.

Mary Jeter's church and state both felt the effects of her leadership. Her husband became co-editor of *The Religious Herald*. From that point on, Mary became editor of the woman's page and was highly influential in sharing missions news. Dr. Tupper asked the capable Mary Jeter to spearhead a drive to gather funds for a house for the Moon sisters in Tengchow, China. She invited women from each of the seven churches in Richmond, and in April 1872, the Woman's Missionary Society of Richmond was organized. This became the precursor of Virginia's Central Committee. Again, Mary Jeter was asked to be chairman, but the women preferred the title "president," which they used in their minutes.

Chapter 5

NORTH CAROLINA

Mattie Callendine Heck

Dr. Tupper approached North Carolina women in April 1877. The name of the woman chosen as the first president of a Central Committee was one that became famous in WMU history. It was Mattie Callendine (Mrs. J. M.) Heck, whose daughter, Fannie Heck, lived to be the longest serving national president in Woman's Missionary Union history. (At the time, young Fannie was 15 years old and greatly interested in what was going on among North Carolina women.) By the time of the Baptist state convention in November 1877, they reported 17 new societies. However, the Convention's response to the report was mixed. First Baptist Church Raleigh's pastor, Dr. T. H. Pritchard, presented resolutions commending the women's work. As Fannie Heck later recorded, "A very storm of discussion between the brethren who favored encouraging women in missions and those who opposed it rose to such a height that the little bark, the unwitting cause of the storm, was crippled and sank out of sight." The Committee had been killed for the moment, but the women's determination remained. They might be down—but certainly not out.

KENTUCKY

Everyone Knows Eliza

Any Baptist in Kentucky surely must know the name of Eliza Broadus.

Daughter of renowned theologian Dr. John A. Broadus, Eliza Broadus carved her own name into the history of Kentucky WMU. She was primarily educated by her father, and her leadership qualities stood out in sharp relief; no part of Baptist life escaped her interest and support. Woman's Missionary Union held a special place in her heart. She poured a lifetime of service into WMU's formative years. In Kentucky, leading Baptist men had input into the formation of the Central Committees. In 1878, Pastor J. L. Burrows of Broadway Church in Louisville, and Dr. C. H. Toy, professor of Old Testament at Southern Seminary, were asked by Dr. Tupper to appoint a Central Committee for the state.

Of those first six women selected, two names became very well known in Baptist circles—Agnes Osborne and Eliza Broadus. Osborne became the first secretary of the group and Broadus was the representative from her church's society.

These ladies first sent letters to every pastor in the state, encouraging their churches to begin a women's society. The ladies reported a "very disappointing" result. They had letters from fewer than half a dozen pastors! Next they directly contacted active Baptist women in the various churches and had better results. By their second report, there were 29 churches with societies, and by the third, there were 45. Now with more societies and requests for more material, the talented Agnes Osborne was named editor of the *Heathen Helper,* a missions magazine. It was a stroke of genius, for the *Helper* became influential throughout the Southern Baptist Convention. Eliza Broadus served on the Central Committee and later the Kentucky executive committee for an astounding 50 years. She was chairman of the Committees for 32 of those years.

Chapter 5

ALABAMA

Organized—Dissolved – Organized Again!

Alabama had a Central Committee appointed in 1878, but there is no record of it in state Baptist minutes. However, the *Foreign Mission Journal* did list the Alabama committee in 1878 and named Emma Hutchinson Hawthorne as chairman. Hawthorne's husband was Dr. J. B. Hawthorne, influential pastor of First Baptist Church, Montgomery. This could be a reason that no furor was raised at the Alabama State Convention, for criticizing Mrs. Hawthorne would be construed as criticizing her prominent husband. It looked like things were going well for the women in Alabama.

Then came the real blow. In 1888, the state Baptist convention actually abolished the Central Committee. And thereby, Alabama became the only one of the organized states to be without a central committee. Change wasn't too far away. A pastor went to bat for the women, and it worked. November 11, 1889, was a big day for Baptist women in Alabama. Rev. John W. Stewart of Evergreen brought a resolution recommending that a State Central Committee be appointed to cooperate with the new Executive Committee of Woman's missions societies in Baltimore. The motion passed, and Amanda Tupper Hamilton (daughter of Henry Tupper) was named president of the committee.

Then one of Alabama women's best friends, *The Alabama Baptist,* stepped forward. The newspaper gave the Central Committee space in every issue, usually on the front page. Amanda Hamilton wrote the news, and it became a popular feature of the newspaper. In 1890, Alabama women applied for membership in Woman's Missionary Union, SBC, and were happily accepted.

GEORGIA

Martha Eleanor Loftis Wilson and Friends

Following the appeal of Dr. Tupper for women to organize Central Committees, those in states where leading men wanted to encourage women to get involved in sending the gospel were fortunate. Georgia had a few good men, and several of these led out.

November 19, 1878, was a red-letter day for Georgia Baptist women, for on that historic day, at Atlanta's Second Baptist Church, they formally organized the Central Committee of Georgia WMU. Martha Loftis Wilson, a real leader among the women of the church, was selected president. Originally from Alabama, Wilson was the wife of a surgeon, the mother of five, and an accomplished author. For ten years, she headed up the work of Georgia WMU.

Wilson and the ladies of Georgia didn't believe in wasting time and drew up a strong constitution right away. They decided to meet each year when the state Baptist convention met in some nearby church or basement. Before long, the meeting had become the annual meeting of the missionary societies. Fannie Heck related with good humor an account of what happened at the first of such meetings. When some of the brothers of the churches learned what was afoot, they protested with vigor, but the women already had the plans in place. Some of the ladies were understandably nervous. However, Martha Wilson and the women carried on. There were large crowds at all three sessions—including a number of men. A certain brother and deacon in the host church declared: "These women are going to break up our churches." At once, a brother standing nearby retorted, "It might be well if some of them were broken up!" The deacon's prophecy didn't come to pass, for that meeting marked the beginning of rapid growth for missionary societies. By 1884, Georgia WMU had 76 societies.

Women across the South began to discover just what God could do through committed women. Over a span of 10 more years, Baptist women grew closer and closer to national identity.

CHAPTER

For the Living of These Days

"We want no 'rights' but to obey God's word."
— Mary Quinche, Mississippi, 1877

MISSISSIPPI

Julia Anna Toy Johnson and Mary J. Quinche

FOLLOWING THE DEVASTATION of war, Baptist women in Mississippi began to regroup. They were fortunate in having a number of strong men who did not fear the missions zeal of women of faith, men like Dr. H. F. Sproles, pastor of First Baptist Church, Jackson. There were actually a number of societies in various Mississippi churches, but no associational or statewide organization. An indication of the approval of some pastoral leadership is evident in the 1875 resolution passed by the state convention—to approve women's missions work, and further, to encourage each pastor to organize women's groups.

Now enter ladies of grace and leadership, inspiring other such Mississippi women to heed the Great Commission. In 1878, Foreign Mission Board (FMB) secretary, Dr. Henry Tupper, requested Mrs. Julia Anna Toy Johnson and Mrs. Mary

J. Quinche to head up the Mississippi Central Committee, serving as president and corresponding secretary respectively. These were brilliant choices. Julia Ann Toy had been friends with Lottie Moon in college in Virginia. In 1860, Toy and her husband, John, were appointed for Japan, but she grew seriously ill. Their plans changed, and Dr. Johnson became a professor at the University of Mississippi. Julia Ann Toy's heart never wavered from its commitment to missions, and the Central Committee provided a platform for her leadership.

Likewise, Mary Quinche, also a professor's wife, brought great skills to her position. As both leader and writer, she shared some interesting observations on Baptist men and women and God's leadership. She wrote a paper on "Pioneer Work of Baptist Women in Mississippi" and spoke of the great work of the societies "notwithstanding the opposition they encountered, chiefly from their Christian husbands!" Quinche concluded that the ladies had met opposition everywhere, "and their failure was predicted; but they persevered, and we are thankful for the example they set for *all* Christian workers."

MISSOURI

Persuasive Courtesy and Mrs. Caroline Moss

Another redoubtable woman, Caroline Moss, was instrumental in the beginning of a state organization in Missouri. It was basically a man's world. But, more and more women quietly and steadily made their voices heard.

Moss was depicted as "persuasively courteous" in making her voice heard. An initial meeting was held in Hannibal in October 1876, and the women decided to schedule a mass organization meeting for the following April in Liberty, where they agreed to have their first annual meeting in Lexington on October 27, 1877. They elected Caroline Moss (Mrs. Oliver Perry) as their first president.

Moss combined intense enthusiasm with great tenacity of purpose. She was still in her forties when beginning to serve as president and was fortunate to be surrounded by a strong group of committed women. The women's societies of Missouri were reporting the formation of 28 new groups by the end of that first year.

TEXAS

Fannie, Ann, and Lucinda

As in Missouri, Texas had a number of forward-thinking women. One such leader was Fannie Breedlove Davis. When the call went out in 1878 authorizing women in each state to organize, Texas was eager to get involved. The Texas Central Committee was appointed in November with Mrs. Fannie Breedlove Davis of Independence as president. Davis's name became synonymous with Texas WMU. The first secretary of this committee was Ann Luther Bagby. Three years later, Bagby became the first foreign missionary to go out from Texas!

Soon the committees in Texas came together to form the Woman's Missionary Union of Texas. Their first president? Fannie Breedlove Davis. A host of strong women were part of Texas women's work. One was a well-known name in Dallas. Lucinda Williams and her husband, J. L. Williams, had actually founded First Baptist Church, Dallas, in 1868. Lucinda Williams organized a missionary society in 1872 that in turn helped establish missions in several parts of Dallas. An early history of Dallas stated that "the congregation owed its very survival to Lucinda Williams. She persuaded 18 ladies to form a ladies' aid society." Williams commented on what Texas women who were organizing societies faced. "Our dear women did not generally get encouragement from their pastors," she said. "In not a few cases they were given downright discouragement."

FLORIDA

Ann B. Hester Bailey

Florida Baptist women did not organize as quickly, but their growth was rapid. The remarkable Ann Bailey was responsible for drawing together the Baptist women of Florida to move forward. Born in Tennessee in 1841, Bailey lived only 45 years, but she left an indelible imprint on the hearts of the women of Florida. Ann Bailey married Napoleon Bailey just two weeks after her 17th birthday. The couple worked in churches in Georgia and Alabama before moving to Florida. Ann Bailey was always frail in health but passionate in spirit. In their new church in Micanopy, she quickly organized a woman's missionary society.

In some areas, Florida outpaced other states. At their first Convention meeting in 1881, Ann Bailey was one of four women permitted to serve as delegates. Then Florida appointed Bailey as secretary for Women's Mission Work. That first year, in spite of serious illness, she organized 26 missionary societies and began a "Little Helpers" children's band in her own church. It was through Bailey's heroic efforts that the women of Florida became a strong union. Her last official report was in 1885 at the state convention when she noted that in four years, the work had increased to 109 societies and bands. Bailey was re-elected in 1885 but died six months later. At the 1886 meeting, women and men alike mourned the loss of Ann Bailey. State Baptist secretary William Chaudin lamented, "She was a choice spirit. She died in harness." Lucina Telford, a former foreign missionary, succeeded Bailey as secretary.

TENNESSEE

Starting, Stopping, and Starting Again

July 18, 1882, turned out to be an important date for Baptist women in Tennessee, when a small group of ladies met at Nashville's First Baptist Church to organize the state's first Central Committee. Jennie Fish was chosen as president. Since Nashville was quite centrally located, it seemed to be a logical place for the committee to have headquarters. The ladies immediately went to work, and almost as quickly, opposition surfaced. It became loud enough that by 1885, the committee decided to become inactive.

This didn't mark a total stop, but more of an interruption. The women simply tried a new approach. This time, the Woman's Central Committee would function as an auxiliary to the State Board. Evidently, this idea sounded more acceptable to the brethren. The woman selected to head the new committee was Fannie Nelson (Mrs. Anson), a superb Bible teacher and talented musician. She was quite reluctant to take on yet another cause. However, Nelson had what she called "a crisis in thought and purpose," and she decided to accept the job. In a shrewd move, the women invited the dynamic Sallie Rochester Ford of Missouri to preside. The gathering was a huge success.

Chapter 6

LOUISIANA

Mother and Sister, In Answer to a Letter

One thing hasn't changed through the years: Word of mouth is still an important means of communication. "Missions" seems to run in families, too. Ellen Hartwell Edwards, sister of J. B. Hartwell, a missionary serving with Lottie Moon in North China, wrote an important letter after her visit with Ann Baker Graves in Baltimore. Corresponding with her mother and sister living in Louisiana, Ellen told of the wonderful meeting in Baltimore and how she was now home in South Carolina to promote women's societies. She urged both her mother and sister to contact their pastor and organize the women in their church. Their pastor went a step further and called the first meeting in his own home in the spring of 1874. Societies sprang up, and in 1884, a Central Committee was formed. By the time the women of the South officially organized, Louisiana had 66 societies regularly reporting.

ARKANSAS

Eagle and Early

Further West, Arkansas had quite an unusual beginning for its Central Committee. A man who recognized the value of women promoting missions called the first meeting. Dr. M. D. Early was vice-president from Arkansas for the Home Mission Board. However, his wife, Margretta, was a woman of multiple talents and was likely the powerful motivator of her husband's efforts with women in missions. The big day for Arkansas women was September 19, 1883, in Russellville when a transplanted Kentuckian became the spark plug who served as their first president. Mary Eagle, the wife of James P. Eagle, one-time governor of the state, was not even 30 when she was elected president. A gifted young woman, Mary Eagle was a multifaceted leader who threw her whole heart into developing the organization, serving as president until 1902! Working closely with her was Margretta Early, who became secretary. Distances were far and travel difficult in the 1880s in Arkansas, but within about three years, some 50 societies were reporting.

CHILDREN'S BANDS

"Let the Children Come Unto Me."

During the early years women led children's groups, impressing on young minds God's call to mission. One of the earliest was the Juvenile Missionary and Education Society of First Baptist Church, Charleston. Pastor Richard Furman organized and led the group himself. Note again the missions impact of Richard Furman. There were also early reports of children's missions groups in Virginia, North Carolina, South Carolina, and other states, going by such names as Little Reapers, Rosebuds, Juvenile Cent Societies, and Children's Bands.

One of the most effective workers with children came out of First Church in Charleston. Eliza Hyde was the niece of Henry Tupper. In 1883, she began her volunteer work among underprivileged children in the city. Hyde's work flourished, and she was asked to lead band work for the state. In her first report, there were 60

bands, 30 of which had been organized just that year.

JESUS WANTS ME FOR A SUNBEAM

Anna Elsom and "Cousin George"

George Braxton Taylor, son of early missionaries to Italy, became pastor of a strong country church in Fairmont, Virginia. Taylor found a real ally in Anna Elsom, a woman described as cultured, lovely, educated, and deeply dedicated to Christ's mission. In just a corner of the church, with no equipment, the Sunbeams program was born. "Cousin George" (as he was known to many) began writing material for the children, and soon it was being printed in the *Foreign Mission Journal* and the *Religious Herald.* In 1887, the *Herald* reported that Sunbeams had also organized at Mt. Shiloh, with 18 children and 6 missionary hens!

Each issue included "Sunbeam Dots," listing the various bands and what they had contributed for a particular project. Hundreds of the little ones in those early bands grew up to become missions leaders, pastors, and missionaries themselves. In 1896, Sunbeams became part of Woman's Missionary Union.

WOMEN AND THE MISSION BOARDS

Following the Civil War, the leaders of Baptist agencies began to understand the importance of women in providing funding. By 1873, contributions to the FMB increased by as much as 75 percent, and years later, Board leaders recognized that the gain in giving came about because of the initiative of Baptist women. On the other hand, the Home Mission Board had only reluctantly recognized the importance of women's involvement by 1877 and was lamenting its lowest giving since the war.

One of the home board's problems revolved around their methods. The two Boards seemed to be competing for the same funds, and the home board's methods were viewed as suspicious. They operated by having paid agents who collected contributions and at the same time skimmed a healthy percentage off the top.

Things changed in 1882 when Dr. Isaac Tichenor was elected to head the Home Mission Board. A gifted man Tichenor left the presidency of Auburn University in Alabama to head the Board, and things started to turn around One of his first moves was to enlist the help of Annie Armstrong of Baltimore in a project to organize women to provide clothing for Native Americans in Oklahoma. And thus began the amazing contribution of Annie Armstrong to Baptists and the founding of a Southwide union of women. Tichenor himself was forever remembered as a friend and partner with women in missions.

During the decade of the 1880s, the economy of the South began to exhibit signs of renewal, and committed women were carefully, prayerfully laying the foundation for a Southwide women's missions organization. The tenacity and courage of no small number of women of grace and grit was about to prove equal to the challenge.

Send the Light

"He who "bought us with a price" surely has something for us to do."
—Sarah Ann Chambers, Alabama, 1882

PROLOGUE TO 1888

BAPTIST WOMEN IN the 1880s battled indifference, ridicule, and often downright opposition. Historian Catherine Allen, making a study of the climate of hostility facing Baptist women in the 1880s, notes that most church leaders imagined a woman's missions organization to be a competitor, not a partner. Women in the 1880s however, steadfastly pulled towards their goal of a Southwide organization.

THE HEATHEN HELPER

A true catalyst turned out to be the "power of the page." Forward-thinking women in Kentucky brought out the first issue of the *Heathen Helper* in 1882, and it proved to be a compelling tool for unity. Editor Agnes Osborne had the backing of her brother Thomas, editor of the influential *Louisville Ledger.* A remarkable number of state paper editors became loyal friends to the *Helper,* with one notable exception. T. T. Eaton, editor of the *Western Recorder* there in Louisville, was *not* happy about the *Helper,* which he considered his competition. The editors of many of the state papers had wives and daughters who were active in women's mission societies. Each state contributed to the *Helper,* and through the paper, women shared ideas and projects.

The powerful *Heathen Helper* monthly gave a voice to Alabama's Martha Foster Crawford, long an effective missionary in North China. She wrote about the crucial need for men and women to work together to advance missions. So widely known was Crawford that her word carried a lot of weight. This *Heathen Helper* was a bright, eight-page sheet containing reports, missionary letters, and pithy editorials.

The *Heathen Helper* had a sister publication—in more ways than one! The *Baptist Basket* originated in Kentucky as well, beginning a little bit later than the *Helper.* Its editor was also an Osborne, Mrs. Thomas Osborne, the wife of Agnes's brother. This sister paper also had a staff of editors, one from each state with a Central Committee. The main thrust of the *Basket* was to encourage giving, stressing the importance of tithing. (In addition, the *Basket* printed a model constitution, plus a similar one for children's bands.) Each month, the magazine included a full women's program complete with hymns, Scripture, prayer concerns, and material for missionary study.

Then a name appeared which was to have profound impact on the beginnings of a Southwide union of women in missions—Sallie Rochester Ford. Ford was never elected to a national office but she, as much as any one person, made May 14, 1888, in Richmond, Virginia, possible. Sallie grew up near the home of her minister uncle, who gave her free access to his library. In 1855, she married Samuel H. Ford, a brilliant minister who wielded a powerful pen. Samuel Ford, who was part of the editorship of Kentucky's *Western Recorder* and Missouri's *Christian Repository,* soon purchased the *Repository,* encouraging his wife to contribute articles. A biographer later called Sallie Ford "the medium through which Dr. Ford gave the world the best products of his brain."

Sallie Ford wrote with force and skill. In short order, she was established as a distinguished author. She was also a beautiful woman and a dynamic speaker, holding strong and sound convictions. Ford was convinced that Southern Baptist women had a right to organize, and she was confident that, if united, the women could raise more money for both boards which were struggling. The various states began inviting Ford to preside at their meetings. She modeled for hesitant and inexperienced women the proper way to conduct a meeting and encouraged women in each state to think towards organizing.

1883 — WACO

Texas has long had a reputation for giving big welcomes. And in 1883, women were specifically invited to a missions gathering. The attendance was the largest the SBC had ever seen. Fannie Breedlove Davis led in planning, and Sallie Rochester Ford presided with grace and poise. It was Ford who introduced the one who electrified the crowd. Martha Foster Crawford was on furlough from China. This seasoned missionary who had already served 32 years in China, was riveting. Onlookers said, "Her face lighted up like an angel's." The gathering was known ever after as "Mrs. Crawford's meeting."

This was the first time a woman had made a speech to a crowd of Baptist men and women. She was sensitive to culture and relaxed the audience by commenting that this was very informal. This meeting surpassed the greatest expectations of the planners and was remembered by many as the meeting that "sent a thrill all through the South."

1884 — BALTIMORE

Nearly a century later, WMU icon Alma Hunt stated that by 1884, women across the South "were developing a frame of mind for a general organization." In Baltimore, women voted "that societies here represented make the Union meeting permanent, to meet annually during the sessions of the SBC." On this occasion, women from each state had been invited to gather in an upper room of one of the hotels to pray and plan. Only three were there—but a special three: Fannie Breedlove Davis of Texas, Ann Bailey of Florida, and Martha Wilson of Georgia. Martha Wilson reported that it was enough to claim the prayer promise. Those women made a covenant to pray on the morning of the first Sunday in each month for the success of woman's missions work. This was printed in state papers and widely circulated.

1885 — AUGUSTA

Women at the 1885 Augusta meeting said that "fear and curiosity were the prompting factors in men's attendance on their meetings," and they adopted without reservation a resolution offered by Sallie Ford that "henceforth the meeting shall be for women only." There was one positive move on the part of the Convention itself; it voted to recommend that state conventions foster Central Committees. The evolution of the union was painful, but it was in process.

In light of the existing misunderstandings and lack of trust, Dr. Tupper, that true friend of women in missions, had advice for both groups. To the women he gave support by saying, "Refuse to be discouraged by opposition. No good thing has ever failed to arouse opposition . . . keep on the even tenor of your way, and by gentleness and kindness disarm criticism." At another point, Tupper defended the work of the women when he said, "It is wiser to stimulate the men than to restrain the women."

1886 — MONTGOMERY

Baptist periodicals sometimes lent fuel to the fire of opposing views. Sallie Ford held the women's fellowship together during this uneasy time. She issued a public denial that the women were plotting treason by planning a separate organization. Ford had corresponded with the Central Committees and put together an entertaining all-woman program, with the exception of three men invited to speak.

1887 — LOUISVILLE

Once more, Sallie Ford drew the women together for the Louisville meeting, some 300 of them. Again, no men were included. Some of the women present wanted to go ahead and select officers and determine an ongoing program during the meeting. However, two strong voices—Annie Armstrong and Mattie McIntosh—suggested they delay. At this meeting, Armstrong addressed the group publicly for the first time and made a strong impression on those who listened to her carefully considered ideas. Mattie McIntosh was quiet and reserved but nonetheless compelling in her understanding and clarity of purpose. It was actually this 1887 gathering that focused attention on these two women who would come to profoundly shape the WMU of the future. It is nearly impossible to think about the founding of Woman's Missionary Union without thinking about the remarkable impact of these women on its development.

As a body, the women planned their strategy for the coming year. They asked each central committee to appoint three ladies to be delegates to meet during the 1888 Convention to decide upon the advisability of beginning a General Committee. Then, if it were so decided, the delegates would plan how to provide for its operation. Armstrong and McIntosh felt the gravity of the decision. They pushed for an organization so finely tuned that it could not be destroyed. Part of the strategy would be to clearly state that they had no desire "to interfere with the management of the existing Boards."

The time was drawing nearer for the actual birth of a new missions organization. Forces were coming together to make 1888 the year when this was likely to occur.

One came from a great distance. Lottie Moon, 10,000 miles away in the Shandong Province of China, was very close in spirit and purpose. Moon, a prolific letter writer, realized the importance of the women's support to the viability of the Foreign Mission Board. In a September 1887 letter to the Board, she declared, "Until the women of our Southern Baptist churches are thoroughly aroused, we shall continue to go in our present hand-to-mouth system . . . (and) I am convinced that one of the chief reasons our Southern Baptist women do so little is the lack of organization." This remarkable woman not only realized how vital the organization was, she envisioned what the structure should resemble. Moon wrote, "What we want is not power, but simply combination in order to elicit the largest possible giving."

In this same letter, Moon made the plea which became forever after quoted, as she asked the Board to recommend to the Woman's Missionary Society to observe the week preceding Christmas as a "week of prayer and self-denial." That tiny woman became a potent influence leading to union in the year to come.

One of the truly powerful factors was the "power of the pen," in this case, the pen of Ruth Alleyn, also known as Alice Armstrong, the older sister of Annie and a prolific and persuasive writer. It was a busy year for Alice Armstrong's journalistic output. She used vivid imagery as she wrote, "There is a sound of shaking in the tops of the trees, and we feel abundantly persuaded that the wind which is stirring the peaceful commotion is none other than the spirit of the living God." Alice Armstrong flooded the state papers with a series of educational articles on the history and promise of women's work for missions. The bottom line was that the mission boards needed money, and women's organizations make money.

It had not happened quickly. It had not occurred without pain or sacrifice. It did not just fall into place. Years, tears, devotion, sacrifice, courage, commitment, and thousands of hours of prayer went into the formation of the organization that was to forever change the face of missions for a denomination. This was a body waiting to be born, as women across the South looked ahead to the following May in Richmond.

CHAPTER

In the Fullness of Time

"At our very doors is the work we crave."
—Lottie Moon

MAY 11, 1888

EXPECTANCY WAS IN the very air. You could feel it as more than 200 women filled the lecture hall of Broad Street Methodist Church in Richmond, Virginia. It was located just a block from First Baptist Church, where the Convention was in session. This gathering didn't begin with fanfare. The women filed in quietly, sensing that something important was about to happen. The outcome would be epic in scope, far exceeding what even the most optimistic of those leaders could have imagined.

It was a rainy Friday morning, May 11, 1888, a day that had been in the making for more than half a century. It had just been a year since Annie Armstrong and Mattie McIntosh had encouraged the women gathered in Louisville not to act hastily but to spend a year laying groundwork. Nothing about that Friday was haphazard; it was the culmination of an inspired plan whose time had come.

Of the more than 200 assembled, only 32 were actually delegates representing their states. Some were timid, others bold and courageous. One fact was clear: All these women had a singleness of purpose.

The leaders had considered the right woman to preside. Sallie Rochester Ford was likely considered too controversial in light of the weighty decisions lying ahead. And she was not one of the delegates from her state of Missouri. A wise plan proved to be the choice of a pastor's wife, Annie Whitfield (Mrs. Theodore). A newcomer to Virginia, Whitfield had been active in the women's society. Her relative anonymity ensured that she would not polarize the group. Whitfield was most reluctant to undertake such a role when Dr. Tupper approached her with the request. "I pray thee, have me excused," she pleaded. He quietly replied, "It is your duty." And preside she did, with poise and a healthy dose of nerves.

Virginia, as host state, planned the program. Ironically, they felt constrained not to vote when the call came, because "the men of the Virginia Convention" had not yet given their approval.

FROM ACROSS THE SOUTH

The delegates were varied in age and background. Some were seasoned women's society leaders. North Carolina women did not feel they had the "necessary approval" to actually vote, but they did have an unofficial representative. Mrs. Mattie Heck had been asked to preside, but "illness" prevented her from attending. (Heck, at 46, was expecting another child.) Instead, she sent her daughter, 25-year-old Fannie, as an observer. How fortunate that Fannie, was there—she who was destined to lead the union to unprecedented heights. Several women, sensing history in the making, brought their daughters.

Abby Manly Gwathmey of Virginia (who later became president of WMU) intentionally brought her twin 10-year-old daughters so they could observe history in the making.

F. M. ELLIS: FRIEND AND ADVOCATE

The program itself had been carefully planned out. Only two men were included as speakers, one of whom was Dr. F. M. Ellis, Annie and Alice Armstrong's young pastor. Dr. Ellis was described as the "orator of the Convention," because following his presentation to the women, he returned to the Convention and delivered its keynote message. Ellis presented the SBC with two prophetic solutions to the funding problems of the boards: systematic, proportionate giving and approval of women's missionary societies, referring to the potential influence of women as "the great power by which the gospel is to be sent to the ends of the earth." The women had no finer friend or advocate than Ellis.

ANNIE WHITFIELD AND JENNIE HATCHER

The women were ready for the day's program. Annie Whitfield's voice did not betray her nerves as she calmly welcomed the delegates from the 12 states and the assembled visitors. Virginia Hatcher, the pastor's wife at Richmond's Grace Baptist Church, graciously welcomed all who had come and concluded, "May wisdom and grace guide our deliberations."

FANNY COKER STOUT

Serving as secretary for the meetings was the *Heathen Helper* editor Agnes Osborne. Annie Armstrong and Martha "Mattie" McIntosh had been charged with preparing the sessions.

McIntosh's close friend Fanny Stout loved missions and knew how to present her ideas forcefully. Hers was the first presentation. She declared, "Much will depend on the spirit which we show," affirming that in the end, the men would recognize the pure motives of the women's missions' efforts. This in turn should convince them that their anxiety over women organizing was unnecessary. She concluded with the affirmation that "we shall all work together in unity."

THE BUSINESS OF THE HOUR

Annie Whitfield next called the roll of states, allowing each to express their opinions. Annie Armstrong rose and offered a resolution: "That the subject of organization be considered, and there be an informal and free interchange of views in order to be able to decide what to do." Armstrong was surely an impressive figure. Tall and stately, she was a 38-year-old woman with real presence. Her presentation was serious—but never dull. As soon as Armstrong brought a resolution concerning organizing, Fannie Davis of Texas rose to second the motion. The Mississippi delegation appeared to misunderstand, thinking that Armstrong was calling for a vote. She explained that the purpose of such a resolution was just to pave the way to discussion. Typical of Armstrong's personality, she remarked: "Let us leave sentiment now and act upon the recommendation."

Just as before, Fannie Davis agreed and seconded the motion, proposing the roll of states to hear their sentiments. There was a general buzz in the hall as many sensed a tense atmosphere. The roll call was not alphabetical but occurred spontaneously. Armstrong spoke first: "Maryland heartily approves of an organization." (No surprise here!) And the states began responding. Mississippi and Virginia could not have a real voice since they were not free to vote. Lucina Telford of Florida had not been instructed one way or the other, so she responded, "I approve of the method by which the most can be done. Think not of prejudice, for when God is for us, who can be against us?"

Not surprisingly, there was not 100 percent agreement on every issue. A debate began as to whether it might be better to wait on the approval of the "brethren" in the states that were holding out. This suggestion was not well received by Annie Armstrong, among others, and she rose to her full height (quite impressive, at six feet tall), stating that she was compelled by her convictions to oppose any delay. She declared, "Is it our work, or not? Religious work has not always been advanced by a majority. Carey stood alone a long time." Some thought they needed to be careful, while others felt the time for action was now. Susan Tyler Pollard of Baltimore "calmed the waters," reminding the delegates that, "A whole year's thought has or should have been given to the consideration of this mighty subject, and you delegates have been asked to come prepared to decide. Is that 'undue haste?' "

A vote was taken as to whether or not to act immediately. The motion failed. Annie Armstrong saw an opportunity for compromise between the "right now" and the "let's wait" trains of thought. She proposed that they have an extra meeting at 10 A.M. on Monday, at which time all questions could be answered. In the meantime, she suggested they carry on with the excellent program the Virginia women had planned. Armstrong asked the chairman to appoint a committee, one from each state, to draft the constitution and report on Monday. She declared, "When the Duke of Wellington was asked what obligations Christians were under to send the gospel to Burma, he answered: 'What are your marching orders?'" The motion was successful, and at the end of Friday's program, Baptist women awaited that crucial gathering just two days later.

MAY 14, 1888

There could not be a woman in that meeting on Monday morning who did not realize that something important was taking place. Many of the women had attended the Saturday session of the Convention, sitting in the gallery, which was permitted. The women gleaned one overall impression from that Saturday: the Convention's feeling regarding women's work was, "Do as you please, only send us your money."

Monday morning, a determined group of women gathered in that hall, deeply conscious of the years and tears and prayers bringing them to this moment. Annie Whitfield presided again. Agnes Osborne read the minutes of their preceding session, and Martha Wilson (Mrs. Stainback) of Georgia asked that the two papers presented by Fanny Stout and Alice Armstrong be printed for distribution. There was unanimous agreement.

The moment had come. The air was fraught with expectancy as chairman Mattie McIntosh rose to give the committee's report. Deeply aware of the gravity of the moment, she called for prayer. McIntosh then rose again to call for a vote: "On roll call of delegates, each state will be asked to vote on the advisability of organizing a general committee. If the majority agree, we have a plan of action drawn up and a constitution ready to adopt." At this point, Virginia Hatcher asked that the plan of action and constitution first be read, and then proceed with a roll call.

The proposed constitution revealed that it had been well planned and constructed. It was largely the work of Annie and Alice Armstrong. In preparation of such an important document, several with special skills and expertise had been consulted. Surely God's grace and wisdom had guided this clear and well-structured plan. The preamble stated: "We, the women of the churches connected with the Southern Baptist Convention, desirous of stimulating the missionary spirit and the grace of giving among the women and children of the churches, and aiding in collecting funds for missionary purposes, to be disbursed by the Boards of the Southern Baptist Convention, and disclaiming all intention of independent action, organize and adopt the following."

The entire document was read, and things grew tense when Virginia Hatcher asked for permission to consult with the Virginia women present. Hatcher told the women that pastor friends were working to gain cooperation from other pastors and asked that they wait on voting. The women reluctantly agreed, realizing they would very likely soon be able to be a part of the new union.

And then came the roll call. Ten states gladly and solemnly voted to form a general committee. The first official members of what would come to be known as Woman's Missionary Union, auxiliary to SBC, were Arkansas, Florida, Georgia, Kentucky, Louisiana, Maryland, Missouri, South Carolina, Tennessee, and Texas. Thankfully, within a short time, Virginia, North Carolina, Alabama, and Mississippi were also able to apply for official membership.

Now the air was filled with a sense of relief and even a bit of euphoria. So much had been accomplished, but then, it had been so many years in the making. This brand-new organization had just approved a constitution. Now it needed officers. Applause filled the hall as the women quickly nominated and unanimously chose Martha E. McIntosh as president. Nearly overwhelmed, McIntosh responded: "I had felt that my official connection with the general work must cease with this meeting and that I should return to my loved state work with the feeling of an uncaged bird, but now I feel constrained to accept the position."

The choice of a corresponding secretary would be equally important. It was vital that a leader with skills in organizing and implementing plans be selected for the new union. Annie Armstrong was a young woman uniquely gifted and prepared to undertake such a responsibility. These two officers were destined to have a profound influence on the course of Woman's Missionary Union. The first recording secretary was Susan Tyler Pollard, a real pioneer in mission societies and a skilled writer. Also from Baltimore was Mrs. John F. Pullen, the first treasurer. It seemed fitting that Baltimore be established as headquarters. The missions reading room was there, as well as Annie Armstrong. It was deemed a logical choice for the new organization's office. Vice-presidents of the new union were made up of a representative from each constituting state.

With the possible exception of Annie Armstrong, the new officers likely had little idea of how to proceed. Everything had a sense of freshness and vitality. Their executive experience was minimal but there could be no uncertainty about their motives and fervor. Their passion was fulfilling the Great Commission that had brought them to this hour. Exciting days lay ahead for the infant auxiliary.

CHAPTER

We've a Story to Tell

"What are your marching orders?"
—ANNIE ARMSTRONG, 1888

ANNIE AND MATTIE AND COMPANY

MARCHING ORDERS INDEED! A new era was beginning on that significant May Monday in 1888, and Annie Armstrong and Mattie McIntosh were standing at the helm, no doubt feeling all sorts of mixed emotions. This new Union was boldly speaking for all Baptist women across the South, although it is likely that no more than 12 percent of Southern Baptist churches in 1888 had a woman's missionary society. But, had the women waited for a majority of churches to organize groups, and for the brethren's full agreement, they would be waiting still.

Emotions were running high. On that afternoon of organization, Annie Armstrong and Mattie McIntosh were commissioned to "wait upon the boards." This was a Union, desiring to be an auxiliary (note this key word), not just in name but also in actuality. For some time, Baptist women had been referring to themselves as the "Union," but officially, they were now the Executive Committee of Woman's Mission

Societies, Auxiliary to Southern Baptist Convention. Years later, Dr. W. O. Carver, known as the Convention's leading professor of missions, declared the idea of "auxiliary status" to be nothing short of the inspiration of the Holy Spirit. He asserted that their very freedom to think and devise means to promote missions allowed them to make progress.

The word *auxiliary* has never appeared more powerful than it has for Baptist women. History reveals that *auxiliary* status has been key to WMU's success for more than 100 years. It was taken literally by those women, for they sought definite guidance from the boards in forming their direction and pattern of work. At the same time, the Home Mission and Foreign Mission boards agreed to share equally all expenses for printing and postage and to pay for any special effort made for either board. Here were boards who believed in what the women were planning and were prepared to back them up.

The makeup of the women constituting the early leaders of Baptist women is not a look at a cross-section of American society. Among those 32 official delegates, at least half a dozen were the wives of prominent pastors. Additionally, daughters of staff members represented the Home Mission Board and Foreign Mission Board. Several came from wealthy homes; most were better educated than the vast majority of ninteenth-century women; one was a missionary, another was a former missionary, and others were married to prosperous professional men. This did not mean, however, that the organization ever intended to be exclusive. It was just the opposite—beginning with the avowed purpose of reaching out and including all women, regardless of background, wealth, or status. This fledging new union did not seek exclusivity but rather *inclusivity.* Here is a true minority—wishing to encompass the majority. That goal has never wavered.

Officially organizing didn't conclude business. Following the election of officers, a request from Dr. Tichenor, secretary of the Home Mission Board, was read, asking the women to raise $5,000 for a church building in Havana and the enlargement of the cemetery there. The Home Mission Board provided "Cuban Brick Cards" as a means of gathering money for the project. The delegates responded immediately to the idea, and all took cards home from the meeting. Annie Armstrong sent out more than 11,000 cards from her Baltimore office to the state central committees. Thus began a missions promotion, the first of thousands planned and successfully implemented by the Union. The women became famous for their skills in raising money for ministry.

BACK TO BALTIMORE

Number 10 East Fayette Street, Baltimore, Maryland, became a familiar address to thousands of Baptist women, children, and even some men. Maryland Baptists had established the Maryland Baptist Mission Rooms there in 1886. Annie Armstrong was chair of the committee in charge of those Mission Rooms, so it made sense to use this as the location of the women's auxiliary. Maryland's Woman's Mission to Mission office was there also. Women donated missionary biographies and other missions material and prepared a "curiosities" cabinet, holding interesting items from around the world. A unique piece of furniture in the room was the couch upon which Ann Judson had lain during her period of recuperation back in America in 1823.

Chapter 9

ANNIE, MATTIE, TUPPER, AND LOTTIE

Annie Armstrong and Mattie McIntosh went to work with a will, each feeling her way in a job with no precedent to serve as a guide. Turning 40 in 1888, McIntosh had the heavy responsibility of leading an untried organization along uncharted paths. She had long dreamed of being a foreign missionary, and for many years, this seemed impossible. Now she poured that passion and concern for the lost into this brand new union that shared her passion. Amazingly, that early wish for mission service eventually came to be in an unusual way. McIntosh gently, firmly, and with patient efficiency guided the Union those first four developing years. And one of her first projects was truly dear to her heart—China and its teeming millions.

This first project that McIntosh and Armstrong steered through to completion was the beginning of a tradition that has become a hallmark of Woman's Missionary Union and of the Southern Baptist denomination. One of Armstrong's first moves after the May meeting was to go to Richmond to "wait on Dr. Tupper for direction in foreign mission work." Tupper began sharing with her letters he had received from Lottie Moon. Moon was a tireless and keenly effective correspondent, knowing how to express herself with clarity and persuasion. Tupper had told her, "You have the power of making people see what you think." It was this talent that galvanized a denomination through the medium of WMU. When Armstrong returned to her office, she received a letter from Tupper, enclosing Lottie's letter of September 15, 1887, a letter which greatly influenced the course of Baptist missions history. It was published in the *Foreign Mission Journal* in December of that year.

Dr. Tupper referred to Lottie Moon's proposition that several woman workers be sent to the Pingtu region, stressing the importance of work among the women. Tupper wrote, "It has occurred to me that your Executive Committee might give special attention to this matter, until it should be accomplished. What do you think? Here is a clear work for Woman's Mission to Woman. The only hope of China is through the women. Might this not be successfully pressed?" He added a postscript: "This letter is suggested by your kind offer to present to the women of the country some special work of our Board." This was, of course, that famous letter so often quoted, where Moon pleads, "Need it be said why the week before Christmas is chosen? Is not the festive season, when families and friends exchange gifts in memory of The Gift laid on the altar of the world . . . the most appropriate time to consecrate a portion from abounding riches and scant poverty to send forth the good tidings of great joy into all the earth?" Historian Catherine Allen declares that: "Probably no other missionary had the imagination to propose or the magnetism to inspire what Lottie Moon brought to pass in 1888. She had been warning that Southern Baptists would continue existing on a hand-to-mouth basis unless the women were organized."

Lottie Moon and her pen were a force that unified the missionary spirit of Southern Baptist women, and over a period of years, involved the entire denomination in missions giving. This type of promotion was one of those areas in which Annie Armstrong excelled. She first brought Dr. Tupper's suggestion to the meeting of the newly formed Executive Committee in October 1888. The women felt it was an urgent need, one that Baptist women embraced. The Committee decided to set the first goal at $2,000, quite a substantial figure for the 1800s. It would take $2,000 to send two women to Pingtu. The committee agreed that the undergirding force must be prayer. Their plan was to have an ingathering of the Christmas offering on Wednesday during the January World's Week of Prayer.

Mattie McIntosh's first step was to send out a circular letter to all the presidents and corresponding secretaries of missionary societies. Considering nineteenth century communications, this was an enormous task. Meanwhile, Armstrong prepared the Wednesday program and offering envelopes. From the Baltimore office, packages of literature and envelopes urging the women to pray and give were mailed. McIntosh and Armstrong wrote literally thousands of letters. The first Christmas offering envelopes were printed and sent all over the South, and the response was extraordinary. The final figure was $3,315.26, enough to send three missionaries. And those missionaries were ready: Mary Ann Thornton from Alabama, Fannie Knight of North Carolina, and Laura Barton of Texas.

Success! Dr. Tupper's confidence in the heart and zeal of Baptist women was not misplaced. And the following year, Moon wrote to Armstrong, "I write to thank the Executive Committee for the hearty response they have made to my appeal for more workers for Pingtu. I urge that the new missionaries be sent out immediately." She concluded her letter, "If 'the joy of the Lord' be their strength, the blessedness of the work will more than compensate for its hardships. Let them come 'rejoicing to suffer' for the sake of that Lord and Master who freely gave his life for them. Hoping soon to welcome them to the field, Yours for the work, L. Moon." It would be close to impossible to overestimate the influence of the life and words of Lottie Moon on the founding and impact of Woman's Missionary Union.

MORE STATES JOIN THE ORIGINAL TEN

Mississippi women had scarcely had time to get home and unpack following that May meeting before they sent a telegram to the new national office. The Mississippi Convention Board had met, and the women telegraphed: "Mississippi Baptist women have wheeled into line by unanimous vote." They were state number 11. Then, in March 1889, Virginia voted to enter the Union. Thus, within the first year, 12 states officially belonged to the new Union. Not too long passed before there were two more. On April 11, 1890, Alabama came in, stating: "Alabama laments the time that has been lost, but setting her face toward the brightening future, she would 'press forward,' animated and inspired by the example of her sister states." North Carolina also "found this year to be the fitting time to come forward and unite her efforts with those of her Southern sisters." They were recognized for the first time at the Birmingham, Alabama, annual meeting.

OUR REASON FOR BEING

Why a missionary union? This was a topic often asked of women about their societies, and as they came to organize into a national body, they spent an increasing amount of time considering just what their objectives were. Two purposes seemed most obvious, and were frequently stated in regard to the reason for having a Union; collecting funds and stimulating the missionary spirit, but not necessarily in that order. The early years had found the women too busy to spend much time trying to articulate a purpose, and "purpose statement" was a term not yet coined. Many more purposes became defined through the years, but those first two statements of intent have been paramount through the years and honed to a fine art. Even before this first meeting adjourned, the Union had undertaken a project to assist the Home Mission Board. Before the year was out, the first Christmas offering for foreign missions was launched. It exceeded their wildest expectations. These missions offerings have become a way of proving that old ungrammatical adage: If it ain't broke, don't fix it.

The intent of "stimulating the missionary spirit" is a bit more difficult to classify and articulate. Those intrepid early women emphasized involving women in serving and acting. Annie Armstrong was the perfect person to encourage mission spirit through literature. The publishing business "spread the spirit," although the earliest leaders didn't see themselves as either a devotional or an educational organization. However, they evolved into both. The great bulk of their emphasis those formative years was on projects that met needs, like packing missionary boxes and inspiring participation in projects designed to fund a particular cause.

Another by-product of Woman's Missionary Union probably never realized by those early pioneer Union women was learning to lead. Women in nineteenth and twentieth century Baptist churches in America sensed or acknowledged the restrictions placed on them by culture and denomination, but in looking at the status of women in "heathen" lands or at their non-Christian neighbors, they were grateful for the privileges they did enjoy, even if limited in number and scope. From the earliest beginnings, these women never sought a visible affiliation with any organization or cause dealing with women's rights. Instead, they were working and praying for the rights of people everywhere to learn of God's love, especially women who needed the freedom available to them through faith in God.

The women of missionary societies throughout the South looked forward to their first annual meeting as a recognized auxiliary of the Southern Baptist Convention. Those who were able would be going to Memphis, Tennessee, to join Mattie McIntosh, Annie Armstrong, and the Executive Committee to plan the business of missions promotion for the years to come. They had embarked on an exciting venture.

CHAPTER

O God to Us May Grace be Giv'n

"God demands not success but effort, leaving the results to Him."
—Eliza Broadus, 1889

MEETING IN MEMPHIS 1889

ONCE MORE IT was May, and time for Baptist women to gather. At the first meeting of the Executive Committee the previous June, Mattie McIntosh had led the committee to select a motto. Their first choice was "Go Forward," and it has stood the test of time. It is used today as the Girls in Action motto. There was no official watchword, but years later, Fannie Heck referred to "We are laborers together with God" (1 Cor. 3:9) as a watchword selected long before.

MATTIE REPORTS

Mattie McIntosh was an optimistic woman, able to find the positive in situations that were frequently challenging, sometimes even daunting. Neither Mattie McIntosh nor Annie Armstrong was inclined to be intimidated by the unknown nor cowed by adversity. McIntosh's first address to those gathered in the city's First Presbyterian Church gave a buoyant report on the successes of this first year, assuring them that "the future will open up before you as rich in fruit as it now is in promise." McIntosh explained how the mission boards were serving as "counselors of your Executive Committee," She regarded the board's cooperation and assistance as vital, as this cemented the auxiliary's relationships with the Convention.

McIntosh referred to the unstinting prayers of member women as having been their "greatest comfort during this year of untried work." After all, they had nothing by which to measure progress. She indicated that her greatest regret was the lack of having made progress in promoting children's work in the churches, because so much of their energy had been channeled into "work to do and things to learn." Emphasizing children's work was going to be one of their first recommendations.

Armstrong gave what would in future years be known as the Executive Director's Report. She referred to her presentation as a "grateful record of fulfilled promise." Armstrong first looked back upon the actions taken the previous year in choosing a president and a corresponding secretary, plus a vice-president from each participating state, as the beginning of effectiveness in bringing about God's kingdom in answer to His commission. The first special offering endeavors, the brick cards for Cuba and the Christmas offering for China, were still in the process of being collected, Armstrong reported. She noted the two boards consented to allow the women to place monthly reports in the *Foreign Mission Journal* and *Our Home Fields*. The *Baptist Basket* also carried the monthly reports.

Armstrong was delighted to report the success of several pieces of material that the auxiliary had published. The women now had their "Sketch and Constitution of Woman's Missionary Societies" in printed form. Those two very effective papers presented at the organizational meeting had been published and disseminated across the Convention: Fanny Stout's "Shall Baptist Women Organize for Mission Work?" and Alice Armstrong's "Woman's Special Obligation to Spread the Gospel."

Annie Armstrong was a firm believer in the power of the press, and her experience with publications was a boon to the new auxiliary. "Chips from Many Workshops" was one of the first "how-to" leaflets ever prepared by and for women. It outlined a sample constitution for women wanting to organize and promote giving, and it spelled out methods for raising money. Armstrong was pleased to report that Christmas offering envelopes and a sample program had been mailed for use by each society. The sample program outlined a suggested meeting and included portions of a letter from Lottie Moon

There was also a beginning of help for those wanting to organize children's groups; Armstrong reported the printing of a pamphlet similar to "Chips" but titled "Garnered Gleanings." It was aimed at young people's bands. Armstrong reported that her office had sent out more than 600 letters and noted giving had risen significantly.

Annie Armstrong rejoiced in announcing that there were now 12 states officially part of the auxiliary. They represented 600,000 women. However, Armstrong reported that the $30,773.69 given to foreign and home missions averaged out to only about 5 cents per woman, and she challenged them to greater giving. Armstrong concluded by affirming, "this first, initial, experimental year has passed. It is not a failure . . . the Lord has been with us and blessed us. . . . Let our motto 'Forward,' be blazoned upon our banners."[4]

Jennie Hatcher of Virginia brought a report from a committee of ten, outlining suggestions for developing children's organizations and emphasizing the importance of missions education.

Another report, presented by Missouri's Mrs. Eliza Hyde, urged each state to use the annual prayer card and each associational and district committee to undergird all the work and aid in establishing new societies. Ways to raise funds and ways not to raise them were included. Bazaars and fund-raisers were discouraged. Rather, country women were urged to have rows of potatoes or beans or a portion of eggs or butter designated for missions giving. Those in towns were encouraged to put aside money by foregoing entertainments or by employing creative ways of accumulating discretionary money.

The conclusion of one year of Southwide organization for Baptist women revealed their success at raising funds for missions—a skill they have honed to perfection for more than 100 years. The result of the first Christmas offering was enough for *three* new missionaries to go out. WMU never looked back, and from that first venture grew what came to be the world's largest single annual offering for missions.

From its earliest days, WMU sought to expand, to involve as many women and children as possible in the cause of missions. Mary Gambrell of Texas put it succinctly when she stated, "The most important words in the Bible are *come* and *go*." The organization has always revolved around prayer and missionaries. The two are inseparable, for they are interdependent. Nothing has so motivated women as the need to train, enlist, and pray for their missionaries.

Annie Armstrong was clear in her belief that every Christian must be a missionary. If one wasn't called to go, one sent out and supported those who were. Those early prayer cards give evidence of the value placed on prayer. Prayer was actually one of the few areas where the earliest, timid societies of women felt safe from criticism. In that first 1888 constitution, the women made one amendment. Martha Wilson of Georgia moved that Executive Committee meetings always open and close with prayer. And so it has been from that day on. Martha Wilson would be delighted to see the offerings for foreign and home missions revolving as they do around weeks of prayer.

The missionary calling has also been a major focus of WMU, central to the organization's strategy. The organization avowed God does the calling, not people. Women saw no reason to believe that God would exclude them from His call. If God called a husband, the wife needed a similar call. WMU celebrated women missionaries as homemakers and also in whatever other capacity God directed, be it doctor, teacher, or evangelist.

FORT WORTH — 1890

Annie Armstrong and Mattie McIntosh felt a bit more at home in their roles and gave their annual reports with confidence when the women gathered in Fort Worth. More than 43,000 Christmas offering envelopes had been requested. Giving was something women did superlatively. Armstrong never failed to encourage the women to do more, and in her report she asked: "Do we appreciate in this golden age of opportunity that not to advance is to retrograde. . . . Un-entered doors do not remain forever open." During this time, Alabama became the 13th state to join the Union. The Fort Worth meeting had another first as Mrs. C. Robb, a Choctaw Indian, addressed the gathering.

While the women developed a network through the committees and annual meetings, they grew more familiar with the work of the state organizations. As early as 1881, Mississippi had employed Mattie Nelson to work in New Orleans, and Texas had a team of a half-dozen Bible women who worked with Hispanics. These women were also WMU officers. Mina Everett is probably the best known of those. She took collections and spoke in audiences where men were sometimes present. This intrepid woman was the first Baptist missionary to Mexicans and at the same time was corresponding secretary of Texas WMU.

BOXES AND BARRELS

Discretionary cash was not a ready commodity of Baptist women in 1890, but goods were another matter. Practically every woman was skilled at sewing and crafts, and "box work" took off with great success. The boxes were often called missionary barrels. Here was "hands-on" missions, women able to share the fruit of their own labor with missionaries in frontier areas who had few conveniences and very little money. Annie Armstrong well remembered her first experience with sewing suits for the Indian students in Oklahoma. That was where her lifelong loving bond with

Indians of many tribes had begun. The office in Baltimore was "box central," as missionaries sent lists of their needs, and societies in various states then got assignments of "their" missionaries.

The ladies placed a dollar value on their goods sent and these were counted as part of their contributions. All sorts of needed staples, plus little things dear to the heart of a lonely woman on the frontier or of a little child with no neighbors, were tucked into the missionary boxes. Those boxes, filled with love, became a source of much-needed help to struggling pioneer missionaries. The women packing the boxes could picture in their minds the response of that family as they opened up their treasure box. These boxes made missions and missionaries personal to women as they would tuck a piece of their hearts into a corner of their box. In 1890, more than 5,000 boxes had been mailed.

The Fort Worth meeting was significant in yet another way. The Executive Committee of Woman's Mission Societies officially became Woman's Missionary Union, auxiliary to Southern Baptist Convention (WMU). And, in a leap of faith, WMU agreed to raise enough money to support all women foreign missionaries. Unknown to those women, a time would come when the women's support even exceeded that lofty ambition, even so far as to literally save the boards from bankruptcy. Each step of faith was leading to yet greater service and ministry.

CHAPTER

To Follow in Their Train

"The one who leads must show she is willing to do more than she asks of anyone else."
—ANNIE ARMSTRONG, 1894

BIRMINGHAM, ALABAMA

AT THE ANNUAL meeting in Birmingham in 1891, North Carolina became the 14th state to join the women's union. Also during the meeting, the women began planning for the Carey Centennial. The SBC asked WMU to help raise funds. The women agreed and exceeded their set goal, but the SBC fell far short of theirs. After the women surpassed their goal, Fannie Heck paraphrased William Carey's famous lines to state: "We have attempted great things for God. Now we are called as earnestly to fulfill the other half. Expect great things *from* God."

LOTTIE

The Birmingham meeting vibrated with excitement when the women realized that Lottie Moon was in their midst—this little woman who had waited at her missions post until reinforcements had arrived. Lottie Moon symbolized for Southern Baptists the meaning of commitment and sacrifice. Fannie Heck had the privilege of introducing her. As Moon spoke, the women sat breathlessly still, absorbing every word. The appearance on the platform of Lottie Moon—less than five feet tall—standing next to the regal six-foot-tall Annie Armstrong would have been riveting.

At this meeting, WMU also incorporated principles of working both "with and for" African Americans. Forward-thinking Armstrong was a leader in this endeavor and set the pace for a denomination woefully lagging in such ministries. Armstrong and Maryland women had already begun efforts with African American Baptists in Baltimore. Armstrong believed there was great emerging leadership potential among African American women; it needed to be encouraged and supported. Later minutes of the National Baptist Women's Convention spoke of "words of good cheer and encouragement" from Armstrong as she met with them, and how she succeeded in waking interest in this work "among her sisterhood. . . . We praise God for these friends, who have so kindly helped us."

FANNIE E. S. HECK

The year 1892 was a time of transition as Mattie McIntosh, beloved and highly respected, refused to be considered for re-election. The next national president went on to serve longer than anyone in the history of WMU. Only 29 years old when elected in 1892, Fannie E. S. Heck has often been called "the most beautiful Southern Baptist woman." WMU leader Ethlene Boone Cox later said of Fannie Heck: "Hers is the predominant personality in the life of Woman's Missionary Union."

Alma Hunt, one of the most dominant personalities in WMU in the century to follow, said of Heck: "The fine features, luminous brown eyes, tall, erect figure, always perfectly groomed, were outward graces of small significance compared to the treasures of her heart and mind." Writer, speaker, creative thinker, editor, leader—Heck's gifts were abundant, growing and mellowing through the years.

NASHVILLE, TENNESSEE

Meeting in Nashville in 1893, Fannie Heck presided for the first time. In her captivating address, one of her most famous lines emerged: "Give us the children of today for missions and we take the world for Christ tomorrow." Heck closed with this reminder: "He sees the end from the *beginning,* we one step behind and none before. Honest work for God knows no failure." This meeting must have been a high spiritual moment because for the last time, Lottie Moon was present and led in prayer following Heck's message.

DALLAS, TEXAS

It was back to Texas in 1894 for the women of WMU. Fannie Heck's address was read in her absence. Heck had been devastated when her father died, and being quite ill herself, she refused to be re-elected. The women sadly acquiesced to her request. In Heck's place, the delegates chose a woman of lofty credentials. Abby Manly Gwathmey was the daughter of Basil Manly, Sr., outstanding Baptist statesman and educator. Her doctor husband had long been a mission supporter and was for many years prior to his death the recording secretary of the Foreign Mission Board. The Civil War decimated the family fortune, and now the widowed Gwathmey was raising nine children while working with the *Foreign Mission Journal*. She was so convinced of the importance of WMU that she had insisted her twin daughters be observers at that first historic meeting in Richmond. Annie Armstrong herself had labeled Gwathmey "as decidedly the most able state officer connected with WMU."

At this meeting, WMU worked on ways to help pay off the Foreign Mission Board's debt. WMU hated debt. As one leader put it: "Like all other women, I hate the three D's—Debt, Dirt, and the Devil." Dr. R. J. Willingham, secretary of the FMB, pleaded with the women to raise $5,000 toward the Board's debt. Immediately, Armstrong issued a promotional leaflet, and the states divided up the goal—and of course, reached it.

Excitement stirred through the gathering as Agnes Osborne conducted a model Sunbeam band demonstration meeting. Missionaries Jane Lowry Graves, wife of the first Baptist doctor to China, and Dr. R. T. Bryan, pioneer missionary to Shanghai, spoke on missions in China.

WASHINGTON, D.C.

In 1895, the nation's capital served as host of the WMU annual meeting. By the following year, the Baptist women of D.C. had a state organization. Abby Gwathmey had such pressing home circumstances she could only serve as president one year. This year saw the first Week of Self-Denial and Thank Offering for Home Missions (now known as the Annie Armstrong Easter Offering). Armstrong commented about WMU as a whole, saying: "This child is no weakling!" She concluded her report, "Go Forward is the motto on our standard, and let us never allow it to trail in the dust."

TRAINING WOMEN FOR MISSIONS

The women of Texas wanted a new item added to the agenda, but Armstrong stated: "It is not time yet to discuss the subject." It was destined to become a divisive but important part of WMU: the establishment of a woman's training school to equip women for service. The highly respected Mina Everett was herself a returned foreign missionary. Six years earlier, she and E. Z. Simmons, missionary to China, had talked about the need for such training for women. Upon hearing of the situation, the president of the Baptist Woman's Missionary Training School in Philadelphia invited WMU to use their school until they had one of their own. In spite of Armstrong's refusal to bring the matter up at the 1895 meeting, Texas WMU sent the same request to the Executive Committee meeting and got the same refusal. The issue remained untouched for several years. The training school finally became a successful reality, but not without a great deal of angst and some hurt feelings.

PRAYER

Prayer has always been an important part of WMU, but under Heck's leadership, it grew even more as an integral role in all the women did. WMU leaders modeled for Baptist women how to make prayer a vital part of daily life. As Fannie Heck returned to leadership, she emphasized the role of prayer. Heck had just gone through deep bereavement and keenly felt her dependency on prayer. She wrote her mother, "Do you ever pray for me as though I were in very great need of help? You would if you knew my needs. . . . I am just now in great need of help that God alone can give."

CHATTANOOGA, TENNESSEE

WMU took an important official step in 1896, when, at the request of the Foreign Mission Board (FMB), it became responsible for Sunbeams. Cousin George had relinquished his role of leadership, and the women stepped in. They loved the task, and Sunbeam Band work flourished.

In Armstrong's annual report, she drew attention to the women's remarkable achievements in giving and noted that Southern Seminary's president, Dr. W. H. Whitsitt, had studied WMU's history and was prepared to advocate its methods.

WILMINGTON, NORTH CAROLINA

During 1897, the WMU headquarters moved to 304 North Howard Street, Baltimore. The year's annual meeting of WMU was ostensibly a calm one, but it marked the beginning of a sharp division in the opinions and interpretations held by the two chief leaders, Annie Armstrong and Fannie Heck. It was really just one of a number of differing views held by the two. The Sunday School Board asked the women to cooperate in enlarging the Bible fund. There was much discussion on the floor of the meeting. Heck both privately and publicly opposed the recommendation, feeling that it distracted from the giving to the mission boards. Armstrong warmly advocated approving the recommendation. The final motion asked only for the cooperation of WMU. The disagreements between the two came to a crux during the year.

NORFOLK, VIRGINIA

When the women gathered in Norfolk in 1898, the delegates made an important move concerning missions promotion by associations. Several states had WMU organizations using the associational approach and finding it successful. Thus in 1898, WMU recommended a plan for each state to have associational vice-presidents. Each would be in charge of the general promotion of the work in her area's churches.

There continued to be underlying tensions between the two leaders, but none of this was made public at the Norfolk meeting. No doubt both women realized that soon something would have to be resolved.

THE ANNIE — FANNIE FEUD

Armstrong and Heck's first years of working together in leadership were very smooth, with each woman recognizing and affirming the talents of the other. However, even in those beginning years of shared leadership, their basic view of their respective roles differed—a problem indeed. Armstrong's interpretation of the constitution held that the organization's president was essentially to be a gracious figurehead who would preside at the annual meetings. Not so in Heck's view. She read the constitution as stating that the president would be a hands-on partner in ministry, actively involved in the various aspects of WMU leadership. While the two women shared the same ultimate goals, their ideas about how to *reach* those goals diverged widely. Both were capable, determined, courageous, and stubborn. Their personalities were very different, their ultimate goal the same—service.

Later in 1898, Armstrong and Heck agreed to meet with the leaders of the Foreign and Home Mission Boards to discuss the situation. The men were naturally concerned about how the feud would affect their bottom line—funds. Part of their solution involved Heck's determination not to be re-elected the following year. Armstrong had consistently left Heck out of the loop in business and decision-making matters. Heck at one point referred to her job as "the office I am now so unfortunate as to occupy." She completed her 1898-1899 term and then stepped down, not returning to office until 1906, the year Armstrong resigned as corresponding secretary. It is a tribute to the depth of character of both women, and to their deep love for WMU, that they never aired their dirty linen in public, nor let it taint their leadership.

LOUISVILLE, KENTUCKY

At the annual meeting in 1899, WMU recommended that the states adopt a graded system of missionary education, working towards the goal of having an organization for each age level, beginning with "Baby Bands." Additionally this year, Fannie Heck refused to allow herself to be re-elected. The women chose Jessie Davis Stakely, a young woman of many talents and deep convictions. Her husband was pastor of Washington D.C.'s influential First Baptist Church, and the D.C. women had entered into organizing WMU work soon after Stakely's arrival on the scene.

HOT SPRINGS, ARKANSAS

WMU went west in 1900, meeting in Hot Springs, Arkansas. The SBC had initiated a "New Century Movement" to raise money for the mission boards. For the first time, the SBC spoke directly to WMU, asking the organization to "induce every church to take regular collections for missions and every member to make regular contributions." Only an estimated one-tenth of the membership gave anything to missions. The New Century committee had decided that the best way to get regular contributions was to establish WMU organizations in every church. The women of WMU agreed to help pastors conduct New Century Meetings (another name for missions rallies). Armstrong herself compiled the first list of churches and church clerks, including addresses—a gargantuan task. She sent more than 5,000 letters to churches, describing the movement and detailing how to organize missionary societies. More than 2,000 pastors responded, and the end result was 616 new women's societies and a growth in WMU contributions of nearly 30 percent. Also at this meeting, Armstrong suggested WMU raise funds for the Church Building Loan Fund, started by the HMB in 1883.

SALARIES AND TRAVEL

Annie Armstrong had steadfastly refused a salary. When she became secretary, the family's income was substantial enough to make this a reasonable decision. However, her family circumstances became more strained, so WMU tried again to get Armstrong to accept a salary. She again refused. However, she reluctantly agreed to accept funds for travel expenses. In fall 1900, Armstrong made the long train trek to Oklahoma and Indian Territory. Home missions had ever been dear to her heart, and the most special corner of that generous heart was reserved for her beloved Indian work. It was the first of numerous trips.

In the span of just one century, the women of Woman's Missionary Union had gone from the seed of an idea in the heart of a paralytic in Boston to beautiful bloom as a thriving, enthusiastic army of committed women who determined in this new century to meet with eyes of faith the challenge of the Great Commission.

CHAPTER

We've a Message to Give

"If you have succeeded without suffering, it is because those who have gone before you have suffered without succeeding."
— Edward Judson, 1914, referring to his father Adoniram Judson

ANNIE'S AWESOME ACCOMPLISHMENTS

THE NEW CENTURY, and decade, would mark the final years of Annie Armstrong's leadership. The fledgling organization had grown exponentially in those first years. The strength and depth of the foundations already laid were in great part attributable to Armstrong's leadership. It is also true that some of the problems she had with new challenges and situations that arose were due to her way of handling conflict.

In 1900, Armstrong brought to reality the Church Building Loan Fund. The Home Mission Board had wanted the fund, but for years the idea lay basically untouched. Armstrong began enlisting people to make an all-out drive to raise $20,000 as a memorial to Dr. Tichenor, the HMB secretary who had recently died. With the exception of about $2,000, all the money for the fund that first decade was from women. Seventy-five churches were assisted through the fund. Likewise, WMU women in 1901 launched the Annuity Plan, another brainchild of Armstrong. Through Armstrong's efforts, WMU was able to establish this funding plan for all three Convention boards. Armstrong never did anything by halves.

Armstrong repeatedly stressed the role of giving as an indicator of the depth of a person's spiritual commitment. Some had criticized her because she thought the call to stewardship was to all believers, even (the) nearly destitute frontier women. In answer, Armstrong declared: "The widow was called on to feed the prophet when she had only a little meal in the barrel and a little oil in the cruse. If we always took out the Lord's portion first, do you not think our experience would be the same? God would look after us." WMU in this first year of the new century had raised over $88,000.

Armstrong's travels that year totaled more than 10,000 miles. She had visited every Southern Baptist state except for two. Especially dear to her heart was a trip to Oklahoma Indian territory. Work among the Indian tribes was conducted by both the New York Home Mission Board and the SBC Home Mission Board. The women in Indian territory were free to choose whichever group they preferred. Missionary Mrs. W. H. Kuykendall, president of the WMU affiliate, was speaking that evening when Armstrong was there. She asked how many of those attending had been able to come because of the help of WMU. More than 20 men and their wives stood. They were dressed in clothes from the missionary barrels.

It was evident that WMU was one of the few places where women were the leaders and where nineteenth- and early twentieth-century Baptist women could gain experience as leaders. At the 1901 Annual Meeting in New Orleans, vice-presidents from each state were made members of the Executive Committee, and for the first time WMU delegates were given badges and seats on the main floor of the Convention. (Two special visitors joined the delegates in New Orleans—Mrs. Kuykendall, missionary in Indian Territory, and Willie Kelly, beloved missionary from Alabama, who was home on furlough from Shanghai, China. (Kelly didn't go to China until age 31 but remained a missionary for 44 years; her Chinese language skills were legendary.) President Jessie Stakely's address was titled "The Genesis of Missions," and she challenged the women with her concept of the prerequisite to missionary progress: "Let us advance on our knees."

In early 1897, the National Baptist Convention secretary Dr. L. G. Jordan brought his assistant, Nannie Helen Burroughs, to meet Armstrong. Jordan recognized in Armstrong the conduit to Southern Baptist funds and cooperation. At the same time, Armstrong realized that this man was the key to developing a woman's auxiliary in the NBC. Armstrong and Burroughs began visiting African American churches to organize women's societies, and Armstrong began writing women's pages for their journals. Armstrong had deep respect for African American leaders, men and women alike. It was like a personal victory to Armstrong when the Woman's Convention, auxiliary to the National Baptist Convention organized in 1900. In 1901 and again in 1905, Armstrong attended the National Baptist women's meetings. In 1905, she addressed the women there, but only after the men left. In her view, it was important that she speak to women only.

The 1902 WMU Annual Meeting was in Asheville, North Carolina, and Jessie Stakely was beginning her final year as president. She challenged the delegates to recall always: "Christ's work is best known by the character of its workers." Stakely and Armstrong reported on two projects they had taken to the Home Mission Board. They laid out a strong case for female missionaries in the mines of Oklahoma and for African American women to work with the brand new National Baptist Convention. Only after state WMU organizations and private individuals agreed to give the money for such missionaries was this project approved. Today, such a project sounds like a given—but in 1902, supporting minorities in their ministries was new territory. Women were working in Cuba and in Indian territory, and Maryland women had employed Marie Buhlmaier, a German immigrant, to work with immigrants. Buhlmaier was a popular, groundbreaking woman who worked with grace and skill. All of these women were supported by funds from the women of WMU. Again this year, Dr. Willingham of the FMB asked WMU to provide the $45,000 needed to support the women missionaries on all fields.

A different issue loomed large in the years ahead. Training women for missions had been discussed by missionaries and WMU members in several states, but never had the convention-wide organization addressed the question. It became a major obstacle for Armstrong and proved to be one of the big factors in her decision to retire. Many Baptist women were realizing the need for women to be trained for missions, and thus far, Armstrong had put off having an open forum.

E. Z. Simmons, furloughing from China, took every opportunity to support the idea of training women. He made the point, "When women come to China, they readily learn the language, but they do not know how to teach the Bible, for they do not know it themselves. There should be a school for training women." Leading Baptist educators approved the idea, as did many women. Simmons felt that Southern Seminary would be logical since there were classes already in place. The seminary would need to give credit, and WMU could provide and staff a home for the single women and offer classes specifically geared to women's needs.

Armstrong appeared to consider the idea and wrote agency heads to ask their opinions. That is when she discovered that all these men had presumed the willingness of WMU to cooperate. She was unhappy that she had not been consulted; nor did she want WMU to handle such a contentious issue. It didn't help that the press reported about a women's school in Louisville in order to help male students find wives to go with them to the field. At the 1900 annual meeting, Armstrong had been able to keep the issue from being discussed, but she couldn't do that forever.

Texas women were insistent about having a school, and in 1902, they recruited Annie Jenkins, a young woman from a prominent Baptist family, to head it up. She prepared a paper that her sister, Josephine Jenkins Truett (Mrs. George W.), read at the 1903 annual meeting in Savannah, Georgia. The name of George W. Truett was known around the world, so this was support of the highest kind. Lillie Barker, the new Southwide WMU president, appointed a committee to work with the SBC to study the issue. Meanwhile, Armstrong visited existing training schools in New York, Washington, Philadelphia, and Kansas City. It appeared that she was learning how to operate a women's school, but instead she was absolutely opposed. It would be this issue more than any other question that would dog Annie Armstrong and eventually lead to her retirement at age 56.

Jessie Stakely was not at the 1903 meeting in Savannah but was at home in Montgomery, Alabama, giving birth to her fifth child. The women elected Lillie Easterby Barker of Virginia, the first former missionary to serve in this position. The issue of a training school for women proved to be quite controversial. It actually led to Barker's resignation a few years later. Barker proved to be a highly intelligent and committed leader. WMU was 15 years old now, and women were comfortable presiding, praying, giving reports, and speaking. So leadership training became a by-product of WMU.

The first officers of WMU did not receive salaries. Some considered accepting a salary as inappropriate for a woman. Some may have felt that working with no pay allowed them a bit of moral leverage over the salaried officers of the missions boards. The women of WMU wanted to pay Armstrong, but she had always refused. Armstrong was strong-willed yet quite sensitive, making for occasional fireworks. She was also very upfront, once admitting: "I know I am peculiarly sensitive to criticism, and I have felt that as I was not a salaried officer I was, in a measure, independent. All of this must be changed if I take this money." However, at this 1903 Savannah meeting, the Union voted a salary for the office. Armstrong still refused to accept the money. Barker and the other women respected her decision and did not force the issue.

The 1904 meeting in Nashville was meaningful time for both WMU and African American Baptist women who attended. Shirley Layten, president of National Baptist Women, spoke. The delegates were invited to attend an assembly of African American women in a local church, where both groups encouraged one another and "Tears flowed freely from the eyes of many white and colored women and many hearty amens were heard."

That same year, the Baptist World Alliance (BWA) held its first meeting in London, although no WMU officers were able to make the trip. The only American woman taking a prominent role in the meeting was Nannie Helen Burroughs, the remarkable woman Armstrong had been mentoring. Burroughs went on to lead National Baptist women for nearly half a century.

Armstrong made a surprise announcement at the 1904 meeting; a woman had made a $10,000 gift for the establishment of a home for the children of missionaries needing to study in America. The generous donation came about because of a visit Armstrong had made to a woman who expressed interest in helping with special needs. The home was to be named "Margaret" in honor of the donor's grandmother, mother, and daughter.

The matter on the minds of most leaders in 1904, however, was the question of a women's training school. Opinions varied widely, but more and more felt that such a school was both needed and highly desirable. Armstrong was not of this majority opinion. One of her reasons must have been tied to strong feelings about the role of women, and the issue of women speaking in front of men. It didn't help that many of the critics kept referring to such a school as a "marriage bureau." Armstrong found this insulting. In October, two events occurred nearly simultaneously on opposite sides of the country. On October 3, Texas women opened their own school with the leadership of outstanding Texas Baptists.

And on October 31, Maryland Baptist Union Association voted to organize a school in Baltimore, where nine students were accepted. Armstrong opposed these decisions.

Meanwhile in Louisville, Eliza Broadus, one of the most respected of all leaders, had previously appeared to oppose a training school. However, now she was heading a movement to establish a home for women attending Southern Seminary. In the summer, leading women formed a committee and set to work, with a representative from each of Louisville's 19 churches. Joining Broadus, Anna Eager provided strong leadership. Eager, Alabama's highly capable vice-president for seven years, had recently moved to Louisville. Her steady sense of determination inspired the rest of the women when the going was rough. It was largely through her influence that the Union came to adopt the idea. Eager and Armstrong were at the opposite extremes in their views about such a move.

Still not sponsored by Southwide WMU but rather by the Louisville local committee, the home for women seminarians in Louisville opened on Thanksgiving Day 1904 with four students. Three of the four became foreign missionaries. When news of the home reached Baltimore, the result was described by one historian as an explosion. Olive Eager, sister-in-law of Anna Eager, was the presiding officer of the local executive committee. The negative sentiment in Baltimore was so strong that Olive resigned. As president, Lillie Barker told the five state vice-presidents who were pressuring the committee to support the school that she would not put the matter on the agenda for the upcoming meeting in Kansas City. If they wanted to, they could bring it up from the floor. That is precisely what they did.

Inevitably, the 1905 annual meeting was unusually tense. Feelings ran high about the training school, and very few attendees were neutral. Of course, the most contentious part of the meeting revolved around the training school issue. Armstrong grew angry, and because of her opposition, the vote to adopt the home for the training school in Louisville failed 25 to 22. This was followed by a resolution calling for individual states to support the school if they wished. The resolution passed. Soon the Louisville committee leased a large old house and began preparations. Annie Armstrong did not remain silent, arguing that the seminary permitting women in its homiletics class was unscriptural, since they would be teaching women to be preachers. The issue hung in the air, with tensions all but tangible. The question needed a resolution, and that resolution was not long in coming.

CHAPTER

We've a Savior to Show

"Enlarge the place of thy tent — lengthen thy cords and strengthen thy stakes."
— ISAIAH 54:2

THE END OF THE "ANNIE ERA"

ANNIE ARMSTRONG HAD wanted to resign in 1905, but for the sake of the Union, both she and president Lillie Barker had agreed to serve one more year. In her heart, Armstrong realized that she had lost in the struggle over a training school. The crisis did not abate, and local Executive Committee members declined renomination. Letters flew back and forth between states, the women of Louisville, and seminary leaders. Armstrong stated, "It is a fearful thing to be misunderstood." Letters to WMU from the seminary came from such men of influence as W. O. Carver and the president of Southern Seminary, E. Y. Mullins. But Armstrong moved in committee that no notice be taken of the letters. By this point, she could no longer view the issue objectively.

In March 1906, Lillie Barker came to Baltimore to preside at the Executive Committee meeting. The lack of unity was glaring; six voted with Armstrong and five were opposed. At another meeting in April, the same stalemate prevailed. Come May and the annual meeting in Chattanooga, Tennessee, the crowds were unusually large. People were very aware of the hanging question about the training school. So many men tried to attend sessions that Barker repeatedly asked the gentlemen to retire. Her president's address was poignant; as her last opportunity to speak in this capacity, Barker hinted at the future success for the training school. Some were surprised, as she was on record as being opposed. Barker asked the women to be careful, "lest, by an untoward deed, we jeopardize the welfare of the organization."

Armstrong's report took a very different approach. The women loved this tireless corresponding secretary who had led so faithfully since the very beginning. The crowd listened with great admiration and respect as she summarized the history of Woman's Missionary Union. Armstrong made absolutely no mention of the training school issue, keeping all her personal frustrations and grief hidden in her heart. Because of a constitutional policy, the official vote would not be possible for another three months, but a committee of one member from each state was appointed in anticipation of the training school coming under the auspices of WMU. Its time had come, and concurrently, the Armstrong era was ending after 18 years of dedicated service.

"Annie the Planner" would be an accurate title for her. She excelled at finding innovative ways to promote missions. Armstrong had been a master architect when it came to building consensus between denomination leaders. She far exceeded any of these male leaders in such skills. One of her successors to the position of corresponding secretary (now called executive director), Alma Hunt, asked the question of Armstrong's tenure of service: "Was it 'foreordained' that Miss

Armstrong's ability and capacity for work should be dedicated to God's glory through Woman's Missionary Union? The years unmistakably testify in the affirmative."

FANNIE HECK

Armstrong must have looked on with mixed feelings at the unanimous election of Fannie E. S. Heck as president of WMU. She and Heck had so often disagreed. Yet at the same time, Armstrong knew the remarkable skills and spirit of Fannie Heck and had to realize that all the years of her own efforts and passion would not go to waste. Heck was experienced, totally committed, and incredibly gifted. At this 1906 meeting, an offer was extended to 47-year old Cynthia Westfall (Mrs. J. O.) Rust of Nashville, Tennessee, president of Boscobel College, to be the new corresponding secretary. She did not accept, but the work of the Union continued quite seamlessly. There was an army of dedicated and capable women across the South "on board" to continue the work of the Union. Heck announced that "there shall be no lapse in the work because of the present vacancy in the office of corresponding secretary." The Baltimore address for WMU also would remain the same.

Armstrong may have thought that the Union would falter without her, but, as a tribute to the enduring foundation she had established, the work continued without a hiccup. Armstrong's endeavors had never been to build up her own ego but rather to strengthen the overall ministry. Sometimes her personality got in the way, but her intent and purpose were always to build up.

Fannie Heck went to work quickly. In June, she took to Baltimore the material for the first issue of *Our Mission Fields,* which became the "mother" magazine of WMU. It was later to be called *Royal Service,* and still later *Missions Mosaic.* There were also more changes afoot. Annie Armstrong asked the boards to return the assets of the Mission Literature Department to Maryland Baptist Union Association. No longer would she serve as its secretary. The end result of this was actually beneficial. WMU found a way to bring in needed operating funds, beginning with the facile pen of Fannie Heck. In 1906, WMU magazines began to roll off the press and circulation quickly grew. Soon WMU was self-supporting. The first *Our Mission Fields* sold for 5 cents a copy.

Heck had three immediate goals. She launched the first magazine, prepared to launch the Training School, and determined to begin more missions organizations for youth, "picking up the dropped stitch," as she called it. There were, of course, women's societies and children's bands, but nothing for the young women. Another topic was a regular missionary calendar of prayer so women could pray for missionaries on their birthdays. Women in Chattanooga asked for the calendars, and the literature department began printing them. The Prayer Calendar became a ministry that has endured.

FANNIE PRESIDES IN RICHMOND

Meeting together in 1907 in Richmond, where it all began, must have been exciting, especially for those who had been present in 1888. There was a certain sense of loss without Annie Armstrong, but she had done her job well. Fannie Heck presided, a task at which she excelled. Heck suggested that the Union use a specific theme each year, and for 1907 and 1908 she proposed the themes Larger Things and Higher

Things. Another enduring idea was also proposed for the first time in that year: in order to assist the seamless flow of business, there would now be a semiannual meeting of the Executive Committee and state vice-presidents.

In her presidential address, Heck urged that each state employ staff members. Right after Armstrong's retirement, Executive Committee member Elia Brower Nimmo began to receive a small stipend for her work as chairman of the newly established Literature Department. Such moves were removing a stigma from women receiving salaries for ministry work.

Because there was not yet an official corresponding secretary, Heck gave her usual president's address and followed this with a survey of the year, making a point of expressing renewed appreciation for the invaluable contributions of Armstrong's 18 years of leadership. She also paid tribute to the local executive committee that literally worked throughout the year. Heck reported that the receipts for the Christmas offering were the highest ever, exceeding $17,000, which was more than $3,000 higher than the previous year.

Optimism permeated the meeting in Richmond as several new ideas were presented. In 1900, Heck and Mattie McIntosh had heard plans presented for an interdenominational committee to prepare and publish a uniform course of mission study. Both women felt the need of such study. However, the Union declined to join such a confederation, some fearing being part of something ecumenical. The concept of a systematic study of missions did not go away. Heck started such a study in North Carolina, and Eliza Broadus did the same in Kentucky. Now, in 1907, the Union decided to move forward with mission study plans of their own. T. Bronson Ray had joined the staff of the Foreign Mission Board as educational secretary. His job was to produce educational literature and foster mission study. He found his strongest allies in WMU. Mission study became a WMU highlight, educating and inspiring women and youth, and often entire churches.

Heck had been working during 1907 to pick up "that dropped stitch" and establish a permanent organization for young women. Present at the Richmond meeting were a number of young women eager to see what would happen. One gave a description of Fannie Heck as she presided. Heck was in the customary hat and gloves. Picture her in a lavender lace dress with high neck, large sleeves, fitted waist, and long skirt. She was gloved in white, and on her silvery white hair was a lavender hat with plumes. The observer commented: "Her voice was full, strong, forceful, rich . . . As one listened, one felt as if one could lay down her life for the cause she presented." The delegates enthusiastically adopted the proposal to promote young women's groups, giving the organization the name already in use in Alabama, Young Woman's Auxiliary.

Without doubt, one of the high moments was the election of Edith Campbell Crane of Baltimore as new corresponding secretary. She was actually a member of the same Eutaw Place Baptist Church as Armstrong. Although Crane had no WMU experience, she was an executive officer in New York City's YWCA and a capable young businesswoman. Praise for her skills mounted quickly as she displayed a keen grasp of her new position.

All the delegates anticipated the vote on the Woman's Missionary Union Training School (WMUTS). Fannie Heck called for the vote that made WMU actual owners of an academic institution. It had been a long time coming and would make an eternal difference in many lives. Anna Eager, one of the driving forces in bringing the school to fruition, rose to call for a message of love to be sent to Annie Armstrong—a poignant move considering the antagonism Armstrong had felt in her relations with Eager and with the whole idea of WMUTS. Southern Seminary yielded total control of the women students to the Training School, allowing them all the advantages of the seminary classes. The SBC approved all the plans of WMU and actually gave a gift of close to $5,000 for the school.

FANNIE FORGES AHEAD – HIGHER THINGS

WMU's theme for the year—Higher Things—was also its goal. Fannie Heck was not a woman of small goals, and she constantly challenged Baptist women with what "could be done." In her annual address in Hot Springs, Arkansas, in 1908, Heck reported that there were a million women connected with Southern Baptist churches and "it is a large estimate to say that 100,000 of these have been touched and awakened to the mission demand through the Union." Edith Crane then gave her first report as corresponding secretary. The work had progressed almost seamlessly, and Crane had visited many of the states in order to bring herself up to speed in an organization that was new to her.

At this Hot Springs meeting, the delegates enthusiastically adopted the motion that called for WMU to organize missionary societies for boys, using the name the Order of Royal Ambassadors. The year 1908 also saw the beginning of camping and it proved to be one of

WMU's most effective means of missions education and inspiration. Virginia had its first camp this year, and other states were soon to follow. From these camps grew WMU's own camps for

young people.

Another matter high on the agenda in Hot Springs was the first report from the Training School. It had begun with a beautiful and competent principal in the person of Maud Reynolds McLure of Alabama. Reports of the first year were glowing. The delegates listened eagerly to news of the daily routine and classroom achievements of the training school students. In the 1908 Old Testament class, all 14 women made a grade of 90 or higher, and 3 made 100. Out of 108 men, only 1 made 100. Not shabby stuff! Furthermore, the school was growing so rapidly that this first building quickly needed to be expanded.

FANNIE IN LOUISVILLE

WMU had come to its twenty-first annual meeting, and with the broadening of the number of delegates from each state, attendance was increased along with enthusiasm. The presence of a number of the Training School students at this 1909 annual meeting was exciting to the delegates. Many of them took advantage of the trip to Louisville to visit "House Beautiful," as the training school was called.

Heck seemed able to gaze into the future and pinpoint those things that were necessary to keep WMU viable. More than 100 years later, her insights are as fresh as this morning's pot of coffee. She challenged: "The pages of history are strewn with the wrecks of organizations which died of inflexibility"

WMU added an organized Personal Service Department in 1909. The name has changed through the years—community missions, then mission action—but the essential purpose of personal involvement in ministry remains the same. Heck appointed Lulie Wharton of Baltimore as chairman of personal service. Growing up, Lulie and her family had lived and breathed personal service throughout Baltimore long before the phrase was coined. Wharton's mother had been the first recording secretary of WMU, SBC.

The idea was sound, and, as one historian put it, "Fannie Heck cut her social action teeth in WMU." Instead of sending out the two or more dozen women missionaries WMU was sponsoring around the country, WMU would "convert itself into a vast company of women who, by their leadership in it, feel called and appointed each in her own community to do such work." At the same time, WMU warned against putting "the ministry of the body before or apart from the ministry of the soul."

The women heard reports of the advances made in the 20 years since their official founding. Edith Crane reported that there were already 992 YWA organizations reporting, with Georgia having the most at 181. Sunbeam bands had grown to over 2,500 groups, and the brand-new RAs already had more than 100 chapters, with North Carolina having formed the first of these. The Woman's Missionary Union Training School had already enrolled 40 students. Women celebrated the fact that 9,251 women's societies were reporting to state officers and nearly 1,500 of these were new. The team of Heck and Crane, along with a stellar Executive Committee, was clearly reaching toward the avowed theme of Higher Things.

CHAPTER

The End of an Era

"He says 'Follow me' to every one of us today, as plainly as he did to the fishermen of Galilee."
—SARAH ANN CHAMBERS, ALABAMA, 1882

FANNIE AND EDITH TEAM UP

WMU WAS NOT far from the beginning of a new era. Fannie Heck and Edith Crane attended the 1910 meeting in Baltimore with a sense of the WMU history that emanated from this great city. The recording secretary described this gathering as the largest in WMU's history; more than 850 were present. Fannie's address centered on the year's theme: Vision.

The Foreign Mission Board requested that the women designate their Christmas offering for the largest field, China. Young Woman's Auxiliaries were to give to hospital work on the fields, and the Sunbeams offering was to support missionaries in Africa. The giving of WMU was quite astounding, considering overall Baptist giving. In 1910, WMU provided a quarter of a million dollars for missions.

WMU excelled at giving, for the spirit of stewardship permeated every phase of its planning and service. In the 1910 Plan of Work, a section recommended that each state Central

Committee stress the giving of one-tenth and systematic collection and also develop a promotion plan. The plan also recommended that the last day of the week of prayer in January be spent in fasting and prayer for tithing. Tithing had become a way of life.

EDITH CRANE — WITH YOUTH AND GLOBAL PROGRAMS

Edith Crane was corresponding secretary for just four years, but she made those years count with her untiring zeal and efficiency. She placed emphasis on the new youth organizations; their rapid growth is indicative of that passion. Crane wrote the first leaflet for YWAs and stressed the need for youth groups to have a specific foreign missions interest to inspire their giving.

Edith Crane and Fannie Heck were both world citizens and desired cooperation with other Baptist groups and other denominations. These sentiments were not common in Southern Baptist circles; Heck and Crane were not aggressive in pushing involvement as a Union but maintained contacts themselves with other entities. Crane attended the World Missionary Conference in Edinburgh, Scotland. Officially, WMU could have no representative, but the FMB named Crane as an accredited delegate. Crane later reported to state meetings and gave women of the Union a new understanding of world conditions and needs. Through Crane, the women of WMU steadily developed their world view.

Crane also kept up with the Student Volunteer Movement. She eagerly attended a special youth meeting held in Rochester, New York, in 1910. The next year was the Jubilee of Missions, the 50th anniversary of organized interdenominational women's work for foreign missions. Edith Crane was selected as the southern advisory chairman for the Jubilee.

1911 — SIGNALING ANOTHER CHANGE

Plans for the second meeting of the Baptist World Alliance included a meeting for women. WMU was requested to appoint a representative to help plan for the event, and Edith Crane was selected. Her efficiency was apparent, and when the Alliance met in June 1911 in Philadelphia, she was elected recording secretary of the Women's Committee.

But right in the middle of extensive plans and promotion, Crane became ill. She asked for a leave of absence for the rest of the year. In January 1912, realizing her condition was not going to improve in a hurry, she resigned, effective immediately. She would be sorely missed. Her tenure had lasted only a few years, but they had been incredibly important years of strengthening WMU.

SOLDIERING ON

At the 1911 annual meeting in Jacksonville, Florida, the women heard reports of a successful year and discussed plans to grow the developing ministries. Edith Crane reported on the plans for the upcoming BWA women's meeting in Philadelphia, announcing that Fannie Heck would be a keynote speaker.

Crane also proposed organization of a Field Workers Council of WMU. It proved a real help to these WMU professionals who held meetings whenever they had opportunity to be together. It was not many years until these state secretaries and other state staff began to meet in conjunction with WMU's Executive Committee, greatly facilitating smooth communications and exchange of ideas. Likewise, the adoption of a Standard of Excellence facilitated efficiency. In the beginning, it called for monthly meetings that would have devotionals, missions programs, a calendar of prayer, periodic mission studies, and a plan for growth. It was a strict standard, and societies who achieved that level of excellence felt a real sense of achievement.

Techniques for personal service were also advancing as ministries in local communities began to multiply. WMU's most ambitious social work project was the settlement house. Methodists had led the way in this ministry. When the first directory of settlement houses was published in 1911, there were no Baptist ministries in the South. Soon, however, settlements were begun by women in Birmingham and Norfolk, and more followed. In time, these grew to be called Good Will Centers and became a mighty force for good.

WMU expanded this year with the addition of Illinois as a sister state. Illinois women had organized in 1908 but with allegiance to Northern Baptist Women's work. However, in 1910, Illinois had sent women to Baltimore to observe WMU in session. These observers went home with favorable reports, resulting in the addition of Illinois as a sister state in Jacksonville.

Two ongoing WMU institutions were thriving: the Margaret Home and Woman's Missionary Union Training School (WMUTS). WMUTS was more than theological training; it provided its students with a cultural and spiritual environment that enhanced life skills. Much of the credit can go to Maud Reynolds McLure who established the majority of the traditions that became part of the Louisville school. Her personal graces and (cultural) polish set a beautiful standard for the young women in her tutelage.

Meanwhile, Texas women never faltered in their desire to have a conveniently located training school. Women were included in the plans for a theological school at Baylor University. When it opened in 1910 as Southwestern Baptist Theological Seminary in Fort Worth, 15 percent of the students were women. Texas women were great fund-raisers and sponsored a special building. The Sunday School Board also contributed to the cost. Soon the Texas school had more women students than Louisville's WMUTS. The two schools shared a slogan: That our daughters may be as cornerstones.

Fannie E. S. Heck was keynote speaker at the BWA Woman's Department's first official congress. She excelled at public speaking, and her message was received with great appreciation. This was the first time Heck had spoken to an international audience, and she graciously disarmed them all by confessing: "We have not realized you. Self-satisfied with our great numbers, our prosperity, our wealth, we have said that in America resided four-fifths of the Baptist of the world and were content." She then touched on the nerve center of women throughout BWA: the heroism of Baptist women in the face of difficulties that those living in free America could not even imagine. She assured those women: "Your faith sets before us in the living reality of today new possibility of service in our own lives."

In 1911, Edith Crane served as corresponding secretary of Woman's Missionary Union for a final year. The pressure of all that was on her, as well as all the possibilities that lay ahead, became almost too much. She was approached about heading up a woman's training school in Europe, and at the same time, she met a lawyer who began courting her. She and her sister were also closing their family home to move into an apartment. All the stress precipitated a breakdown; doctors insisted on complete rest. Therefore, in January 1912, Crane resigned from a position that she had filled so successfully.

Crane left with a heavy heart and great admiration for the organization she had come to love. At the time of her resignation, she actually recommended Alabama's secretary, Kathleen Mallory, as a successor. During Crane's tenure, she had seen Mallory demonstrate the remarkable skills and poise of a young leader.

WMU's nominating committee met quickly; they wanted a new corresponding secretary as soon as possible. Eliza Broadus of Kentucky was chair of the committee, and Mallory was the group's unanimous choice. Fannie Heck immediately wrote Mallory, asking if she would be okay with her name being submitted. Mallory pondered her answer, knowing that it would determine the future course of her life and that of an entire organization. She began to do what she always did when weighty choices confronted her: Pray.

CHAPTER

A New Beginning

"We will find a way."
—Fannie Heck

THE TEAM OF HECK AND MALLORY

WOMEN GATHERED IN Oklahoma City in 1912, anticipating the election of their new corresponding secretary. A few of the "pioneer" leaders could remember the tentative beginnings 24 years before, and new leaders were anxious to learn who would be guiding them into the future. Meanwhile, all relied on Fannie Heck and were carried along by her enthusiasm and passion for the task before them.

Heck challenged her constituents to build up the work of all the youth organizations, a priority if they were to build for the future. Heck also announced that up to the close of the year's third quarter, WMU had given to foreign missions more than half of all money given by the SBC. The same was true of home missions.

The highlight of the meeting was the selection of the new secretary. Kathleen Mallory had pondered long and prayed earnestly before allowing her name to be considered. In her billowing yellow organdy she looked young and lovely. One

WMU matron whispered to her neighbor: "There's just one thing I don't like about her. She's too young."

Just prior to the report, Eliza Broadus sent her card to Mallory. On it she had written, "I think you will like to know that you are the unanimous choice of our committee." Broadus brought her nomination, noting Mallory as "possessing high qualities of mind and heart." The ballot vote was unanimous. WMU had a new leader, one who for decades skillfully charted its course.

Mallory's manner of public prayer was surprising to some. She knelt. Women soon recognized it as characteristic of her genuine humility. Mallory's great strength was rooted in her prayer life. Talking with the Lord was as natural to her as talking with her father. She absolutely believed that a Christian advanced upon her knees.

To equip herself for effective service, Mallory began by traveling many miles, meeting with state leaders, speaking at functions, and learning the inner workings of the Union. Armed with the brand-new WMU Year Book, she set about helping women across the region organize more effectively.

JUBILATE — 25 YEARS OF MISSIONS

Mallory was beginning her tenure at a particularly busy time, for WMU was preparing for its Jubilate in 1913—25 years of organization. She and Fannie Heck became a remarkable team. In Heck's address to the Jubilate Annual Meeting in St. Louis, Missouri, she led the delegates on a memory journey, suggesting that remembering those early pioneers would help them renew *their* purpose after these 25 years. Fannie asked for any who had been at that memorable May 1888 meeting in Richmond to stand: only four others stood with Fannie.

And, beginning with this year, WMU was reporting directly to the SBC; their voice was heard. Also beginning in 1913 was the plan for WMU circles in local churches, a successful system for many years. New printed materials became available for rural and urban WMU groups, geared to their specific needs. WMU's seal was officially adopted, and Fannie Heck's hymn, "Come Women Wide Proclaim," became the official hymn. Heck's history of Woman's Missionary Union, *In Royal Service,* was also published.

THE TEAM OF MALLORY AND HECK IN NASHVILLE

It was a lovely sight, the two beautiful leaders of WMU on the platform together, both with prematurely silver hair. No one knew that this 1914 gathering would be Fannie Heck's final annual meeting, least of all Heck herself. In her address, "Facing a Prophecy," she laid out an ambitious plan for continued growth. Heck had a gift for sharing a vision that in turn inspired others.

Our Mission Fields would become *Royal Service,* and it would be published monthly. The group of girls between the ages of Sunbeam Band and those of YWAs officially became known as Girls' Auxiliaries. This last group to form actually became the strongest of all the youth organizations over the next 100 years. The women also voted to form businesswomen's groups for those who worked outside the home.

FANNIE'S FINAL MONTHS

Every report was overshadowed by the burden on every heart in attendance in Houston, Texas, in May 1915. Fannie Heck lay gravely ill in a Richmond hospital, and her close friend and a loved leader, Mary Thomas (Mrs. Julian P.), gave her message to the delegates. In WMU history there is no more honored literary effort than Fannie Heck's final message. Her eyes were so painful that she could not see clearly to write, so her friend Mary Thomas wrote down the message as Heck related it. When Thomas read Heck's message, the women stood to hear it. Her final words are the most quoted lines in WMU history:

> See to it only, that you listen to His voice and follow only where Christ leads.
>
> Be prayerful in your planning.
>
> Be patient and persistent in your fulfillment.
>
> Endeavor to see the needs of the world from God's standpoint.
>
> Plan not for the year but for the years.
>
> Think long thoughts.
>
> Train the children for worldwide service.

Heck concluded:

> "Most earnestly I pray — God be with you till we meet again."

Minnie James (Mrs. William Carey), the woman who succeeded Fannie Heck as president, is the one who wrote her definitive biography in 1939. James recounted the final months of Fannie Heck's life. One Sunday morning in 1914, as Heck was preparing to go teach her Sunday School class, a sharp pain struck. She managed to get through the class by leaning on surfaces. Heck described it as like a lightning bolt that hit her. She went to her room and did not leave it for two months, and then only to enter a Richmond hospital.

Her biography does not name the illness, but certainly it must have been cancer. In spite of the pain, Heck continued to write. She received thousands of letters, cards, notes, and gifts. Kathleen Mallory sent her a note every day—never missing—recounting little snippets of interest that she knew would encourage Heck. Witnesses said her room looked like a bower of flowers. It was her "Room of the Blue Sky."

In August 1915, Heck asked to go home. Just moving was agonizing, but she insisted. The last weeks of her life, she stayed in the parlor of her home, surrounded by family. All of her brothers and sisters and her close family members were nearby. On the evening of August 25, Fannie Heck breathed her last breath.

KATHLEEN, MINNIE JAMES, AND A MEMORIAL

A sense of loss hovered over the 1916 meeting in Asheville, North Carolina. Heck was gone, but her spirit of optimism and courage emanated through all the proceedings. Mary Faison Dixon was chosen to head young people's organizations, becoming the first full-time professional staff member other than officers. And women approved the sale of the Margaret Home since it was no longer needed as a home for MKs. It sold for three times the original price. Interest from the invested money would be used for scholarships for missionaries' children; it has helped educate thousands of MKs since.

There was no president's address because the delegates the year before had determined to re-elect Heck. In her report, Kathleen Mallory commented: "Enfolding the year like a robe of white has been the conscious absence of our faithful leader, Miss Fannie E. S. Heck, who on August 25 entered the Promised Land where 'till the day break' she waiteth for us."

James Franklin Love, new secretary of the FMB, brought before the women the Board's financial plight, citing their debt of some $180,000. Love later called that meeting "the holiest hour we ever saw." Love and George W. Truett explained the situation, and women began rising and making pledges of money and jewelry. One woman promised $5,000 as a thank offering for her husband, who (she felt sure) would give the money! By the end of the session, gifts and pledges exceeded $17,000.

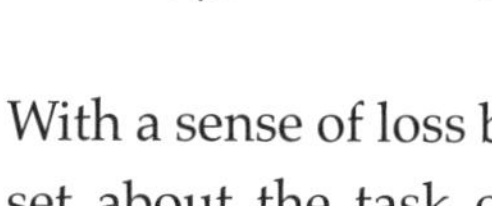

With a sense of loss but also of new beginnings, the delegates set about the task of selecting a new president. Blue-eyed Minnie James caught the attention of Virginia WMU when her husband became a pastor in Richmond. Within two years, she was elected state president. Upon their first meeting, Minnie James and Fannie Heck charmed each other. Heck soon assigned her to some key leadership roles. Minnie James possessed great powers of intelligence and poise, using these to head up the important Jubilate committee. The results impressed everyone.

The highlight of the Asheville meeting was the memorial service held for Fannie Heck on Sunday afternoon. The head of each board of the Convention had a part, but the main address was delivered by Maud McLure, principal of the Training School. She eulogized Heck as a leader of rare vision and foresight, as one "who saw the end from the beginning."

MALLORY AND McLURE AT THE SBC

One of the highlights of 1916 was the appearance on the platform at the Southern Baptist Convention of two women who spoke to the body. This was history. The matter that made the moment revolved around the Training School. It had outgrown its quarters, and the need for more space was critical. A committee had determined that an additional $98,000 was needed. (This didn't sound quite as daunting as $100,000 would have!) Said Mallory, "The brethren simply must come to our aid!" Maud McLure concurred. They would present the plans to the SBC.

Usually a man presented the WMU report to the convention. At the evening session, B. D. Gray, secretary of the Home Mission Board, informed the convention that he was giving the first 30 minutes of his time to WMU, and with no fanfare, introduced Mallory and McLure. McLure presented slides showing the proposal for the much-needed facility. Speaking of herself in the third person, McLure later related: "With shaking knees and pounding heart she very simply explained the rather crude, innocent, slides as they were pictured on the screen, then sank into a chair to revive again."

Then it was Mallory's turn. A news report later recorded:

> *"As Miss Mallory stood before that great congregation in her dainty gown of white, I wondered if it occurred to her . . . that she was smashing a cus-*

> *tom that was sixty-five years old and maybe more. I wondered, as she made her graceful speech, if it occurred to her that she was the first woman to speak to the Southern Baptist Convention."*

And Gambrell, in the *Baptist Standard,* wrote:

> *"One of the thrills of the Asheville Convention was brought on by two of our very finest women who spoke about a work important in their hands — my insistence is for the liberty wherewith Christ has made us all free."*

Thus, 1916 stands as a moment of departure and the beginning of a new sense of the importance of women's work for missions.

CHAPTER

O Zion Haste

"Thy Mission High Fulfilling"

WAR, WOMEN, AND GOING FORWARD

AS 1917 ARRIVED, the specter of world war loomed and set the tone for the annual meeting in New Orleans. This was the year Kathleen Mallory compiled the first *Manual of WMU Methods* providing flexible planning for women's societies. But, as women made plans, they knew world evangelism would be influenced by what happened on the battlefield. By 1918, American troops were going to Europe by the thousands. WMU's personal service chairman, Lulie Wharton, involved local WMU organizations with their nearest Red Cross chapters.

Several innovations were introduced at the 1918 Hot Springs, Arkansas, meeting, including putting the Calendar of Prayer into monthly issues of *Royal Service.* Mission study and tithing were both emphasized this year.

This year the Christmas offering received its name. Annie Armstrong actually broke her silence that had lasted since retirement in 1906 and suggested that the offering be named in honor of Lottie Moon. When the biography of Lottie Moon was written by Una Roberts Lawrence telling about Lottie's life of service and sacrifice, the offering grew exponentially.

In 1918, the Convention voted that women could be messengers to the Convention. It had been a controversial topic since 1885, and WMU leadership kept out of the fray. The constitutional amendment for such a move was approved by the Convention. The Union took the high road and voted to thank the brethren for their courtesy in granting the privilege of being messengers. In May 1918, the new Woman's Missionary Union Training School (WMUTS) building was completed. At the WMUTS graduation, a woman gave the address for the first time—Minnie James, president of WMU.

ATLANTA, GEORGIA AND $75,000,000

Atlanta in 1919 came right on the heels of the armistice ending WWI. A stark new awareness of reconstruction needs in Europe and the Near East, combined with a new consciousness of the spiritual poverty there, led Baptists to "attempt one of the greatest undertakings ever attempted by any denomination." The FMB asked the Convention to consider a survey of these needy areas with the thought ot entering new fields. The presentation of needs led to a unanimous vote launching the $75 Million Campaign. The SBC took on the job of raising that huge sum in just five years. This was the first joint SBC and state agency fund-raising drive. WMU's Executive Committee met in July and pledged WMU's cooperation, promising to raise $15,000,000. The ladies appointed Georgia's Mrs. Isa-Beall Williams Neel to chair the drive. Women chose nine o'clock each Monday as a call to prayer for all women, realizing that without prayer they would never reach the goal. Their slogan was Millions for the Master. On December 8, 1919, Kathleen Mallory received a telegram from Neels: "WMU $15,000,000 quota is over subscribed by $3,000,000. Let Jesus Christ be praised."

Mallory and James were named to the Committee on Future Program, marking the first time women were appointed to a non-WMU Convention committee. Based on pledges, SBC agencies borrowed money, and the FMB sent 84 missionaries and their children to the Orient. This was thought to be the largest group ever sent at one time. Problems arose as agencies became possessive, causing the campaign that had begun with such high ideals to turn into a disaster. Sure enough, the campaign disintegrated and the agencies reverted to their former, unilateral methods.

On top of that, economic recession hit the nation in 1920. However, WMU's cooperative network held firm from the local level up. A typical problem arose at Woodlawn Baptist Church in Birmingham where the deacons recommended keeping part of the WMU campaign money to pay a new staff member's salary. In pointed discussions the ladies declared: "The men know nothing about missions, not having made a study of it." The vote was finally taken and the men reversed their request, forwarding all the money to campaign headquarters. In the final tally, the overall $75,000,000 goal was not reached, but WMU gave more than 100 percent of its own quota.

WMU moved forward in other areas, including beginning an involvement in literacy. The president of the Neighbors League of America trained women at the Atlanta meeting in how to teach English to foreigners. Going forward, literacy became part of WMU's plan of work.

Ethel Winfield joined the staff and became an indispensable executive assistant in 1919. She helped with editing, correspondence, and proofreading, and her responsibilities continued to expand. She faithfully served more than three decades.

WASHINGTON, D.C., 1920

WMU met in Washington, D.C., in May 1920. It marked a special anniversary for Elizabeth Lowndes, who had been elected WMU treasurer 25 years earlier. The meeting focused on involvement in personal service through Good Will Centers. The HMB offered to provide a building for a center and in 1921 employed Emma Leachman as the center's director. By WMU's decision, Leachman's salary came through the home missions offering.

By this time, other countries were establishing WMU organizations. WMU groups were active in China, Brazil, Nigeria, Cuba, Mexico and Japan. WMU was reaching out around the world.

THE QUESTION OF HEADQUARTERS

A geographic move was about to take place. For more than 30 years, WMU's headquarters had been located in Baltimore, which meant the organization was dominated by one region. There was a widespread feeling that headquarters should be more centrally located. In February, an Executive Committee meeting was called in Nashville, and the Maryland local members were not present. The Alabama and Georgia representatives called for the headquarters to be moved. Mary Hill Davis of Dallas, Texas, chaired the study committee recommending a change, with 13 of the 17 states favoring the idea. Baltimore was not the center geographically or psychologically. Opponents of the move were concerned about the cost. The proposal seemed a bit shocking at first, and the women voted to defer a decision for a year.

Four cities invited WMU to have their headquarters in their city: Atlanta, Nashville, Birmingham, and Memphis. Nashville sounded appealing since the Sunday School Board was there and they had offered free offices. Birmingham was also a pull, as the SBC Education Board had recently established offices there, and their head was the husband of WMU president Minnie James. When the vote came, the officers living in Baltimore abstained, as did Minnie James and Kathleen Mallory. When the votes were counted, there were 203 for Nashville, 203 for Birmingham! James did not want to cast the deciding ballot, and the treasurer, Elizabeth Lowndes, and the brand-new young people's secretary, Juliette Mather, were asked to vote. Birmingham was chosen.

JULIETTE MATHER JOINS THE TEAM

Baptists gathered in Chattanooga, Tennessee, in 1921, and WMU arranged their meetings so as not to conflict with SBC meetings. Now WMU requested that a quota of female representatives be included on the SBC Executive Committee and boards, and the Convention voted to elect members based on qualifications, regardless of gender. Times had changed! Something very difficult to change, however, was a perennial issue: race relations. Baptists were not big on cooperating with nondenominational movements, but there were Baptist women who saw the importance of such groups. Racial tensions in the nation were getting uglier, and a Woman's Committee of the Commission on Interracial Cooperation invited all denominations to participate. Just three Baptists attended the planning caucus. But by the Committee's first meeting, several Baptists joined, and Minnie James was a main speaker. It was clear that the Southern Baptist effort at relieving racial tensions was anemic compared to other denominations, and James had to work hard to preserve WMU ties with the Commission. At least from this era until the Commission dissolved in 1943, WMU greatly increased the visibility of work with African Americans, even including some strong women taking a stand against lynching.

Prior to the Chattanooga meeting, Minnie James traveled to the training school to interview three young women, hoping to find the right fit for the young people's secretary. By April 8, the Executive Committee was ready to elect that right fit: Juliette Mather. James was impressed with her find. Mather, a direct lineal descendant of the Mathers of colonial fame, was eminently qualified in scholarship, spiritual depth, WMU knowledge, and personality. For many years, she was the innovative and dynamic leader of the children's and young women's organizations, and she left a lifelong imprint on their formation and success.

MOVING TIME

WMU's big move was approaching. Mrs. Lowndes as treasurer would continue living in Baltimore, but the rest of the operation moved to Birmingham in October 1921. WMU was located in the Comer Building, which at that time was reported to be the tallest building in the South. Kathleen

Mallory set up her small desk with cardboard accessories and never changed it. Membership soared, and the publication business grew each year, but still they stuffed everything into the same small space. It would be more than 25 years before WMU faced the question of a move to larger space.

THE ARMORY IN JACKSONVILLE, FLORIDA

In 1922, women decided to make literacy work a part of personal service. "Star Classes" would reach uneducated adults, and individual tutoring was offered. It was hands-on ministry and the women loved it. They also loved the new young people's secretary. The creative Mather presented her first annual report in Jacksonville in the form of a pageant. Mather was quick of step and quick of skill, launching the first quarterly magazine for youth in October 1922. It was for all age groups and was so popular that it became a monthly publication in just two years.

KANSAS CITY AND CP

The 1923 annual meeting in Kansas City was memorable for the beginning of plans for a Cooperative Program. A number of women on the committee brought the plan to fruition. Minnie James led in a discussion of how to develop a plan for systematic and proportional giving by churches and individuals, which had long been a dream of WMU. This year SBC appointed a very large Committee on Future Program. It included Mallory, James, and a WMU officer from each state. One-third of the committee was made up of women, the highest female representation ever achieved on an SBC-appointed committee or board.

The result was the formation of the Cooperative Program, which has literally been the lifeline of Southern Baptist work. James felt that this might be the most important piece of business she conducted during her entire career as president. WMU literally loved the program into being; the CP was implemented in 1924 and received its official name in 1925.

The skills of Minnie James had not gone unnoticed. Later in 1923, she attended the Baptist World Congress in Stockholm, Sweden, speaking on behalf of the women of the Southern states of America. She included greetings from the Woman's Missionary Unions around the world. James was elected president of the women's meeting of the BWA. As a result of this trip to Europe, she became interested in helping European young women receive training for missions. At the close of her service as Union president, WMU honored her with the establishment of the James Memorial School in Bucharest, Romania.

ATLANTA, GEORGIA

In Atlanta, in 1924, Lulie Wharton resigned as personal service director. She had served as director for some 15 years and as recording secretary since 1921. She remained in that secretarial role for an amazing 16 more years. Juliette Mather's dream of a camp for YWA members became reality this year. It was the first regularly sponsored Southwide Baptist event at North Carolina's Ridgecrest Baptist

Assembly. It would be held annually and would draw up to 1,200 young women.

THE JAMES ERA ENDS

Minnie James presided for the last time in Memphis in 1924. She had been part of progress on many fronts during her nine years. Alma Hunt later called James "the woman for her time." James truly believed the abilities of women should be recognized and used in the Convention. Historian Catherine Allen calls James' leadership style a mix of historic awareness, practical femininity, and serious religion. In her final message to the Union, James concluded: "I know of but one thing that can cause us to fail and that is to lose the vision of the Saviour."

The guidelines for the new Cooperative Program (CP) were released, and WMU had insisted on one thing: "The special thank offerings for state and home missions and the Christmas Offering for Foreign Missions ingathered during the Week of Prayer of WMU for these respective causes shall be recognized as gifts in *addition* to the regular contributions to the CP." This was to prove vital many times in the years to come.

At this Memphis meeting, a relative newcomer to leadership, Ethlene Boone Cox, was asked to be chairman of general arrangements. As the meeting began, Minnie James announced her resignation as president, so the nominating committee asked this inexperienced new leader to become the next president. This was the beginning of a remarkable 27 years of leadership, first as president, then as full-time treasurer. WMU was headed for greatness.

CHAPTER

"To Tell to All the World —*that God is light*"

THE TEAM OF MALLORY AND COX

A NEW DUO led WMU for eight dynamic years, blending the talents and creativity of Kathleen Mallory with those of Ethlene Boone Cox. Cox may have inherited some pioneering skills from her ancestor Daniel Boone, for she added a new dimension to WMU with her remarkable speaking skills. She also discovered some latent aptitude in financial matters, for following her years as president, she became the Union's first full-time treasurer. The end of the 1920s to the mid-30s were fraught with financial landmines, caught in the grip of the Great Depression.

Cox quickly learned the inner workings of WMU and where the needs were greatest. The majority of WMU organizations were in rural churches, so material needed to be prepared to meet those needs. Cox's predecessor, Fannie Heck, had been the guiding light behind personal service, but she realized that it was a revolutionary idea and would take time "to grow in the minds of women." In 1927, less than 37 percent of societies reported personal service participation. Ethlene Cox realized that the Union needed a personal service chairperson in each state, and in 1929, Cox asked Missouri's Una Roberts Lawrence to be the national personal service chairman.

Lawrence stressed personal evangelism. Cottage prayer meetings proved to be one of the best avenues for soul-winning. The emphasis on soul-winning merged with the more usual tasks of sewing, preparing food, and nursing the sick. It proved a potent combination.

A more sensitive issue was race relations. Most societies were in the South, and race had long been a delicate subject. Una Roberts Lawrence formed a close bond of friendship with Helen: Nannie Helen Burroughs, the renowned African American women's leader. In 1932, Ethlene Cox appointed a committee to recommend the direction WMU should take in relationships with National Baptist women, appointing Lawrence as the official representative to their Convention in 1932. A partnership developed, with Una being a contributing editor to their publications and Burroughs a popular speaker with WMU. In this millennium, it is shocking to think of the agonizing difficulty of even the simple logistics of seating and dining because segregation was so entrenched at the time. Sometimes the sheer mechanics of dealing with strict racial ordinances was daunting and heartbreaking. WMU was clearly advanced in race relations as compared to the SBC as a whole. Here again, women led the way in plowing unfurrowed ground.

WMU began encouraging organized and consistent mission study. This new plan involved thousands of women in systematic study, and by 1933, such study was multilevel. Women would choose from 30 books, ranging from study of a particular country or area to biography to soul-winning. Many studied the books in WMU Missionary Round Table or in circles. Lawrence continued as chair for 15 years. An interesting by-product of the Union's emphasis on mission study came when a committee of leaders from the various boards proposed a Church School of Missions. WMU was soon encouraging churches on the associational level to undertake simultaneous schools and bring in missionaries to speak and inspire, a precursor of the twenty-first century's Global Mission Conferences.

40 YEARS AND A RUBY ANNIVERSARY

Women gathered in Chattanooga in 1928 to celebrate WMU's ruby anniversary. Ethlene Boone Cox asked Alabama president Alma (Mrs. J. C.) Wright to be chairman of the planning. Wright, who had become identified with stewardship, led the Union in adopting a $4,000,000 goal for the Ruby Year (40th anniversary) to include contributions to the newly established Cooperative Program. Alma Wright's passion was faithful stewardship as she encouraged women to rise above "Lilliputian giving."

Cox's messages at annual meetings were always a highlight. Audiences were spellbound by her golden, melodious voice, and were moved by her spiritual depth. The ruby anniversary resulted in over 6,400 new organizations, which brought the total to well over 30,000. WMU's Ruby Year saw WMU membership pass the half million mark.

FORWARD STEPS AND MOVING FORWARD

As young people's secretary, Juliette Mather came up with a winner in 1928 when she presented a plan of Forward Steps for GAs. It became an immediate success. The girls memorized assigned Scriptures, studied the work of the denomination, and worked on various missions projects. GAs fell in love with the recognition ceremonies, which became a highlight of their GA year as they wore formal dresses and received badges, crowns, capes, and scepters. Their five ideals closely echoed WMU's aims. A ranking system, involving some 50 projects, had been developed for RAs as well and included a badge and regalia. In 1928, Juliette Mather wrote the first book-length manual for leaders of youth organizations.

ETHLENE BOONE COX AND THE PODIUM

New ground was plowed in women's platform leadership during the tenure of Ethlene Cox. Prior to 1929, the only women to speak from the podium of the SBC had been Kathleen Mallory and Maud McLure in 1916, for an unannounced presentation of the needs of the training school. Thirteen years had passed, and the old hidebound tradition of "men only" as speakers seemed firmly in place. Then along came Ethlene Boone Cox, WMU president. Her reputation as a spiritually profound speaker of unusual persuasive skills was becoming widespread. Her beauty no doubt added to the aura that was part of her appeal. She addressed the women's meeting of the BWA in 1928, and women began clamoring for her to speak to the Southern Baptist Convention.

So for the first time, a Baptist woman received an invitation to address the SBC. A sprinkling of disgruntled voices of opposition groused a bit, but the vast majority wanted to hear this speaker about whom they had heard so much. George W. Truett, who greatly admired Cox, was presiding that day. It is possible some of his admiration was due to the realization that in Ethlene Cox, he had met his oratorical match. Her presentation surpasses the expectations of that vast audience of thousands. A reporter, just a couple of months earlier, had written: "What a winsome personality is Mrs. Cox. She had a clear, musical voice that is easily carried to the utmost limits of any auditorium. . . . I was so spellbound that I found when she had finished her matchless address that I had only the most meager notes. I was so swept away with the power of her eloquence that . . . I completely lost sight of the fact that I was supposed to be covering her address."

Ten years later, Cox and Truett were again sharing a platform; this time it was the BWA Congress meeting in Atlanta, Georgia. Margaret Mitchell's book *Gone with the Wind,* and also the forthcoming movie, had taken the author's city of Atlanta, as well as the entire nation, by storm. Cox had thoroughly prepared her message and was backing up her memory with a manuscript. Just as she had thanked Dr. Truett for his introduction, a gust of wind swept across the outdoor platform and playfully scattered the top pages of her manuscript across the stage. Immediately, the dignified Truett dropped to his knees and captured the drifting pages. The poised Mrs. Cox, not missing a beat, gave a graceful sweep of her hand and declared, "Gone with the wind! And what more appropriate place could it have happened than in Atlanta?!"

GONE WITH THE WIND – PROSPERITY THE GREAT DEPRESSION

The Great Depression came close to burying the work of the denomination. Even in 1925, WMU had to fight tooth and nail to keep the offerings for foreign missions and home missions from being absorbed by the new Cooperative Program. WMU adamantly insisted that guidelines say: "The special thank offerings for state and home missions and the Christmas

Offering for Foreign Missions shall be recognized as gifts in *addition* to the regular contributions to the Cooperative Program." This revealed the core intent of WMU's missions heart. WMU had contributed approximately 43 percent of all the money given to SBC causes, even though WMU had organizations in fewer than half the churches. The Union also decided in 1926 to have the Week of Prayer Observance in early December rather than January, and the change resulted in larger giving.

More trouble surfaced in 1927. As FMB debt continued to grow, leaders discovered that the Board's treasurer had embezzled over $100,000. The FMB announced that the deficit meant its missionaries would soon have to be called home. WMU took immediate action. Mallory led the way, asking for the women to designate the first $48,000 of the next offering to pay for the return of 40 missionaries to their fields and WMU would guarantee their salaries for the coming years.

The 1928 offering went hand in hand with WMU's Ruby Anniversary emphasis on giving. At the annual meeting, delegates had decided that "debt retirement" had lost its appeal as a motivator. A more targeted goal would be an incentive, so they asked the FMB to restrict part of the 1928 Christmas offering for sending out 20 new missionaries. Furthermore, WMU would help in the selection process, and priority would be given to training school graduates. The proposal worked so well that it was employed again in 1929, and that year's offering returned 60 foreign missionaries to their fields. WMU women were now contributing not only to the two offerings each year, but also leading out in promotion of the Cooperative Program.

Then news came that the Home Mission Board had suffered the same fate as the FMB, but to a far greater degree.

In 1928, long-term embezzlements by the HMB's treasurer came to light, and the Board was now stumbling under a $2 million debt. WMU immediately made a formal request that every penny of that year's special offering be spent on missionary support. This staved off clamoring creditors and guaranteed the Board's survival during the Depression. Women found other ways to help, like reviving the efforts of the frontier boxes. This, in turn, allowed home missionaries to survive in hard times.

The Convention continued to do its best to force the special offerings to become part of the total Cooperative Program (CP) allocations, and WMU continued to maintain its ladylike but unmoving insistence that it remain separate and designated. WMU's 1929 report to the SBC stated: "WMU is radically opposed to any budget system which would preclude or discourage the offerings."

A few positive sides to the SBC's handling of the CP emerged, however. In 1931, they recommended that the expenses of state WMU organizations be considered as a deductible promotional expense before state conventions divided funds with the SBC, thus recognizing state WMU organizations as major promotional agencies for the Cooperative Program. The following year, WMU representation was restored to the Promotion Committee of the SBC. Furthermore, in 1933, WMU's corresponding secretary became a member of the SBC Executive Committee by virtue of her office.

The 1920s came to a grinding halt with the United States facing the most colossal financial collapse in its 150-year history. Depression blanketed the country in despair, fear, and anxiety. Money grew scarcer while bread and soup lines grew longer. The work of the Boards and agencies was close to a standstill, and the denominational integrity of Baptists was at stake. In 1933, WMU adopted a plan to reduce the debt of the FMB, suggesting that the SBC devise some means of saving the Convention and its agencies. After literally months of negotiations, the SBC adopted the Hundred Thousand Club, and WMU agreed to support it. Approximately 100,000 persons pledged an extra $1 a month to pay off agency debts. Mallory's new letterhead read: *For a Debtless Denomination by 1945.*

The proportion of Southern Baptist giving coming through WMU channels is shocking. Unemployment was a staggering 25 percent by 1932, and WMU members were responsible for guaranteeing the support of 100 foreign missionaries through the Lottie Moon offering. At the end of 1932, the WMU offerings made up 70 percent of the FMB's income. WMU's contributions were essential to the survival of the boards. By 1934, when WMU membership made up only 13.3 percent of total SBC membership, this small minority was supporting the majority of the work of missions.

In 1934, WMU voted to name the Home Mission Offering after Annie Armstrong. It proved a great shot in the arm, reversed the falling trend of home missions giving, and put 36 new missionaries on the field. WMU never wavered in insisting that special offerings dollars be spent solely for missions rather than debts. The bottom line: Without WMU, the two mission boards would not have survived. By the end of the Depression, the tallies showed that WMU had given over 60 percent of all debt payment money.

There had not been a moment when the women of WMU had bowed to defeat and ceased their struggle to overcome. Their faith emerged stronger for all its testing, and the Union looked forward to what God had ahead for them.

CHAPTER

How Firm a Foundation

"We stand tiptoe on the edge of the future.

— FRANCES LANDRUM TYLER, 1938

ETHLENE BOONE COX CHANGES ROLES

THE GREAT DEPRESSION remained a challenge for WMU and its leadership, especially for Ethlene Boone Cox. Her husband, Wiley, had suffered deep financial losses and fallen victim to crippling heart disease. Ethlene Cox was faced with several crises: Wiley needed her presence and help, and she needed a job. She found it heart-wrenching to leave the presidency. The annual meeting in Constitution Hall, Washington, D.C., marked her final message as president. In her usual dynamic style, Cox challenged her beloved Union to recall WMU's three-fold chord: prayer, study, and missionary education of young people. The audience was rapt as she concluded with the words of a pioneer missionary: "I summon you to fresh vision and a mighty advance for worldwide missions."

The women were loath to lose Cox. But they kept her in the fold as they asked her to prepare the history of WMU for release in 1938. When WMU's long-time treasurer Elizabeth Lowndes retired, the Executive Committee requested Ethlene

Cox to became WMU's first full-time employed treasurer. She knew nothing about bookkeeping, for she loved words and people, not mathematics. It worked beautifully, however, because her friend Mattie Morgan of South Carolina, who was trained in finances, offered to help. Morgan started by volunteering to help Cox get going and ended up not only training her but also assisting her for years to come. Wiley Cox lost his fight with heart disease in 1934.

Thanks to friend Mattie Morgan, Ethlene Cox was able to serve as treasurer and to answer the many calls to speak. Mallory often said that WMU had a double bargain in Cox, calling her "a treasure and a treasurer." Her reports were never dull figures but moving accounts of people and facts reflected in figures. For some 19 years, Cox served as treasurer and a trusted advisor to WMU.

LAURA DELL MALOTTE ARMSTRONG AND KATHLEEN MALLORY

Laura Dell Malotte Armstrong, the first president to come from west of the Mississippi, became national president in 1933. Her credentials were impressive, and so was her service. A preacher's kid, Laura was active in all the missions organizations. She taught school and then married a young attorney, Frank Armstrong. While serving as a legal clerk, Laura Armstrong gained invaluable skills that she readily used in her work as president. It could not have been easy to follow the silver-tongued Ethlene Boone Cox. Armstrong had something of a halting delivery but compensated for this with profound depth and spiritual wisdom. She and Mallory worked together in great love and respect and were able to call upon the sagacity of Cox as well. The 1934 annual meeting in Fort Worth was the first at which Armstrong presided. The home missions offering was officially renamed the Annie W. Armstrong Offering. Annie Armstrong opposed the idea but relented when friends convinced her that it would make a difference in the giving. It did indeed.

The first years of Laura Armstrong's presidency were extremely difficult as the nation tried to pull out of the Depression. An unusual number of anniversaries took place during her years as president—a total of five between 1936 and 1938. Armstrong presided at the women's meeting of BWA in Berlin in 1934. Her legal expertise revealed itself in her unbiased decision-making and ease in handling parliamentary procedures. And her calm confidence was a special boon to delegates who came from tense areas standing on the brink of world war. At the 1935 WMU meeting in Memphis, Armstrong presided over discussions and decisions concerning convention-wide mission study. WMU and the two mission boards agreed to plan a cycle of graded, correlated mission study books. FMB published the first one. Known as the Graded Series, the books proved extremely effective in churchwide missions education.

1936 AND THE BEGINNING OF JUBILEES

More than 2,000 Baptist women gathered in St. Louis in 1936. This was the year WMU began Focus Weeks. WMU's longtime friend Nannie Helen Burroughs was a guest speaker at the St. Louis meeting. A gifted presenter, Burroughs always delivered messages that resonated with the women. WMU presented Burroughs with a gift to establish a Literature Department for the National Baptist Convention; it became an annual gift and aided in supporting that ministry for National Baptist women.

As usual, money was on the women's minds — how to raise it for missions needs and how to promote tithing. A 1936 study reported that Southern Baptist per capita giving to missions, education, and benevolence was the lowest among denominations — a meager $1.87. However, when studied separately from Convention statistics, WMU per capita giving for the same period was $4.49. In spite of the crisis of the Depression, WMU did not ease up on its support. In the nine years from 1928 through 1936, the percentage of HMB re[illegible] coming from WMU ranged from 59 pe[illegible] to a whopping 91 percent of the Board's [illegible] receipts. Small wonder it was noted that [illegible] had saved both mission boards, first from [illegible] ing bankruptcy due to embezzlement and [illegible] because of the Great Depression.

A CENTENNIAL AND A JUBILEE

Of the five anniversaries to be celebrated in just three years, the most outstanding was the Golden Jubilee, WMU's 50th anniversary. Baptists were also commemorating the Convention's Centennial, as well as 50 years of WMU publications, the Shuck Centennial, and 50 years of Sunbeam Bands. It fell to Laura Armstrong to select the Jubilee committee. She appointed Cora McWilliams (Mrs. George A.) of Missouri to head the planning committee. The talented McWilliams approached it as a celebration emphasizing spiritual growth. Special plans for giving were also incorporated into the Jubilee's celebration.

The Shuck Centennial had long been anticipated by the women of WMU, whose pioneer leaders had been inspired by Henrietta Hall Shuck's selfless devotion to God's calling as the first American woman to serve as a missionary in China. The Centennial celebration began in the early fall of 1935 and concluded with the 1936 annual meeting. In the Christmas Offering designations, women placed $30,000 to build a school for girls in South China and to provide Bible training schools for women in China. At the 1936 annual meeting, Mallory paid tribute to her life and reported that the money designated to memorialize the work of Henrietta Hall Shuck had exceeded $100,000. Mallory's message was followed by one from Mrs. F. Y. O. Ling, president of All-China Woman's Missionary Union. Ling paid moving tribute to the life and sacrifice of Mrs. Shuck.

The Sunbeam Jubilee was the other highlight of the St. Louis meeting. Juliette Mather, young people's secretary, presided and introduced their special guest, Cousin George himself, the founder of Sunbeams. The entire body rose in tribute to the 76-year-old George Braxton Taylor. Much of the 1937 annual meeting in New Orleans was centered on Jubliee plans. Ethlene Boone Cox's book, *Following in His Train,* was released, recounting the story of the first 50 years of WMU.

JUBILEE!! RICHMOND, VIRGINIA, MAY 1938

Excitement filled the air as women gathered in Richmond, Virginia, exactly 50 years to the week that they had first gathered there to organize a Woman's Missionary Union. In May 1888, a little handful of brave delegates from 12 states had met in the basement of Broad Street Methodist Church. On May 8, 1938, an impressive 3,535 women from 19 states met in Richmond's auditorium, focused on celebrating 50 years of God's guidance for the Union. Retiring secretary Lulie K. Wharton (Mrs. H. M.) was honored by the Union for her many years of effective and selfless service. Her successor was Frances Landrum Tyler (Mrs. Wilfred C.) of Mississippi. Tyler was to serve with distinction for 19 years. As women looked together at a comparison of WMU membership between 1888 and 1938, they were struck again by the blessings of God. Membership had grown from 37,200 in 1891 to 705,399 in this year of 1938. Leadership had surely been the key in such phenomenal growth.

Even as the women celebrated 50 years of history, wars loomed on the world scene. Visitors at this historic WMU gathering had come from many corners of the globe where WMU had made an impact. They were introduced at one of the sessions.

The planned Jubilee was long remembered. In a Parade of States, representatives dropped contribution certificates into a golden chest, gifts totaling $60,000. Golden trumpets sounded at the introduction of the pageant, "The Path of the Golden Years." More than 4,500 people observed some 350 Richmond young people present the Golden Yesterday, the Golden Today, and the Golden Tomorrow. Scores of missionaries were present, as well as a handful of elderly women who had actually been present at that 1888 inaugural meeting. Annie Armstrong, 88 years old and bedridden in Baltimore, sent a message of encouragement for the occasion. Of course, she included in this her final message, the two words that are forever linked to her name and spirit: Go Forward.

Chapter 18

OKLAHOMA CITY

The 1939 meeting in Oklahoma City had a flavor all its own, reflecting the rich Indian heritage of the state. At this meeting, WMU first asked the Brotherhood Commission to take an interest in RA work, including furnishing counselors when requested.

On the first day of the Oklahoma City meeting, nine members of the Fairfax, Oklahoma, Indian Missionary Society appeared in costume. Mrs. John Smith, a Creek Indian, told of a visit from Miss Annie W. Armstrong, who rode on horseback to organize the first missionary society among the Indians. Smith was one of the Indian girls educated by Armstrong and her Baltimore friend. She told of boxes received at Christmas and of their tree above which they put the name of Miss Armstrong. This was followed by a report from Mrs. Lena Rivera, an Osage Indian; Mrs. Eula Eshleman, a Pawnee, sang a solo to conclude their presentation.

The 1939 meeting, the first after the death of Annie Armstrong, was filled with tributes to the great leader. Kathleen Mallory's report was built around statements that Annie Armstrong had made through the years. Mallory stated: "Miss Annie W. Armstrong, who 50 years before, did more than any other one person to consummate the organization now known as Woman's Missionary Union. . . . It is gratefully believed that she laid at Christ's feet a golden sheaf from her long life of sowing and tending in His many fields."

As 1939 ended, the specter of global war of proportions never before imagined loomed on the horizon. WMU sent contributions for relief in areas already wartorn; yet could not help but look with foreboding at what might well lie ahead. Within just two years, their worst fears were realized.

CHAPTER

"A Mighty Fortress Is Our God —*a bulwark never failing*"

THE TWIN REALITIES: DEBT AND WAR

WOMAN'S MISSIONARY UNION, and indeed the entire SBC, entered the decade of the 1940s with the inevitability of world conflict. A weaker Union would have wanted to fade quietly into the night, but adversity merely seemed to strengthen WMU's resolve. When women gathered in Baltimore in 1940, two topics seemed to permeate the atmosphere: the possibility of war and the ever-present story of the Convention—debt.

Denominational debt was not of WMU's making, but the organization was determined to attack it head on. On Monday, Laura Armstrong spoke briefly on "For a Debtless Denomination by 1945." The heads of the two mission boards and presidents of the seminaries next explained what debt clearance would mean to their ministries. Kathleen Mallory then spoke, and as she drove the theme home, the state WMU executives and young people's secretaries walked across the back of the platform, unfurling a huge banner bearing the motto: For a Debtless Denomination by 1945. Mallory immediately presented the recommendation of the Executive

Committee, that in light of the Convention's $3,000,000 debt, WMU would undertake to raise $1,000,000 of that amount. It was a staggering amount, and yet it passed without question.

Charles Maddry, secretary of the FMB, announced to Baptists at large: "We will have our debts paid by 1945. WMU has promised and you can count on them." Kathleen Mallory personally made the point each day for the following five years by using stationery with the letterhead: For a Debtless Denomination by 1945. In spite of debt, the Convention reached out to Baptists around the world by appointing a Baptist World Emergency Committee. Three from WMU were included on the committee: Kathleen Mallory, Laura Armstrong, and Blanche White of Virginia. WMU specifically provided funds to bring missionaries home from the Orient and supported HMB work among the US military camps.

Several "firsts" occurred for WMU in 1940. WMU officers were designated as the standing committee for WMU work. Up until 1937, the committee had been headed by a man. Women now gave their own reports. A special name also appeared in WMU's Annual Report this year, one that would appear countless times in the following years—Alma Hunt. At the Baltimore meeting, Hunt gave part of the report on YWA work. Little did she know that she would be giving literally hundreds of reports for the next three decades.

In 1940, three interracial institutes were held. Their purpose was to train African American women as leaders of missionary societies. Nannie Helen Burroughs was ill from cancer surgery but still managed to help Kathleen Mallory plan the events. The struggles they went through with Jim Crow restrictions would have flattened the hopes of lesser women, but not the women of the two missions organizations. The institutes succeeded in spite of rank prejudice and discrimination. The life story of Nannie Helen Burroughs, a woman of incredible grace and courage, is a study in heroism.

A money problem of a different kind arose in 1940. The Training School had outgrown its size, and in the fall, WMU laid the cornerstone for a beautiful new building.

Additionally, this year, camping was on the rise. There were more than 25,000 Baptist campers, nearly half of them in Texas. Camps were wonderful tools for missionary education.

However, the looming shadow of war in Asia and Europe was on the minds of each woman at the meeting. One of the speakers warned the women that their sons might be on the battlefront in a matter of months. It proved all too prophetic.

1941 — WAR

America was embroiled in deadly World War II by the end of 1941. WMU continued with the challenges of stewardship. For years, WMU had designated by name the missionaries they supported, but this year, that practice stopped, and a general lump of the Lottie Moon offering went into the FMB salary budget.

As the shadows of war grew deeper, more women were working outside the home. An estimated 2,700,000 women in the South were employed, but probably no more than 6 percent of Southern Baptist women were in that number. The circle plan, working so successfully in missionary societies, easily fit the needs of businesswomen as well. As a result, evening businesswomen's circles were organized. They were soon growing at a faster rate than other circles. By the end of the decade, nearly every state had a statewide BWC organization.

Youth organizations also continued to grow, and something new occurred among RAs. Mississippi WMU employed

J. Ivyloy Bishop to work with RA camps. Bishop, the first man employed by WMU for professional RA work, was soon jointly employed with Alabama and South Carolina as well as Mississippi. Within two years, he moved to the Southwide WMU staff in Birmingham. Mary Christian, who had taught missionary education at the Training School, also came to the WMU staff in Birmingham in 1942 as a WMU representative. The Personal Service division had grown each year, and someone was needed to promote it full-time. Also in 1942, leaders voted to change the name "Personal Service" to "Community Missions," a name that was used for many years to follow.

December 7, 1941, arrived, and the immediacy of war was all too real. WMU could not get designated Lottie Moon money to its allocated places in enemy lands, so they asked the FMB to reserve those funds until the war's conclusion. These reserved funds would give the Board a head start on postwar advance and rehabilitation.

1942 AND SAN ANTONIO

WMU continued its programs as best it could in wartime conditions. The theme for the 1942 annual meeting in San Antonio was Expect—Attempt, the two great words from William Carey's famous quote: "Attempt great things for God; Expect great things from God," in honor of the sesquicentennial of the Modern Missionary Movement and Carey's arrival in India. Laura Armstrong rejoiced with the Union that nearly 42,000 WMU organizations were active, but she challenged the women to reach out to the churches where there were no WMU organizations. Kathleen Mallory noted that over 11,700 Southern Baptist churches did not have any missions program.

Young People's Secretary Juliette Mather had acquired quite a reputation as a "pageant maker," and at the Friday evening session presented the celebration of the Sesquicentennial of Carey's arrival in India. The pageant featured scenes from Carey's life, first as a boy, next as a schoolteacher, and then the publication of his famous tract, "Enquiry." Children, women, and men of various ages participated in the pageant that was the grand finale of the annual meeting.

DECLINING DEBT

WMU was relentless in working towards its goal of a debtless denomination. Its efforts did not go unnoticed. In 1942, the SBC Executive Committee gave "especial mention and grateful appreciation to the WMU for their gracious, sustained, and increasingly substantial help. If our men will rally to this cause in a similar way we shall surely have a Debtless Denomination by 1945." A prime mover in the process was Alma Worrill Wright, an outstanding state president in Alabama who went on to head the stewardship committee of WMU for 10 years. She led the women to adopt the slogan "Debt-free in '43, Count on Me." This tireless woman was the "General" of Stewardship, speaking most effectively all across the convention, inspiring women and men as well to personal responsibility in stewardship. A veritable army of WMU foot soldiers took Wright's slogan personally: "It depends on me."

The denomination did not become debt-free in 1945—it was 1943. On March 11, 1943, the FMB sent a cable to every mission saying it was free of debt. When the figures were tallied, WMU had given a full 61.2 percent of all the debt payment money since 1933. A convention leader commented: "Women just hate debt."

1943 — WITHOUT AN ANNUAL MEETING

War conditions were so pervasive that attempting to hold the usual annual meeting was not a good option. Mallory, Armstrong, and the Executive Board decided instead that each state would receive the published book of reports. Birmingham urged each state to promote local and regional gatherings.

OKLAHOMA CITY AND LAURA ARMSTRONG

The 1944 annual meeting was not an ordinary one for several reasons. Because of war conditions, no city could handle both the SBC and WMU meetings at the same time, so WMU met in September in Oklahoma City. During the war, WMU had been helping start churches and WMU groupings near military installations. And, as soon as Italy surrendered, WMU started sending food and clothing to Italian Baptists. As various areas were liberated, relief quickly began.

Dr. Theron Rankin, secretary-elect of the FMB, was presented by Laura Armstrong. The audience stood, expressing loyal cooperation to Dr. Rankin as he assumed his duties. Following Laura Armstrong's election to serve another year as president, she stated that it would be the last year she could accept the office. For several years she had been suffering increasing problems with high blood pressure but could not bring herself to slow down the pace of work. Less than a year later, a cerebral hemorrhage proved fatal.

Before her death, Armstrong, at Kathleen Mallory's request, selected a committee of women in February 1944 to study how the Union could best carry forward its purpose in promoting missions in the dawning of a second century of Southern Baptist work. Cora McWilliams (Mrs. George) of Missouri was named chair of the survey committee and was to report its findings to the delegates. The purpose was to "present plans and policies of the WMU."

The committee surveyed pastors, missionaries, state WMU leaders, and WMS members in churches. The committee's recommendations reflected its members' vision for future work. They brought the report in January 1945. Some of the findings were disturbing, and some of their recommendations were startling. Discussing the report actually strained some friendships that had been solid for many years, as opinions widely differed. One new idea was for the president to appoint a budget committee annually because the findings showed that the Union must expand in order to accomplish its maximum growth and that would clearly require a larger budget. Furthermore, WMU needed a stated budget outlined and then implemented.

The committee recommended restudying the Standard of Excellence that had been in place for 34 years. The survey focused attention on the missionary fundamentals of stewardship, community missions, and mission study. This committee ushered in an era of analysis for greater efficiency. Because of the scope of the survey, its plans would actually fall on the shoulders of another president and another executive secretary.

One of the last contributions of Laura Armstrong to her beloved Union was a study of the report with Kathleen Mallory. She then appointed committees to set in motion the survey's ideas. In just a matter of weeks, Armstrong lost her battle with high blood pressure.The overall impression of the report was that just about everything about WMU needed overhauling. The report was actually so controversial that Kathleen Mallory sealed it in a vault to be read only with permission. Some felt the report implied lack of confidence in the officers, so it became a test of WMU's ability to handle differences of opinion. The committee felt that WMU should have a closer relationship to the church's overall program and that workers with youth and children should have more status. Meanwhile, Mallory quietly implemented many of its proposals.

For the second time, no annual meeting was held. Much was going on across the globe in hot spots of war. Even through the worst of conditions, the vision of WMU remained a focus. The Lottie Moon Christmas Offering exceeded $1,000,000 for the first time that year. WMU also began the Mission Round Table, a plan by which WMS members shared in buying and studying books with missionary significance and interest. As Southern Baptists reflected on their centennial in 1945, they looked to ways to better evangelize the nation. They soon proposed a plan to win a million converts in observance of 100 years of ministry. As usual, the women joined in the drive. The Texas evangelism secretary gave a report that gives insight into the impact of WMU on the campaign. Women comprised 90 percent of the attendance at morning revival services, 95 percent of those at prayer meetings, and 75 percent of those at evening services. Plus, they were 95 percent of the evangelism workers. Mallory, in her usual kind, understated way, declared: "It is humbly believed that quite a few of the baptisms were in part at least (a) . . . result of community missions."

Sadness loomed over WMU in 1945. Laura Armstrong, their beloved president, had died, and because there was no annual meeting that year, the Executive Committee met in Birmingham in July to select a president. Olive Martin (Mrs. George) Martin, long-time Virginia president, was chosen. She began 11 years of service and led WMU in a difficult postwar era, serving with distinction alongside two executive directors. Olive Martin left her stamp on the Union she dearly loved. The onset of a new era was just ahead for Baptist women.

A New Era Begins

"It is so old a story, yet somehow always new."
—HEINRICH HEINE

MALLORY AND MARTIN AND MIAMI

AFTER THE TRAUMA of world war and the lack of opportunity for annual meetings, the women of WMU were excited about the 1946 annual meeting in Miami. Olive Martin had been selected president by an emergency meeting of the Executive Committee and needed all her platform skills to remain poised and confident in her first meeting. Her vibrant voice enhanced her effectiveness in presiding. Martin was officially elected by the delegates in Miami, and the women stood in support of their new president. Laura Armstrong was eulogized at the gathering, as WMU recalled her gifts of leadership. The Union honored her memory with a $50,000 gift through the Lottie Moon offering to establish the Armstrong Memorial Training School in Rome, Italy.

Mallory's report was presented to a large crowd. Mallory might have been small and slender in frame, but she had become a woman of stature in the Southern Baptist Convention. It was WMU's 58th year, and the list of attendees looked like something of a who's who of Baptist statesmanship. The secretaries of the two mission Board also participated.

Dr. Rushbrooke, president of the BWA, was present, as were two of America's most famous pastors, C. Roy Angell of Miami and R. G. Lee of Memphis. R. G. Lee reminisced about his years as a Sunbeam.

Even in the buoyancy of spirit experienced in a post-war atmosphere, WMU faced the usual problems with SBC leadership over the Union's relationship with the Convention. There were men who continued to desire to alter that relationship and thus gain control over the functioning of WMU. In one such effort in 1945, the Executive Committee had voted that WMU must submit reports and budget requests for the Training School, since SBC agencies were likewise required to report. The Training School graciously complied.

An ever-present "thorn in the flesh" was the issue of percentage of CP funds going to the FMB and HMB. The Convention Executive Committee continued in its efforts to have WMU's two missions offerings count as part of the overall percentage of funds going to the two missions boards, and WMU continued to oppose such a move.

CONCLUDING AN ERA

WMU was beginning its 59th year as an official organization in 1947. Only a handful of those who had been the youngest present at the 1888 meeting were still alive to remember those days, but the pioneer spirit remained. Kathleen Mallory and Olive Martin, as well as the hundreds of women in WMU leadership, were students of their own history, recalling the paths on which they had walked.

The scope of world conflict seemed to usher in a new reality of the global implications of WMU's closeness of heart and purpose with sisters of common faith across the world. The war had shattered the women's committee of the BWA, and it was basically not functioning at the time of the 1947 Congress in Copenhagen. Olive Martin was asked to preside over the women's meeting. Close friend Blanche S. White of Virginia went with her. Martin was one of three women (also Mrs. Ernest Brown of England and Miriam Bates of Canada) selected to form the women's committee. Much of the forward thinking came from Blanche White, who had tapped funds from Virginia's Lottie Moon offering to organize BWA's women. Returning to Europe the next year, Martin and White brought about the appointment of a new BWA women's committee. While there, Martin helped European women form the European Baptist Women's Union (EBWU), just the first of several continental unions she helped organize.

World War II had changed the old order in America as well. Racial tensions were high. As usual, WMU women were among the first in the SBC to lead out, and the Union's educational materials grew increasingly open in stating that white women must respect African Americans as equals. However, on one of two occasions an article appeared that sounded patronizing, with a bit of "equal but separate" flavor. This was quickly brought to a halt. In 1947, Nannie Burroughs was featured on the cover of *Royal Service*. From that point on, segregation was never defended in WMU materials. The new generation of young WMU leaders wanted to integrate WMU conferences and began a trend in that direction.

The 1947 meeting was highlighted by the 40th anniversary of both the Woman's Training School and Young Woman's Auxiliary. Olive Martin spoke of "These Forty Years," and

Juliette Mather presented the program featuring YWA. Mather had been young people's secretary for 25 years, and all the youth organizations had grown exponentially during her tenure. Several hundred YWA members were seated on a raised platform behind the speakers, forming a living YWA emblem in black against a background of white. The effect was striking. Numerous women in leadership, including Alma Hunt, dean of women at William Jewell College, spoke of the contributions YWA had made in their lives.

The Executive Committee had considered changes that would strengthen WMU's overall ministry. WMU headquarters was crowded, and, in January 1948, the committee recommended that the Union purchase property in Birmingham in order to build a headquarters building. Studies by other committees brought other proposals to the attention of WMU. Many leaders were convinced that a new day in growth was in the offing. The Executive Committee concurred with the finding of the Survey Committee in feeling that an editorial department needed to be expeditiously established. There would need to be a constitutional amendment made in order to create such a department. The new office of editorial secretary would be vital. In short order, the eyes of the committee fell on Juliette Mather, who combined writing gifts and people skills with creative genius.

This was a tough decision for Mather, however, who loved her role with the youth organizations. All her years of experience with youth and her expertise in writing and editing made Mather the perfect candidate. After all, she had given birth to several of the existing magazines! With Juliette Mather accepting this new position, various changes in other areas would also take place. It meant the national executive secretary would no longer be required to edit *Royal Service,* an exacting and time-consuming job. Mather would now be giving up her traveling to promote the young people's' work she had loved these more than 26 years. Instead, she would plan and edit the women's magazine, as well as those for young people. One leader commented that Juliette Mather with a new title was like a bride with a new name. She had spent so much time on the road in her first job that she was taking engagements only to keep "from growing to her editorial chair."

CHANGES IN THE MAKING

Things were changing in a hurry, and Kathleen Mallory looked with clear vision at what lay ahead. Here were plans for building a new headquarters. Here was an editorial department with a number of magazines to produce. Here was a need for new equipment to facilitate the handling of magazines and literature orders. She had been working in close harmony with Juliette Mather as young people's secretary for over 26 years and there would be adjustments necessary when a new secretary was chosen to replace her. Mallory looked back over her 36 years to the young and inexperienced Alabama WMU secretary who had come to this office to lead the Baptist women of the nation. Memories flooded her heart of challenges, of trials, of staggering disappointments and surging joys, as she had worked with women of all temperaments and talents and loved them all. Her heart told her that the time had come to step aside from being the heart of this WMU family that she loved as her own, and let God's next woman for the job come to her desk.

On that evening of January 30, 1948, after the Executive Committee meeting had ended and the members had returned to their homes, Kathleen Mallory typed a letter of intent and quietly mailed it to members of the Committee, state executive secretaries, and other leaders. In it, she basically stated that she felt the new secretary for young people should have the privilege of starting her work with the executive secretary who would be counseling her from the very beginning. She also felt the next executive secretary should be the one with input into the plans for the new building. Thus, the new editorial secretary, young people's leader, and new executive secretary would essentially all begin at the same time. Mallory concluded her letter: ". . . and because I love the Union better than I love my own life, I find it easier than otherwise it could possibly be to ask the WMU Nominating Committee to refrain from submitting my name for re-election in May."

Meanwhile, the chair of WMU's nominating committee, Cora McWilliams of Missouri, had been searching for a new young people's secretary. While on a trip to her former church in Liberty, Missouri, during fall 1947, McWilliams visited with Alma Hunt, dean of women at William Jewell College. She knew that Hunt had been one of the leaders for the YWA Conference at Ridgecrest for a number of years and would thus know the young people's secretaries for the different states. Did Hunt have any suggestion that would help the nominating committee? She did. Hunt recommended Margaret Bruce of Tennessee.

It was not until three months later that Cora McWilliams knew her committee would also have the task of nominating a new executive secretary. McWilliams returned to Liberty, this time to approach Alma Hunt with the possibility of her being WMU's next executive secretary. Hunt had been active as a Sunbeam, GA, and YWA. She excelled in YWA leadership locally, in her state, and at national events, so she was well-known to WMU leadership. After years of teaching and working in school administration, Hunt had been selected as dean of women at William Jewell College. When Cora McWilliams told her that she was the nominating committee's choice for executive secretary, her immediate response was, "I'm not a speaker!" Those who knew Alma Hunt in later years would be astounded that she could ever have made such a statement, so gifted was she as a public speaker. However, her lack of confidence in that area made her look long and hard at the possibility of accepting the new position. In the end, Hunt felt confident that God would provide the skills she would need. And did He ever! Many years later, leaders who recalled Hunt's doubts about her skills as a speaker, could only smile and comment, "When Moses cried out to God that he was 'slow of speech and please send someone else to do the speaking,' the Lord appointed Aaron to the task. Alma Hunt didn't need an Aaron!"

On Tuesday, May 18, 1948, in Memphis, Tennessee, Alma Hunt was elected as the fourth executive secretary of Woman's Missionary Union. The slender, blonde-haired woman in the fashionable dress and high-heeled shoes must have looked out of place surrounded by gray-haired women of mature years. Nonetheless, Hunt quickly won the hearts of those who found behind the stylish appearance a depth of spiritual maturity and business acumen that would galvanize the growing ministries and outreach of an organization whose time had come. The women of WMU stood as one to welcome their new leader. In her acceptance speech, Hunt promised WMU two things: commitment to the people of WMU and commitment to its purposes. She never departed from those pledges. At the same session, Olive Martin was re-elected president and Kathleen Mallory was made an honorary member of the Executive Committee.

In the Memphis meeting, thousands of women from across the nation had gathered not only to conduct their business and make plans for the years to come, but also to pay special tribute to their beloved Kathleen Mallory. In a moving tribute by Missouri's Mrs. H. W. Munger, Munger characterized Mallory as the "King's Daughter," consecrated to the King of kings, recounting her many years of capable and devoted commitment to the task of worldwide missions. WMU had literally been Mallory's life. She had left behind a thriving organization on the cusp of a new era. Mallory only lived six more years but continued her faithful prayer support and encouragement. Her far-seeing vision looked beyond the immediate to see that God had new horizons for WMU, and she rejoiced for what lay ahead. Indubitably, 1948 marked the beginning of the greatest growth in WMU history. It also became the period of greatest change. A new era had indeed begun.

CHAPTER

Christ for the World We Sing

"The World to Christ We Bring"
—1950 WMU Hymn of the Year

ALMA HUNT AT THE HELM

AFTER THE ELECTION of Alma Hunt as the new executive secretary that pivotal May afternoon in 1948, Kathleen Mallory called the state officers together, handed her gavel to Hunt, put her arm around her, and prayed God's special blessings on her. It is just as well that Hunt didn't know at that moment the reaction of at least one of the "old guard" of faithful WMU leaders sitting in the audience. As the elderly woman looked up to the stage and saw the fashionable young blonde assume the helm of Woman's Missionary Union, she began to quietly weep. That night she prayed that the Lord would preserve the Union. The weeping woman must certainly have been comforted at the very next annual meeting to hear Hunt declare to the delegates: "We must build on the foundation which has been laid. We must underscore with our heart's blood the eternal, unfaded verities, and in addition make our own contribution."

As Alma Hunt assumed her new position on October 1, 1948, daunting reality confronted her that fall morning in Birmingham. The spacious Comer Building that Mallory and the small staff moved into in 1921 was now piled with boxes and stacks of literature and supplies. Hunt watched as six women with noisy typewriters worked in one small room with no outside window for light. Filing cabinets stood in the hall and bags of accumulated mail waited for staff to have enough time to open them. Boxes of magazines ready for shipment to subscribers lined the hall, awaiting available hands to prepare them for stuffing and mailing. Shortly thereafter, *Royal Service* carried a royal apology, explaining, "Yes, we are ashamed of the delayed service," and proceeded to paint a verbal picture of space too crowded and staff too sparse. The article ended with a plea for patience until the new building was ready.

It would take time; Hunt, staff, the Executive Committee, and a Building Committee estimated it would cost $300,000 for an adequate headquarters building; the Union voted to give the first $100,000 in tribute to Kathleen Mallory's 36 years of service. The architect designed a building, revised his drawings, and then, with money considerations as a reality check, revised them yet again. Meanwhile, Hunt and the staff coped as best they could.

Much of Hunt's first month was spent with the lawyer, the auditor, the real estate agent, the equipment salesmen, and employees. In order to get a handle on what was the best approach in publications, a field unfamiliar to her, she traveled to visit major periodical publishers. Hunt was in search of expertise. When she made her first report to the Executive Committee, Hunt admitted she had set up a dangerous habit, working late into the nights, trying to meet deadlines. In all sincerity, she promised not to keep doing so. That promise was impossible to keep; other than stopping briefly for two surgeries and one summer's collapse due to exhaustion; she lived and breathed WMU for the next 26 years.

CHANGES IN THE OFFING

Alma Hunt soon realized that her administration was a time of adjustment for WMU as well as for herself personally. Olive Martin learned to work with a very different personality in the office of chief administrator, and over her more than 2½ decades, Hunt developed an ability to work in harmony and joy with a vast array of personalities in the office of Union president. The same held true in her dealings with SBC leadership, especially the presidents of the two mission boards. The same year Hunt assumed office, M. Theron Rankin of the Foreign Mission Board issued a dramatic challenge for foreign missions: Advance. It would depend on a larger share of the Cooperative Program (CP) and increased giving to the Lottie Moon Christmas Offering. True to form, WMU proceeded to finance this great period of growth in missions with an even stronger emphasis on the special offerings. It became two streams of funding: the Cooperative Program and WMU's special missions offerings. The first reflected pragmatism, the second, the heart of WMU.

Theron Rankin began calling WMU the Board's "channel to the churches." The three-strand cord involving WMU with the two mission boards has remained the heart and soul of Baptist missions endeavors for more than 150 years. Any information concerning the developments in the two missions boards is clearly reflected in the footnotes of WMU. Alma Hunt came to be known for her frequent declaration: "WMU has no program of its own. Our program is that of the Foreign Mission Board and the Home Mission Board."

The question of making the special offerings churchwide, became a matter of discussion in 1948. Dr. Rankin had first mentioned it to a WMU committee, but they had turned him down. However, several larger churches in North Carolina, Louisiana, and Texas were already observing churchwide offerings. It seemed especially appealing at Christmastime, as an alternative to rampant secularization of the Holy Season. Marie Mathis, president of Texas WMU, had a special fascination with the Lottie Moon offering and was an amazing promoter. She had begun her efforts when serving as Texas WMU executive secretary. By 1951, these efforts led Texas to give 37.5 percent of the entire 1951 offering. Several of the more conservative Virginia leaders, including Olive Martin and Blanche White, protested that churchwide offerings would undermine the CP. In an Executive Board discussion, one of the Board members said to Blanche White, "But Miss Blanche, where do you think we ladies get our money for the offerings? From our husbands!!"

In another area, changes were also occurring. By 1948, Southern Seminary was granting bachelor of divinity degrees in religious education to men. At the same time, they also began putting pressure on WMUTS to grant a religious education degree to women. The Training School would naturally be affected. Many more changes were in the offing—just one more area where Hunt would need all her wits and wisdom about her.

AND WHAT IS "AUXILIARY?"

How many times has the question been asked through the years: what does *auxiliary* mean to WMU? In earlier years, the meaning of the term probably was determined by personality. Olive Martin as president took a strict view, believing auxiliary status gave WMU freedom to dictate policy to the missions boards and the right to control funds contributed by women. Kathleen Mallory was pretty well considered beyond reach of negotiation; she was a force within herself. Then came Alma Hunt to leadership, and she was continually quizzed, largely by SBC leadership among the men, "What do *you* mean when you say 'auxiliary?' " During Hunt's years, she led WMU to return to the original definition of auxiliary. She was disarming in her approach, and SBC leadership quickly came to accord great respect to her skills and discernment. After she took office, Hunt was invited to help form the SBC Inter-Agency Council, serving as its president for several years. Likewise, she gradually withdrew WMU from control of expenditures of the special offerings.

GETTING READY FOR A NEW HALF-CENTURY

The WMU meeting in Oklahoma City in 1949 had several special moments, including the introduction of Mrs. George Veal of Dallas, Texas. Mrs. Veal had been at the 1888 meeting in Richmond when WMU was officially born. This was Alma Hunt's first year as chief executive, and a new generation of women met with great anticipation to hear about missions work around the world.

Hunt was able to report on several "firsts." This year, for the first time, more men than women were counselors for RA (Royal Ambassadors) members. Several new job positions were created, and the WMU staff was increased. Myrtle Creasman, a pastor's wife from Tennessee, became director of stewardship. Besides writing missionary programs for

Royal Service for 17 years, Creasman had authored countless pageants. Employed part-time, Creasman actually worked full-time and was always in demand as a speaker. Her friend Edith Stokely, also of Tennessee, was employed as community missions director, and Mildred McMurry (Mrs. Willian), likewise from Tennessee, was the first full-time mission study director. Speaker, writer, and scholar, McMurry became a worldwide leader of women.

WMU continued to blend the best of the past with the unique challenges a new half-century brought. The box work that had made such an impact in frontier missions in those early years took on a new and creative form—Christmas in August. Although officially taking off in 1950, the seed for Christmas in August was planted in 1927 when missionary Elizabeth Wiley spoke in a church in Virginia, telling about missions work at a school in Shanghai, China. The Sunbeams in the church sent 100 gifts to China and a wonderful tradition was born that has thrived through the years. Membership increased greatly in 1950; for the first time enlistment surpassed 1 million.

A singular moment in the hearts and minds of thousands of WMU women came this same year in Cleveland, Ohio, at the Baptist World Congress. Ayako Hino (who later became secretary of the BWA Women's Department) came to carry the flag of Japan in the Roll Call of Nations. Her body literally shook with fear of carrying her country's flag in the United States so quickly on the heels of World War II. WMU leaders were concerned about audience reaction when Hino appeared with the flag, but at that very moment, BWA president C. Oscar Johnson called out to the audience, "We will all rise for Japan." The audience stood to its feet.

A NATION IN THE MIDST OF CHANGE

Hunt took leadership at a time when America was in a period of great postwar changes. Looming large was civil rights. The racial controversy became so heated that many Southerners were too inflamed to even tolerate the mention of black ministry. To quote Hunt, she felt her job was to "keep the cars from being uncoupled from the train." It was no easy task. Each time racial reconciliation was mentioned in WMU magazines, a barrage of hate mail and cancellations would flood the Birmingham headquarters. Baker James Cauthen, executive secretary of the Foreign Mission Board, constantly reminded WMU that news of racial violence in Southern Baptist territory echoed around the world, seriously undermining the efforts of missionaries. Despite hate mail and snubs, WMU took a progressive stand through its speakers at every annual meeting for the next two decades.

Alma Hunt had the joy of leading WMU into their new headquarters in September 1951. An excellent building ready to be occupied had become available. Hunt was also learning the loneliness of being an executive. Truman's oft-quoted remark, "the buck stops here," came to have personal meaning for her. Soon the message got around that the new leader of WMU had a firm but fair mind. She was not one to be easily intimidated, nor did she intimidate others. She early on stated her belief that if "two people think alike, the organization can get along without one of them."

AN ICON RETIRES

There was an element of nostalgia at the annual meeting in Miami in 1952; an era was ending as Ethlene Boone Cox, that golden voice with the servant heart, retired after years of devoted, creative service. The women paid loving tribute to her magnificent years of service. The Miami meeting was poignant for other reasons as well. Missionary Everly Hayes was present and shared firsthand news of the last days of Dr. Bill Wallace's life in Wuchow, China, and his martyrdom there.

Work was expanding into new states, and WMU had to develop new approaches. In pioneer areas, there were few leaders, and churches were small and scattered. WMU felt the best approach was to allow the state WMU executive secretary to represent WMU among other church programs as well, making it a department approach. Naturally, the obstacle was money, and, in cooperation with the HMB, WMU allocated $5,000 of the Annie W. Armstrong Offering to "WMU promotion of missionary education in weak states." The amount grew with the growth of the work. Additionally, 1952 saw a change in the presentation of the prayer calendar in *Royal Service,* as missionaries were listed on their birthdays, a feature that has stood the test of time.

GAs AND RAs CELEBRATE

GAs and their leaders celebrated 40 years of organization in Houston. Appropriately, the 1953 annual meeting theme was "A Story to Tell." In beautiful pageantry, more than a hundred white-robed GAs with lighted candles participated. A coronation scene was portrayed, and the closing tableau revealed nationals from all continents looking toward a revolving globe, over which rested the shadow of the cross.

In August, more than 5,000 RAs congregated in Atlanta to celebrate 45 years of Royal Ambassadors. In their annual session, WMU had voted to consider the future of RAs in cooperation with the Brotherhood Commission. A move in the direction of aligning RA ministry under the work of Brotherhood was likely one of the most painful decisions the women had ever been called upon to make. There was forward action in literature for youth as well, as *Tell* and *Sunbeam Activities* magazines replaced *World Comrades.* Also for the first time, a WMU conference was held at Glorieta Baptist Assembly in New Mexico.

Alma Hunt rose to the challenges facing her. Porter W. Routh, executive secretary of the powerful SBC Executive Committee, admired her leadership and championed it. He characterized Hunt as one who defined *auxiliary* as "augmenting a basic power . . . not to control policy for the mission boards, but to be a source of help." Routh worked at maintaining WMU's special relationship with the SBC, suggesting that the president of WMU be made a member of the SBC Executive Committee by virtue of office. Throughout Hunt's years, the question of auxiliary was a key point in the organization's relationship with the Convention. WMU had cause many times to be grateful for the profound people skills that Hunt employed in her task of leadership. She and Olive Martin looked to the changes and challenges of the mid-1950s, trusting in God's continued guidance and direction.

CHAPTER

To the Ends of the Earth

"Bring all your powers into the best service of the best King."
—FANNIE HECK

"MEET ME IN ST. LOUIS"

JUDY GARLAND MADE famous the title song of the movie *Meet Me in St. Louis,* and that is precisely what several thousand Baptist women did in 1954. Olive Martin and Alma Hunt led the women in the three-day meeting in the Opera House of Kiel Auditorium. Although the meeting began on a sad note, the event was a celebration of women's role in worldwide missions. Kathleen Mallory had come to St. Louis for her first annual meeting in 1913, and at the 1954 gathering, Hunt sadly reported that Miss Mallory was critically ill. The annual meetings had become quite well-known for beautifully presented pageants, and St. Louis was no exception. At the closing session a pageant highlighting the part Baptist women had played in worldwide missions expansion was presented in music and drama, moving from Mary (Polly) Webb in 1800 to the present time while portraying the working of God's Spirit.

As part of WMU's plan for employing additional staff, leadership for youth was considered a top priority. Directors for each age group were employed to join Margaret Bruce. Additionally, executive board vice-president Marie Mathis (Mrs. R. L.) of Texas was appointed as chairman of the newly expanded department.

CARVER SCHOOL OF MISSIONS AND SOCIAL WORK

Training young women in missions as a life calling had been the original purpose for the founding of the Woman's Missionary Training School (WMUTS). It had proved of priceless value in preparing and equipping many young women for missions service. WTS had grown, expanded, gone into larger quarters, and extended its outreach around the world. By the mid-1950s, a careful re-examination of the school and its future was needed. As usual, WMU turned to their trusted friend through the years, Dr. W. O. Carver. Surely, no man in the entire Convention knew missions as did Carver. He had always championed WMU's cause and was the Training School's first professor. In his lifetime, Carver had taught nearly every training school student. Again the Union consulted this peerless mentor. Following Carver's counsel, WMU decided to magnify the school's original specialties of missions and social work and to drop the antiquated name "training school," admitting students regardless of gender or race.

The school's name became Carver School of Missions and Social Work, in honor of this treasured friend. Dr. Carver died in 1954. The times had brought new challenges: a changed denomination environment, no accreditation, and the proposed establishment of a school of religious education at Southern Seminary. Carver School needed redefining, and naturally, these advances mandated more funding. WMU had asked the SBC for help; they had been receiving 1 percent of Cooperative Program (CP) funds, but the Convention refused further funding because the school was not controlled by the SBC. A compromise was affected, with Carver School to be transferred to SBC ownership in two more years but trustees still to be named by WMU. The arrangement was never altogether successful, and by the next decade, the trustees voted a merger of the school into Southern Seminary, later creating the Carver School of Church Social Work. For half a century, this school had been a part of the very fiber of WMU's being. Graduates had gone out as missionaries—WMU workers, teachers, nurses, good will center directors, social workers, church staff workers and pastors' wives. WMU's unique school had made a significant impact on missions.

MARTIN'S FINAL YEAR

The annual meeting in Miami in 1955 proved to be the final full year of Olive Martin's tenure as president. Having been elected in 1945 by the emergency committee meeting that year when there was no national gathering, she had served a remarkable total of 11 years. Strategist and organizer that she was, these skills sometimes led to problems for others working within the framework of her plans. Martin had her own ideas about WMU's independence as an *auxiliary,* and it led to some heated negotiations with SBC leadership. At this annual meeting in Miami, some in leadership began discussing limiting presidential tenure. As the nominating committee met prior to the following year's annual meeting, Olive Martin was not a unanimous choice. In light of that, she declined to accept the nomination. Her final year in office was an extremely busy one, however, and through all the years to come, her work and involvement in the work of WMU never faltered. She also continued as a leader on the world stage with BWA.

The Miami meeting was filled with progress on many fronts but also a real air of nostalgia and lingering sadness. Kathleen Mallory had died June 17, 1954, and Baptist women from across the South honored her in a moving tribute, describing her life as "a constant pageant of triumphs for Christ." A beautiful portrait of Mallory was unveiled at the meeting and hangs today in WMU headquarters.

It was about this time when the Business Women's Circles (BWC) movement peaked. They tended to focus on meet-and-eat-and-give-money special functions rather than the in-depth study and prayer emphasis of WMS circles. On the national level, the promotion of BWC as a special arm of WMU was funneled into other WMS structures. Another change occurred in terminology during this year. The long-used phrase *Tithes and Offerings* was changed to a more encompassing term: *Stewardship of Possessions.* This year, 1955, the first US-based WMU magazine for Spanish-speaking members debuted; it was a condensed translation of *Royal Service* titled *Nuestra Tarea.* In addition that year, Alma Hunt became the first woman to call SBC agencies to order when she was selected as president of the Southern Baptist Inter-Agency Council.

In November 1955, WMU employed a firm of management consultants in Chicago to review the entire organizational pattern and business approaches and "make certain all elements are as effective and efficient as modern management can achieve." When the report came a number of months later, the analyst wrote: "The Union is a large and impressive organization that enjoys a responsible position in Southern Baptist life. The report noted three significant strengths: "the basic appeal of its program, the completely democratic process of its operations, and the large degree of participation of its lay leadership." Thereupon, a revised pattern of organization was put into effect by 1957.

THE TEAM OF HUNT AND MATHIS

The 1956 gathering was in Kansas City, Missouri. Frances Tyler retired, completing 19 years as national recording secretary. Helen Fling of Texas became the new recording secretary. Olive Martin also concluded her many years as president. The Union paid tribute to Martin's distinguished service and the growth of WMU. Organizations had grown in number from 41,227 to 79,101 while membership had grown from 739,360 to 1,256,254. Martin's outstanding contributions to the development and growth of the Women's Department of the BWA were acknowledged as the women of WMU honored this faithful leader.

The Union's new president, Marie Mathis, had long been a force in her home state, and her contributions to national WMU causes were already greatly appreciated. When Mathis was elected, the officers stood as Martin asked all present to pledge anew their loyalty to Woman's Missionary Union. At the Convention following the election of Mathis, the SBC decided to participate in the Baptist Jubilee Advance. Mathis immediately joined with other leaders to help lay plans that in turn marked her entire term of office.

At Marie Mathis's first Executive Board meeting, the issue of making the missions offerings churchwide was laid on the table. Mathis' strong views in favor of such a move held sway, and the subsequent "opening" of the offerings to churchwide participation led to an explosive increase in giving. Thus, in 1956 the weeks of prayer became churchwide. WMU remained firmly committed to the concept that the special offerings were not to be promoted aside from prayer.

The question of WMU's control over allocations from the special offerings had been around for years. The early years of control had protected the special offerings as a valid channel of support in addition to the CP and had helped the two mission boards to survive both debt and the Great Depression. Baker James Cauthen, secretary of the FMB, regularly reminded his board that the Lottie Moon Christmas Offering (LMCO) and the Cooperative Program marched hand in hand. When the special offering increased, so did Cooperative Program giving. In the fall of 1956, Alma Hunt went on record as the first WMU officer to speak at an FMB board meeting. She announced that the LMCO allocations would be proposed by WMU, but with participation by the FMB staff, and that the FMB would have final approval. She also announced that the entire Southern Baptist family would be invited to give to the offering. The news elicited exclamations of delight from the entire Board and staff. One staff member said that Hunt had added "dignity and beauty and brains to the FMB meeting!" A 13 percent increase in giving to the LMCO that December 1956 spoke to the wisdom of WMU's new plan.

CHICAGO IN 1957

WMU met in Chicago in May 1957, the city where the firm of management consultants employed to review the entity's entire program was headquartered. The suggestions of the firm would be implemented, but first, the Union had several areas of business that needed immediate attention. High on the agenda was the official transfer of Royal Ambassadors to the Brotherhood Commission. WMU only agreed to the transfer because the Commission convinced them that the missions purpose would be retained. WMU officially transferred literature, subscription lists, and 127,656 members to the Brotherhood Commission. This was doubtless the most traumatic single action taken by WMU up until that point in their history. It was almost like losing a child.

By now, reorganization was well under way, with WMU restructuring under two major divisions: Business and Promotion. Restructuring required more personnel, and the national office continued to grow.

Women met in Houston for the 1958 annual meeting and transferred ownership of the Good Will Center in Louisville, Kentucky, to the HMB, with the understanding that the center be continued. Delegates also adopted goals for the five years leading up to Baptist Jubilee Year in 1964. Women, for many years, had not been on any committees of the SBC. Then leaders of WMU were represented on just a handful of committees. However, in 1958, the SBC bylaws were changed to require laypeople on SBC boards, and this meant that there would be more representation from women, although it was slow. Another staunch friend of WMU, Porter Routh, a layman himself, facilitated this change.

LOUISVILLE AND JUBILEE PLANNING

When Baptist women met in Louisville, there was an underlying sense of excitement as they began making plans for Jubilee Advance in the coming five-year period. Marie Mathis was an inspired choice for president at such a time, for she loved planning pageants and promotions. The women set ambitious goals for the Jubilee period, including increasing membership, increasing special offering giving, conducting intensive leadership training, and supporting the Convention movement to organize 30,000 churches and missions. Both Marie Mathis and Alma Hunt were committed to making a renewed emphasis on prayer, considering it key to the success of the ambitious goals being proposed.

WMU EXPANSION

In keeping with the Jubilee planning was the expansion of work into new states. This trend began in earnest in this decade. In 1953, WMU of the Northwest Baptist Convention began affiliates in Canada. Colorado WMU was organized in November 1955. Also, on the east coast, Paul and Ava Leach left a large church in Atlanta in 1957 and moved into a small New York City high-rise. Paul became pastor of a small congregation, Manhattan Baptist Church, and Ava began organizing women's groups, some as many as 350 miles away. The couple's work led to new churches in the area, establishing the Northeast Baptist Association and Northeast Baptist WMU in 1960. Ava asked for help, since needs were evident all over the area. Volunteers brought teams to help, but more were needed. The HMB agreed to provide the funds for a full-time WMU staff member for pioneer areas. Bernice Elliott, with rich experience in WMU young people's work, was hired for the job. Elliott was based in Birmingham but worked across the northeast area. Associational WMU work had long been a staple in most states, and and in this decade, the national WMU office began to share communications and plans with associational WMUs.

MIAMI AND MARIE

Miami Beach was the setting for WMU's 72nd annual meeting in 1960, where Alaska and Hawaii were welcomed as state unions. Baker James Cauthen's message entitled "Southern Baptist Roll Call of the Nations" was presented in dramatic episode, with Cauthen announcing the largest ever single offering for missions in the previous year's Lottie Moon offering—close to $8,000,000. He asked all state WMU presidents and executive directors to stand in recognition of the outstanding leadership of WMU in making such an offering possible.

The women voted to strengthen work with 8-year-olds by giving them the name of World Friends, along with a motto, song, and emblem. Additionally, the *Woman's Missionary Society Manual* was introduced, launching a second plan of organization, one for churches needing more than one WMS. In a certain sense, WMS got its own identity during the year 1960. National WMU also encouraged church organizations to be included in their church budgets. Financial concerns made this an important step. WMU was defined as a WMS plus one or more youth organizations. WMU's leadership was constantly monitoring needs and opportunities, looking to advances lying ahead. With changes coming rapidly, one thing remained absolutely constant: WMU's commitment to fulfilling Christ's command.

Marie Mathis had been elected treasurer of the Women's Department of the BWA at an earlier gathering of the Women's Department. She was delegated to arrange for the 1965 meeting. Event planning was clearly Marie's "cup of tea."

CHAPTER

In the Power of His Might

"The candle lighted by the Lord in the beginning of the century has never been quenched, only shaded by the dark intervening years."
—FANNIE HECK

JESUS WANTS ME FOR A SUNBEAM

WMU KNEW HOW to put on a production; the pageants and dramas used to commemorate special anniversaries were remembered for years. The Sunbeam celebration at the meeting in 1961 in St. Louis was a prime example. Scores of men and women and more than a hundred Sunbeams captivated the crowd as the story of "Cousin George" Braxton Taylor, Anna Elsom, and the Sunbeams came to life in tableaux, music, and drama. The pageant traced Sunbeams through their sponsorship by the FMB until WMU took responsibility in 1896. The audience enjoyed seeing children dressed in the costumes of the world. The children joined hands and circled a massive world globe as they sang "Jesus Wants Me for a Sunbeam," "Jesus Loves the Little Children," and of course, "Jesus Loves Me."

MISSIONS SUPPORT AND GIVING

A highlight every year was the report of giving through the two special offerings. Throughout the history of Baptists in America, WMU had been leaders in giving among the churches. Dr. Cauthen of the FMB called the Lottie Moon offering and the Cooperative Program "twin tracks on which the train of foreign missions" was propelled. Now, in 1961, the Annie Armstrong offering for the first time provided more than 40 percent of HMB income. Shortly thereafter, it also outstripped the CP as the HMB's single largest source of income.

A change in the handling of the Margaret Fund, long a friend to MKs gaining an education, was also discussed. Currently, 164 students were receiving assistance, and it was more than WMU's treasurer, LaVenia Neal, could handle. WMU's board decided to turn over responsibility for the scholarships to the respective boards to administer.

Delegates were uniformly happy to learn that enrollment in mission study classes continued to show phenomenal success. In 1961, more than half a million people had read missions books, and almost 125,000 study classes had been held. WMU increasingly emphasized week-by-week (or month-by-month) study in group meetings. WMU magazines lent themselves beautifully to an educationally sound and balanced approach to missions knowledge.

WMU AS AUXILIARY: WMU AS A DEPARTMENT

As the 1950s and 1960s arrived, WMU had to take a long look at their definition of *auxiliary*, as well as the question of WMU as a department of state Baptist endeavors. It began to look like "one size does not necessarily fit all." Until 1955, all of the

24 state WMU organizations had functioned as an auxiliary, although Missouri and Florida had originally begun as a department of the state Convention. However, each state had its own understanding of *auxiliary*. Some WMU organizations received all or part of their budget from the state's CP funds yet elected their own officers and functioned quite independently. Most also had some other sources of funds.

When the SBC began expanding geographically, the department status of state WMU organizations became an alternative form. Work was small and struggling, and often one woman would serve as both president and executive director. Generally, national WMU advised against this, feeling that the historic two-headed organization worked more smoothly and democratically. Obviously, money was the big obstacle to the traditional form of organization. Several wise leaders foresaw problems in the departmental shift as different states had varying amounts of success with its implementation. At the base of all concerns was the question of control; often it was a question of personalities. Who was strong enough to maintain the proper balance, and who would cave in to traditional forms of control and authority? There was no easy answer and it would continue to evolve.

GEARING UP FOR THE 75TH

For the first time, prayer retreats were suggested as WMU activities in 1962, and the Executive Board set the pace by having a three-day prayer retreat. To begin preparations for WMU's 75th anniversary, the Board designated a 75-day period of prayer to open the anniversary year. Several changes were implemented at the San Francisco annual meeting: WMU decided to no longer vote on Lottie Moon and

Annie Armstrong allocations. Furthermore, all who attended annual meetings were considered delegates and could vote. Henceforth, church letters would report WMU membership. Membership this year of 1962 was 1,496,926.

I'M A VOLUNTEER

WMU women had been giving time and energy to missions projects for years, but these efforts were formalized in the 1960s. In 1962, a board member, Susie Illingworth, indicated her willingness to help and ended up spending her own money and giving her summer to WMU camps and leader training in Colorado. The idea was born, and WMU asked the HMB to work out a women's volunteer plan. This year also saw the completion of the merger of Carver School into Southern Seminary. WMU had made the seminary the beneficiary of a trust of the remaining assets, and the seminary was to use those funds to perpetuate the purposes of Carver School. It marked the end of a special era of direct WMU involvement in preparing young women for service.

50 YEARS OF GIRLS' AUXILIARY AND 75 YEARS OF WMU

GAs had experienced tremendous growth through the years. Their 50th anniversary was celebrated with three GA conventions in 1963 in Memphis, Tennessee. More than 21,000 girls registered. As for the women, Kansas City was the location for the celebration of WMU's 75 years of official organization. The annual meeting was marked by the move of Marie Mathis from president to national staff member and the election of fellow Texan Helen Fling as president. Fling was to preside during one of the most controversial periods in WMU history; she did so with consummate grace and keen wisdom.

Marie Mathis had never reached greater heights in all her splendid pageants than she achieved for the Diamond Jubilee. The meeting's theme, Laborers Together with God, was carried out on the spectacular stage backdrop, in the program covers, and throughout the pageant. Ted Perry of the Southern Baptist Radio and Television Commission wrote and staged the 22 fast-moving scenes of the production. It was a moving experience for the more than 11,000 people attending.

1964 AND JUBILEE

WMU wasn't through celebrating yet, nor were Baptists as a whole. In fact, in Atlantic City, New Jersey, in 1964, WMU, the SBC, and the American Baptist Convention jointly celebrated the 150th anniversary of the founding of the Triennial Baptist Convention in 1814, marking the beginning of organized missions and cooperation for Baptists in North America. Not surprisingly, Marie Mathis was at the heart of creating and planning the dramatic presentation of how it all began. An impressive 180-foot Jubilee platform was the setting, where a magnificent 40-foot-high, 70-foot-wide screen stood. The two-part missionary feature "And Thus It Was Written," featured "Out of the Past" and "Into the Present." The impact of the message was unforgettable.

The release of Alma Hunt's *The History of Woman's Missionary Union* also marked the occasion. WMU membership peaked this year at 1,529,454, with over 99,000 organizations. By popular demand, *Royal Service* again included a Bible study in every issue.

Although women had much to celebrate this year, the entire decade was fraught with racial tensions that impacted everyone. Alma Hunt and Marie Mathis, then Hunt and Helen Fling, were constantly challenged as to how to continue their longstanding relationship with African American women and provide needed encouragement, money, and property for their friends in the National Baptist Convention. WMU stood firm in the face of blistering criticism, even hate mail and vitriolic statements by some extremists. WMU was quite radical in their publications as they encouraged women's efforts toward cooperation and reconciliation. Each article published would be followed by cancellations and criticism. Southern Baptist professor and statesman T. B. Maston noted that "Woman's Missionary Union has generally made and continues to make the most directly challenging approach to the whole area of race."

WMU was located just blocks from where many protests and demonstrations were staged during the civil rights movement. In spite of a volatile atmosphere, WMU managed to take a stand and maintain firm friendships with their counterparts in the National Baptist Convention.

CHRISTIAN SERVICE CORPS IS BORN

No matter what fires needed to be put out, the Union was ever on the cutting edge of moving out into new frontiers of effort. With Susie Illingworth's successful volunteer project as a model, WMU asked the HMB to develop such a ministry. Thus, Christian Service Corps was born in 1965, and volunteer missions became a popular focus. The entire decade of the 1960s saw expansion. WMU began focusing on teaching missions to the whole church and on targeting states outside the South. Women supported the SBC's Thirty Thousand Movement, aimed at establishing that many new congregations by SBC's 150th anniversary. Concurrently, WMU struck out to spread missions education to new congregations. Before 1965 was even reached, there were nearly 25,000 new organizations, which resulted in 6,682 new churches.

Language missions work also grew. WMU organizations expanded in this area of work in many states including Texas, New Mexico, and Puerto Rico. Alma Hunt and the HMB organized the first conference for Spanish-speaking women at Glorieta Baptist Conference Center (now LifeWay Conference Center) in New Mexico.

Additionally, churchwide mission study was a new idea in 1965. WMU proposed that, in cooperation with the whole church, WMU would undertake to teach mission studies. In some places it was highly successful, although not always easy to facilitate.

THE TIMES, THEY ARE A-CHANGING

This was not a simple time for WMU in terms of their cooperative work with churches. Everyone viewed *auxiliary* from their own vantage points, and WMU worked at remaining an auxiliary but also cooperating with total church programming efforts. Sunday School, Brotherhood, and WMU materials reinforced each other's topics. After three years, WMU dropped out of the planning process; it had proved too cumbersome. One of the chief roles undertaken by Helen Fling during this volatile period was that of encourager. Her growing spiritual depth equipped her to be a voice for hope, acceptance, and trust. Her final message was titled: "No Time to Be Afraid."

THE 1960s: CHARACTERIZED BY CHANGE

Alma Hunt and Helen Fling must have wanted to "hold on to their hats" as they rode the roller coaster of a constantly changing denomination and society. Hunt's message at the annual meeting in Detroit in 1966 was insightful. She titled it "Woman's Missionary Union—NOW" and used the life and writings of Fannie Heck to spotlight the past and look to the future. As Hunt followed the path through Heck's hopes and dreams for the future, she noted that Fannie's 1909 message was as fresh as if she had assembled it yesterday. Her words echoed a startlingly new thought: "The pages of history are strewn with wrecks of organizations which died of inflexibility." WMU's official program statement was discussed—a bold paper outlining its history, program structure, relationships, and supporting services. The 15 closely typed pages left no doubt as to WMU's purposes. This meeting featured a beautiful eulogy to Ethlene Boone Cox, who had died the previous August. Marie Mathis brought a moving, paying tribute to Cox's rare combination of beauty, grace, and radiance, noting her unending contributions to the Union.

The forward-looking leaders of WMU clearly understood that more social unrest and further denominational changes were in the offing. Continual adaptations would be required. With strong leadership, WMU looked to the future, not content to see just the present problems but determined to look beyond them to understand God's direction.

CHAPTER

Come and Thy People Bless

"The word to use is not go but come. The one who leads must show she is willing to do more than she asks of someone else."

—ANNIE ARMSTRONG

1967 MEANS MIAMI BEACH

IRENE JORDAN, RENOWNED Metropolitan Opera soprano, sang at the 1967 annual meeting in Miami. Her sister, Dr. Martha Jordan Gilliland, missionary doctor in Nigeria since 1942, was the featured missionary speaker. Their mother, Mrs. Eugene Jordan of Birmingham, Alabama, was present; and Alma Hunt paid tribute to this missionary home with nine children who reflected their Christian heritage, including two foreign missionaries.

The delegates discussed plans for a new cooperative effort between WMU and Brotherhood, with help from both mission boards. The jointly sponsored World Missions Conference was the forerunner of many to come. The delegates also voted to introduce a church WMU achievement guide.

Mission action was the major topic of discussion in Miami. WMU published a *Mission Action Survey Guide* in partnership with the Brotherhood Commission and the Home Mission Board. Guide books for specific needs, such as work with internationals, the economically disadvantaged, and juvenile rehabilitation were also published. Mission action was an instant hit among Southern Baptists. All age levels embraced the idea, and within six months of publication, more than 60,000 copies of the guide had sold.

FLING AND HUNT LEAD IN HOUSTON

The 1968 annual meeting in Houston had a significant impact on the future of the Union; WMU planned for a new look—a "program re-design." Women voted to bring age groups in the youth organizations more into conformity with other church organizations. They understood that change was hard but necessity demanded it. The theme for the meeting in Houston was Hope of the World, and the women planned with hope for ways to remain relevant as the leading missions education entity among Southern Baptists.

THE 1960s AND RACIAL TENSIONS

America was at a boiling point in the late 1960s; the civil rights issue affected everyone in some way. WMU took a strong stand for racial equality and understanding. Helen Fling, determined for Baptist women to make a positive difference, received many venomous letters. Just the year before, in 1967, the FMB had appointed its first African American missionary since the 1880s, and she was on the program in Miami.

Alma Hunt gladly joined with other Southern Baptist leaders in signing the Statement Concerning the Crisis in Our Nation, and the SBC adopted it at the Houston meeting. WMU leaders realized they were paving the way, for at the Houston meeting, Dr. Dorothy Brown, an African American doctor-legislator, spoke on "A Dream in My Heart." She closed: "The attitudes of reason are the only true and effective weapons of oppressed people anywhere, and their use requires a good sense, a spark of courage, mature judgment, a spirit of forgiveness, and personal ability to absorb plenty of threat and abuse, even from members of your own group." Dr. Brown received a standing ovation. Alma Hunt considered 1968 a turning point in Southern Baptist attitudes toward African Americans.

Other issues were addressed in the 1968 meeting, including changing the name of the annual offering for home missions to the Annie Armstrong Easter Offering, (AAEO). There was also the move for Woman's Missionary Societies to focus on teaching women in small groups rather than traditional circles. A group could choose to concentrate on some particular aspect of missions. Naturally, many women resisted the change, believing that "circles" met their needs. WMU leadership quickly recognized that different women—and different churches—might well have different needs.

During this period, WMU began targeting certain issues as well as certain groups. This approach resulted in the current two-year focus on a critical issue.

Marie Mathis was head of the Promotion Division of WMU and was at her best when planning and presenting events. She directed the program for launching the Crusade of the Americas at the 1968 Houston SBC. Between 1968 and 1970, she also worked tirelessly as chairman for the 1970 BWA Congress in Tokyo. She carried out the gargantuan task under the leadership of her African friend, William O. Tolbert, who later became president of Liberia.

MARIE MATHIS AND HELEN FLING: NEW ROLES

Program changes were not enough—it was also time for change in leadership. However, the transition worked beautifully because the new leadership was also "old" leadership, as Helen Fling was led to a whole new challenge in home missions. In 1968, her husband, Robert, made the huge move from leading a large Texas congregation to becoming pastor of a tiny church in Westchester County, New York. Helen's heart told her that she must resign her WMU position in order to fulfill her call in New York.

Helen Fling gave her final address as president at the New Orleans annual meeting in 1969. As she declared, there is "No Time to Be Afraid," noting the end of one era and the beginning of another. She concluded with the affirmation that we are all engaged in one task: world missions. "It is no time to be afraid," Fling told the women, "pray that He will match us to this time. . . . O thrilling age, O willing age! When steel and stone and rail and rod become the avenue of God."

Thankfully, there was no vacuum in experienced leadership for national WMU when Fling decided to step down. WMU looked for a steady hand to work with Alma Hunt in guiding WMU over the rocky shores of structural change. Many women were fearful of what lay ahead. The nominating committee asked Marie Mathis to return to the position. This was a huge challenge, but Mathis met it as she had every major summons to her talents and abilities. She was elected, once again, to the office of president.

TALK ABOUT CHANGE!

At no other period had so much change been faced at one time. So often, the easy thing to do seems to "keep things as they are," but Alma Hunt and the courageous leadership of WMU realized that this was no option for them in light of national changes and denominational changes and shifts. The Denver meeting in 1970 as one of momentous importance as Hunt and Mathis presented the many ideas and proposals to the gathered delegates. The women accepted the challenge and moved ahead. The theme, Living the Christ Life, stated why they were making the moves dictated—in order to fulfill their calling. The meeting's music was a tremendous inspiration. It sounded like a roll call of glittering nationally known musicians, including Norma Zimmer and Jim Roberts of the popular *Lawrence Welk Show,* plus the brilliant Baptist tenor Claude Rhea.

The national WMU staff and Executive Board spent months in laying down plans to take WMU into the future, and those plans were presented in Denver. Two movements had occurred at practically the same time—the woman's liberation movement and a movement of major changes in Southern Baptist entities. It was great timing, or awful timing, depending upon perspective! One fact remained: WMU could have been destroyed had the great majority of members not been absolutely committed to its success. The organization was determined to plan its church activities in consultation with other church programs—hence the need for change. WMU had already established the difference between WMS and WMU, no easy thing to achieve after so many years as simply "WMU."

Had it not been for the inspired leadership of Alma Hunt and the help of Helen Fling, Marie Mathis, and a loyal and talented staff, it could not have happened. Hunt had told the women several years previously that this "is Woman's Missionary Union's hour of opportunity to provide a program of missionary education for NOW." Hunt wrapped the proposal in WMU's own history, quoting from Fannie Heck's classic 1909 message: "The ultimate test of any institution is its present vitality." She followed Heck's statement with the challenge: "Our lane is broad; there are no roadblocks ahead." These proposals presented in Denver were to take effect in October, and leading up to that date, WMU magazines laid out the new plans in detail. Change was difficult. The number of organizations remained steady, but nearly 100,000 members were lost in three years.

In order to align more clearly with other church programs, WMU had to do some drastic age changing of organizations. Baptist Women became the new age-level organization for women ages 30 and up. Additionally, *Dimension*, a quarterly magazine for officers and leaders, was created. Young adults ages 18 through 29 became known as Baptist Young Women, and their magazine was *Contempo*. Change didn't stop there. Girls' Auxiliary became Girls in Action, thus retaining the popular GA designation. Forward Steps became Missions Adventures. The girls' new magazine was *Discovery* and their leaders had *Aware*. GA ages were now changed, with GAs including girls grades 1 through 6.

Girls in grades 7 through 12 became Acteens, and StudiAct was their achievement plan. Preschoolers were regrouped as Sunbeams became Mission Friends. Brotherhood also took over the leadership of 6-, 7-, and 8-year-old boys.

Implementing changes in the basic organizational structure of WMU was enough of a task; however, the BWA also demanded the time and energies of the women of WMU. Marie Mathis was not only conducting her massive duties as national president in 1970, but she was also chairing the 1970 BWA Congress meeting in Tokyo. As treasurer of the

Women's Department, she was responsible for making the travel arrangements and paying hotel bills for nearly 300 women. To top it off, she was elected president of the Women's Department at the conclusion of the Congress. This assignment would take her all over the world for the next 10 years.

Change is exhausting. So much change in society. So much change in the beloved Union. But—no change in *purpose*. Baptist women who loved missions were determined to continue to meet the challenges confronting them around every corner. Annie Armstrong would no doubt have been shocked at all the changes surrounding women in the 1970s, but WMU's consistent determination and unflagging zeal would not have surprised her.

CHAPTER

With World-Encircling Love

"The harvest is very great,
the laborers, oh! so few."
—Lottie Moon

NEW DECADE — NEW STRUCTURE

NOW CAME THE work: implementing change. "Committed" was the theme for the 1971 meeting held in St. Louis. Baker James Cauthen of the FMB, Arthur Rutledge of the HMB, and Porter Routh of the SBC Executive Committee joined Alma Hunt in leading a call to commitment.

Every agency proposed a program statement. WMU was a recognized specialist in missions, so naturally, its program statement involved the promotion of Christian missions. Ultimately, the fine line revolved on how WMU could cooperate and at the same time, stay on task to maintain their identity and auxiliary status.

Many in WMU were slow to accept the changes that seemed necessary. National staff and state leaders, both full-time and volunteer, worked tirelessly to make the new approach appealing. The response of women across the nation varied from excitement to outright rejection. Some felt that the group approach would allow women to concentrate on what really appealed to them. Others thought it unnecessarily polarizing and a possible threat to the unity of the organization. The group concept was to involve all the women in ministry and participation, but some did not see it that way. Others found the changes bewildering. WMU strove to bring about clarity as they provided well-planned materials for each group target area.

CHANGING ROLES OF WOMEN

WMU tried to remain neutral on the issue of women's roles. The movement affected all areas of society—even WMU. As women took jobs outside the home, membership in WMU organizations declined. Leadership worked diligently to adjust to changing times and preserve membership and participation. On the other hand, some Baptist leadership looked at other denominations that were said to have women "storm the pulpit" and suggested that "other soft-spoken women are following a circuitous route to high church positions." WMU, as usual, took the high road. Marie Mathis is quoted as saying, "Don't think we're not progressive," to which Alma Hunt added, "We're just not militant."

Hunt issued a succinct yet forceful memo to the 35 men and 1 woman who made up the interagency program coordination group. She clarified that *unified* does not mean not distinctive in tasks. WMU would not approve a proposed design for small churches that didn't continue to call for age-level organizations. Alma Hunt stated that WMU strongly denied the right of any department to promote or encourage (either directly or indirectly) the weakening of another agency. These vexing issues remained a concern throughout the 1970s.

WMU and its goals and purposes were inextricably linked to missions giving; a few voices of malcontent suggested that WMU's highly successful two missions offerings automatically threatened the vitality of the Cooperative Program (CP). The Home Mission Board decided to see if such was the case, undertaking a project to determine if the special offerings were actually eroding the CP. The survey results were not well received by the naysayers, for the report indicated that churches with higher per capita income were more likely to give generously to both the CP and the special offerings than churches with below-average income.

Some churches wanted to combine the two missions offerings into one event, while others decided they would include a set amount for the two offerings in their church budget and thereby eliminate any hassle. Alma Hunt brought the issue before the FMB in October 1971, stating her "honest conviction that if the offerings are combined, the weeks of prayer will ultimately be combined and we will lose one week of emphasis on missions now well-established in the churches." Cauthen placed his powerful voice and influence right beside Alma Hunt's, stressing the vital importance of maintaining the integrity of individual weeks of prayer and giving. Some churches tried their new plans (and continue to do so). However, extensive research proved that eliminating the special offerings does indeed reduce missions education and prayer. The two missions offerings have stood the test of time.

1972: IN THE CITY OF BROTHERLY LOVE

Freedom's Holy Light was a most fitting theme for WMU's annual session in Philadelphia. It highlighted this important city where religious freedom for the nation had begun to take shape and where the Triennial Convention was organized in 1814. A highlight of the meeting was the message from Apollo 15 Astronaut James Irwin.

WMU paid tribute this year to the inimitable Olive Martin (Mrs. George R.), longtime WMU president and champion of the BWA. Martin had traveled throughout the world organizing continental Baptist women's unions. A chapel at the European Baptist Seminary was erected and named the Martin Chapel in her honor. This remarkable leader died on June 15, less than two weeks after the Philadelphia meeting.

WMU and the HMB had worked in close cooperation to sponsor and develop language missions. In the beginning, it was mostly work with Hispanic-speaking people in America. The work had been headquartered at HMB offices in Atlanta. Alma Hunt and Dr. Rutledge of the HMB agreed that WMU would begin coordinating ethnic WMU organizations. Thus on January 1, 1972, Doris Diaz, editor of *Nuestra Tarea,* moved to the Birmingham office of WMU, along with the entire Spanish WMU management. The HMB funded the work, and WMU directed its expansion.

Traditionally, the HMB and WMU had worked in close cooperation in promoting missions. The year 1972 was a case in point, as WMU and the HMB jointly sponsored 15 national missions action workshops, pooling the talents and resources of both entities to produce meaningful opportunities for training in effective mission action. Also in this year, 900 girls ages 12 through 17 met at Glorieta Baptist Conference Center for the first National Acteens Convention (NAC—now called Blume).

EACH ONE BRING ONE, CULTIVATE ONE

WMU began a two-year emphasis on enlistment and enlargement in 1972 and 1973. These two "Es" were considered the most urgent needs in WMU. Campaigns called Giant Step and Each One Bring One, Cultivate One were launched to halt the gradual decline in membership. WMU concentrated on enlisting and orienting new WMU members through a continuing one-on-one relationship with a committed member. The Giant Step goals continued until 1974. Historically, WMU had been conscious of the need for groups of varying sizes and in varying settings in order for small churches to maintain a complete WMU program. Then the issue of urbanization came into focus during 1973. Families moving to the suburbs created changing neighborhoods in the cities. Churches needed help to minister to the changing environment. Therefore, WMU programs were developed and material prepared to address these evolving needs. Programs such as Big A Clubs were established in 1977.

CHANGING ROLES

A talented young woman from Alabama, Saralyn Collins, was a highlight of the annual meeting in Portland in 1973. She performed a series of monologues about a woman contemplating changes in her role and finding her rightful place of service through WMU. The following year, Alma Hunt looked squarely at the question of the changing role of women as she gave her final address: "I believe Woman's Missionary Union lifts a woman's perspective above the kitchen sink, or above the desk, or above the industry where she works, to see a world in need and to see that she herself can have a part in it. I believe that WMU enables women to be molders of circumstances rather than victims of circumstances."

Happily, 1974 brought a welcome change in trends for WMU. For the first time since the 1963–1964 year, WMU membership increased, as did the number of organizations. Another problem came into focus: world hunger and famine. Through personal service, WMU women had often shared food with the poor, but on a global level, they had only responded when a particular crisis arose. By the 1970s, news stories of famine, especially in Asia and Africa, were prolific. The FMB began to receive hunger-relief contributions, and just short of $300,000 was sent spontaneously. In following years, WMU increased its focus on the worldwide crisis in hunger.

ANOTHER ERA BEGINS

Alma Hunt had been executive secretary for 24 years, and she felt the time had come when God wanted her in another role. Hunt accepted the invitation of the FMB to work as a consultant for overseas women's work. In this new role, she traveled to more than 40 countries to help build up women's organizations.

In Dallas, Texas, in June 1974, Alma Hunt retired and Carolyn Weatherford was elected as executive director. It was WMU's 86th year as a national organization. The Convention Center Arena seated slightly more than 8,000; it was full. Baker James Cauthen led a commissioning service for 22 new missionaries, and Irene Jordan sang the closing solo, "The Lord Is My Light."

Gardner Taylor, renowned pastor of Concord Baptist Church, Brooklyn, New York, brought the meeting's keynote address: "Listen to Your World." Baptist leaders from all entities of the Convention gave tribute to Alma Hunt. Ever the masterful storyteller, Hunt brought the crowd to tears, then laughter, then back to tears again as she related stirring events from her decades in office in her final message: "Retrospect, Introspect, Prospect." She said, "I want to say to you that I think the hope of our future is as bright as the promises of God."

Monday afternoon, Carolyn Weatherford officially became executive secretary-elect of Woman's Missionary Union. Alma Hunt escorted her to the platform, where Marie Mathis presented her to the assembled delegates, who stood in recognition of their new leader. Weatherford responded by briefly relating the journey that had brought her to that point, concluding with her recognition that she could not accept this responsibility "except for the assurance that God has led me to this point and that He always empowers a person for the doing of what He calls her to do."

AND CHANGE CONTINUES

In 1975, Marie Mathis had served as national president for two terms. Knowing that Mathis would not be eligible for reelection, denominational leaders planned a dinner preceding the meeting to honor her exceptional leadership. Mathis was praised for her courage in working in difficult and dangerous fields, for the brilliance of her productions, and for her boldness in denominational leadership.

This 1975 meeting in Miami Beach was highlighted with a commissioning service for 18 new foreign missionaries. WMU also elected Christine Gregory of Virginia to the office of president. In accepting the position, Gregory remarked that the previous fall she had made a vow to God that if "he'd let me get my children through college, that I was going to do something in mission work. Heavens to Betsy, I surely didn't know it was going to be this!"

Once again WMU had two new faces in leadership. The Executive Board reorganized the headquarters staff and created several new positions. June Whitlow would head up planning and research, and Catherine Allen would direct public relations and employee relations. Several others joined the staff, and a Promotions Department was formed. A number of special events highlighted 1975, including WMU's celebration of the 50th anniversary of the Cooperative Program; after all, the Union had played a vital role in its birth. The second National Acteens Convention was held in Memphis, with nearly 11,000 attending.

Massive changes marked this first half of the 1970s. Few could possibly anticipate that greater and potentially more difficult changes were ahead. WMU realized anew how much they depended on the One who never changed; that assurance provided the fortification they would need.

CHAPTER

Stand Up and Bless the Lord

"Bless the Lord O my soul and all that is within me, bless His Holy Name."
—PSALM 103:1

NORFOLK: STAND UP AND BLESS THE LORD

WMU CELEBRATED ITS 88th year as an organization in Norfolk, Virginia, on June 13-14, 1976. It was Christine Gregory's first year as president and also the year of America's Bicentennial. WMU celebrated America's freedom and the freedom found in Christ. Hermione Jackson (Mrs. Lamar), pastor's wife and president of Alabama WMU, had written a drama based on women in US history, adapted for staging by Ed Seabough of the HMB. The entire cast received a standing ovation. The drama continued, as Dr. Baker James Cauthen of the FMB concluded the service with a dramatic meditation titled: "The Living Flame," closing with the declaration that the living flame of missions zeal is burning today in the hearts of Christians.

The same program was repeated in the Sunday evening service in order to accommodate the massive crowds. A noon-day prayer service met on Monday in Norfolk's Scope Plaza with more than 5,000 in attendance. The crowd celebrated US Flag Day and WMU Day of Prayer, Fasting, and Humiliation. Fifteen flags representing successive periods of US history were paraded. The first Kaleidoscope conference for Baptist Young Women was also held, where more than 800 young women were challenged to look beyond themselves to find their personal mission in life.

CHALLENGES IN MISSIONS COOPERATION

The SBC had appointed a Missions Challenge Committee in 1974, and two years later, made two recommendations related to WMU. Each recommendation asked WMU to cooperate with the mission boards, Brotherhood, and the Sunday School Board to reach more with mission study. The next year (1977), Southern Baptist denominational leaders served as a think tank, and from this group came a report that stronger WMU organizations were needed and that new ways of missions teaching should be used, with the pastor being the key to success. It was a documented fact that many of the changes brought about by the SBC had cost WMU significant drops in membership and finances. Through all the changes, WMU had stood firm in its goal of missions education. The same downward trends were evident in every organization of the Convention. In spite of valiant efforts, the percentage of Cooperative Program funds leaving the states for national and worldwide work declined.

Baptists have always been big on committees. The SBC appointed a Committee of Fifteen in 1970 to study SBC structure and goals. Marie Mathis was named to the committee but soon resigned so the group would have freedom to examine WMU's program objectively. While the committee worked, WMU continued cooperating in planning unified emphases. The report suggested that WMU's enrollment drop was due to an over-emphasis on mission action rather than missions education. WMU strongly rebutted such a sweeping yet narrow view. Later, as Marie Mathis sat with a group planning future emphases, she insisted that the SBC must end the decade with bold missions. It was Mathis who coined the phrase that became the slogan used not just for the rest of the 1970s but until the end of the century—Bold Mission Thrust.

Ecclesiastes 4:12 says a cord of three strands is not easily broken. In the beginning, there were three Baptist entities forming three strands: FMB, HMB, and WMU. This three-strand cord has stood the test of time. Alma Hunt declared time and again: "WMU has no program of its own. Our program is that of the FMB and the HMB." As early as 1948, Theron Rankin of the FMB was explaining the relationship in modern terms, calling WMU "the FMB's channel to the churches." This became even clearer as interagency programming cooperation grew yet stronger. A study of the correspondence between the boards and WMU leaders through the years reveals evidence of the mutuality of goals and concerns and of deep respect.

MISSIONS NIGHT OUT, ROUND TABLE, AND BIG A

Several new approaches aimed at different ages and target groups developed in 1977. WMU began producing books suggesting activities for one-day missions education experiences geared toward various groups or toward the entire membership of a church. Campus Baptist Young Women (CBYW) and

Round Table Book Clubs were introduced, and Big A Clubs were created in 1977. The purpose was to teach simple Bible truths to children with no church background. Big A became a vital tool used by both US and international missionaries. The first Acteens national advisory panel was chosen this year, and Beverly Sutton, national Acteens consultant, introduced the first panelists at the annual meeting where they served as pages. Several hundred outstanding young women have served as Acteens panelists over the years, and many have gone on to become missionaries and to assume leadership roles in missions education.

BOLD MISSION

The annual meeting in Kansas City in 1977 opened with Carolyn Weatherford of WMU, Baker James Cauthen of the FMB, and Dr. William Tanner of the HMB together on the platform, presenting Bold Mission as a challenge for Southern Baptists in 1977–1979. A missionary and flag processional with 200 home and foreign missionaries and flags of 84 nations and 50 states where Southern Baptist missionaries serve stirred the audience.

THINK ON THESE THINGS

The 1978 WMU Annual Meeting was held in Atlanta, Georgia, where the women were inspired to "think on these things." This powerful meeting concluded with an address by Grady Cothen, president of Baptist Sunday School Board, emphasizing the magnitude of the challenge for each Southern Baptist to "use Bold Mission Thrust to say to the whole world that God loves the world and sent His son to show you that love of God in the showcase of the human heart."

Several innovations were launched this year including Acteens Activators, a short-term missions volunteer program that began with a pilot project in 1976. Soon teenaged girls were making vital and lasting contributions to missions. The Union also co-sponsored a Convocation on World Hunger, and the following year began their largest focus on world hunger. For three years, women were encouraged to live more simply so others might eat.

WMU and the HMB decided in 1978 to employ a WMU consultant to work with African American Baptists. One new step this year was to sponsor, along with SBC boards and agencies, a Consultation on Women in Church-Related Vocations. The Convention was concerned that fewer women were going into missions. The results of the consultation convinced WMU of the need for a plan of action that would encourage women to consider church-related vocations. This focus, however, was overshadowed by the increasingly touchy subject of women's roles and was reflective of the general situation in the Convention during this period.

With many opinions about women's roles at opposite extremes, Carolyn Weatherford took care to explain that *women in ministry* was a newer phrase for what had formerly been called *women in church-related vocations.* She carefully explained: "the word *minister* doesn't necessarily mean ordination. Each church decides for itself whether or not to ordain particular staff members." WMU consistently used the word *minister* to refer to laypersons as well as in the more traditional use of the term. WMU leaders felt one of their important jobs was to create an environment where persons could hear and respond to God's call into missions. They sought to be honest with girls who might be facing challenges in responding to their calling.

Carolyn Weatherford also addressed a related area of concern for women in missions service. She requested the FMB identify married women missionaries by their own names and allow them to have job classifications other than "home and church," if they wished. The FMB implemented Weatherford's suggestions and received a written thank-you from Weatherford for "taking the giant step of classifying women's positions beyond home and church." Later she noted that WMU, "with women everywhere, will rise to call you blessed!"

THE ENDING OF THE DECADE

The decade of the 1970s was ending, as were the long and effective years of Dr. Baker James Cauthen's tenure as executive director of the FMB. He brought the keynote message at the Houston meeting in 1979, challenging the Union to "rekindle the gift of God that is within you." The assembled delegates honored Dr. Cauthen for his dedicated service with a standing ovation. Carolyn Weatherford's report focused on entering the decade of its centennial. Weatherford commented on the decline in membership, pointing out that various Convention critics suggested that WMU needed to broaden its base and become more things to more women. She stated that the Executive Board had again expressed its determination to retain the singular purpose of missions. Weatherford declared, "While this purpose might tend to exclude some, it should also tend to *include* those women and youth who are looking for meetings with meaning, involvement with results."

CHALLENGES AND UNCERTAINTY

With a goal of enlisting more women and youth in missions, WMU launched a National Enlargement Plan, in 1980, a three-year plan to organize WMU in more churches. Beyond expanding membership and organizations, WMU set as priorities for the next six years: to strengthen WMU initiative in missions; nurture missions in the home; simplify WMU organization; and sharpen the effectiveness of the national office. These goals were challenging indeed.

Tell It Again

"What has been done for the glory of God will remain steadfast as the stars."
—Annie Armstrong, 1891

THE TASK AHEAD

CHALLENGES APLENTY AND daily uncertainty came to be the norm for WMU leadership at this critical juncture in Southern Baptist life. In retrospect, it is easy to agree with the anonymous philosopher who said, "As new questions about the past arise, history is written yet again." WMU leadership had to examine every statement crossing their desks, exercising care in making any statement that could be misconstrued by the hearer. This state of affairs challenged the very foundation of Woman's Missionary Union.

As undercurrents of controversy began to eddy around Convention meetings, WMU leadership felt their task was to remain out of any such discussions or, as national president Christine Gregory so succinctly put it: "My subject is missions." This central purpose had remained unchanged for well over 100 years. In the midst of the turmoil, WMU sought to handle touchy issues with grace and forbearance, trying not to insert personal bias or self-serving agendas.

In one of Carolyn Weatherford's reports to the WMU Executive Board, she reiterated WMU's determination to retain the singular purposes of missions: "Without apology, we can move into the 1980s aggressively, seeking to enroll more women, more girls, more preschoolers in missions participation."

LOS ANGELES AND THE NEW DECADE

Missions work in California was a microcosm of worldwide missions, and various phases of California Baptist missions endeavors were highlighted at the WMU Annual Meeting in Los Angeles in June 1981. The Lottie Moon offering receipts for the year, thus far, were already more than 10 percent higher than the previous year. Additionally, women voted to make a change in WMU bylaws, determining that the office of president would be limited to five years in order to guarantee continuity of leadership. Los Angeles was the final meeting at which Christine Gregory would preside. And, just days after the WMU meeting, Gregory was elected first vice-president of the SBC, the first woman ever to hold that office. WMU elected Dr. Dorothy Sample (Mrs. Richard) to succeed Gregory. Dot Sample held doctorates in both theology and psychology and brought vast WMU experience to her new position.

NEW HOPE MOUNTAIN

National WMU was sorely in need of more space, and new hope was sparked when plans began for a new headquarters building. Property was bought on New Hope Mountain on the outskirts of Birmingham. WMU's new address was perfect: 100 Missionary Ridge. The new building became a labor of love as many WMU staffers, Executive Board members, and interested Baptist women poured untold hours of planning and effort into making the new headquarters a reality. Catherine Allen, WMU's associate executive director, was instrumental in achieving the goal of a modern, functional, and beautiful facility. The 137,000-square-foot building housed offices, conference space, a library, a warehouse, and publishing facilities. The lobby featured a dramatic and unique global fountain. Around the walls were beautiful pieces of East Asian art and missions displays from across the world that had been accumulated over the years—true treasures of missions memorabilia. The items included Lottie Moon's trunk and a newel post from the Methodist church where WMU was established.

Those planning the new structure had history on their minds as they included a copper-lined vault holding historical information about WMU. Individuals and states were all invited to donate a designated amount of money that would allow them to name a particular area in the building. These rooms and areas were then decorated to reflect the person, state, country, or type of work thus honored. It is worth noting that financing this building was the first time in its history that WMU had requested money for its own purposes. No fund-raising campaign was conducted, but the money began to come in. It is remarkable to realize that the entire building was completely paid for by the time WMU celebrated its 100th year of organization.

During the time when WMU's new building was a work in progress, all the usual work of the Union continued unabated. The HMB assisted WMU as it began publishing materials in an array of languages: Chinese, Korean, Japanese, Romanian, and basic English. And in WMU's continuing efforts to support and train African American WMU leaders, a special training conference was held at WMU headquarters in 1981. A follow-up conference was also conducted the next year.

WITNESSING WOMEN

The theme for the 1982 annual meeting in New Orleans was illustrated with Bible studies featuring witnessing women from Scripture, as well as contemporary witnessing women who gave testimonies. A featured speaker was Deborah Dahunsi (Mrs. Emmanuel), president of WMU of Nigeria. Her late husband, Emmanuel, was the first African American to enter Southern Seminary in 1950. She had nothing but praise for Carver School and its love and concern for all people. Mrs. Dahunsi's closing message described the field as the world, affirming that the conditions of our world make it urgent that Southern Baptists proclaim the gospel.

WMU's largest push on world hunger came during 1979–1982. Hunger was a major emphasis, as WMU stressed the importance of a simple lifestyle. Beginning this year, and continuing for several years, thousands of Baptist women attended state and national training conferences conducted by WMU. A highlight was the first national evangelistic conference for women, DaySpring, dually sponsored by the HMB and WMU. In 1983, nearly 3,000 women attended the conference at Ridgecrest, and the following year, some 2,600 attended a similar meeting in Fort Worth.

Chapter 27

PITTSBURGH IN 1983

The 95th annual meeting was held in a new venue—Pittsburgh, Pennsylvania. New England was now the area where pioneer work was being "re-launched" in the twentieth century. The new music drama, "A Call to My People," premiered at the meeting. Each session closed with reflections from actress Sheila Bailey, who portrayed Lottie Moon in the play.

NEW TRENDS AND GROUPS

More and more women were employed outside the home, and overcrowded schedules, led to a trend to a decline in WMU membership. The Union conducted a three-year enlargement plan, beginning in 1980. More than 3,000 churches organized some kind of missions work, with WMU memberships reflecting an increase.

WMU launched Baptist Nursing Fellowship (BNF) in 1983, involving nurses in worship, witnessing, and ministering with their special skills. June Whitlow, WMU associate executive director, was the first executive director of BNF. She is credited with the consistent ministry and vital contributions of BNF from its inception on into the new millennium.

Another 1980s trend was the remarkably steady growth of the Lottie Moon Christmas Offering and the Annie Armstrong Easter Offering. Even in times of economic downturns, these offerings have demonstrated an astounding ability to remain steady and to continue growing.

VISION 88

Referring to the prophet's vision in Habakkuk 1:5, Carolyn Weatherford challenged WMU women to hold high the torch as "we let the world challenge us, scripture inspire and instruct us, and the fire ignite us to draw masses of committed workers to itself." This was also a stellar year for Acteens, as more than 14,000 teenaged girls gathered in Fort Worth in July to be challenged to mission service.

NEW HOPE

With WMU occupying a beautiful new building on New Hope Mountain, yet another "New Hope" was established as WMU launched a new line of books and materials under the name New Hope. The year 1985 was WMU's first year to publish unique missions education products. For the first time, WMU was providing missions materials and other books for an audience that was not necessarily a part of WMU. Topics with a broad range of appeal were introduced under the New Hope label. Some appealed to casual readers, to new parents, or to youth. This new imprint also tried distributing in new ways, including selling through bookstores and direct marketing.

Video publishing was another WMU innovation. The new headquarters building had been engineered to be a telecommunications base. In 1985, WMU began selling videotapes along with printed products, including many mission study aids. WMU cooperated with SBC missions agencies in producing programming that was aired on BTN (SSB network.) WMU was a pacesetter among Southern Baptists in videoconferencing.

CHAPTER

Approaching the Century Mark

"Join our lives in mighty chorus, 'Til we come from every place; with all those who went before us, To the fullness of God's grace."
—WMU CENTENNIAL HYMN:
"GOD, OUR AUTHOR AND CREATOR"

FIRST LOVE

WHEN WMU MET in Dallas in 1985, the theme centered on First Love. The focus was on Revelation 2, the call to "not forsake your first love"—sharing the gospel with the world. Leadership keenly needed this focus, for they were being forced to spend a great deal of time attempting to get a grip on the myriad of changes surrounding the SBC, which consequently affected WMU. The women drew strength from their roots; Dorothy Sample called the women in Dallas into session using the gavel made from the wood of a tree growing over the grave of Henrietta Hall Shuck, the first Baptist woman missionary to arrive in China. In her address, Carolyn Weatherford repeatedly summoned women to recall the challenges extended by the inimitable Fannie Heck just weeks before her death in 1915: "Changes will come . . . but our beloved Union is safe in our Master's care. See to it, only, that you listen to His voice and follow where Christ leads."

A by-product of an amazingly efficient organization was that WMU as a body had unlocked essentially every door now open for women in Southern Baptist life. Interestingly, at no point was this WMU's expressed purpose. Even at that first meeting in 1888, one of the founding members stated: "To say that this is a woman's rights movement is absurd." That early prophetic statement has stood the test of time. The first 100 years of organization reflect a body of women who gained influence through proven excellence in structure and administration. By the 1980s, the WMU Executive Board was meeting twice a year and developing missions programs for local churches. Elected Board officials and state and national professionals were made up of all age groups and members. They continually sought input from SBC agencies in order to facilitate cooperation and effectiveness.

WHAT WE MIGHT YET BE

The theme of WMU's 1986 annual meeting in Atlanta's World Congress Center was a good indication of the positive spirit maintained by WMU leadership in the face of Convention divisiveness, even as new Convention leadership strove to find means of dictating policy and planning relative to WMU. This was WMU's 98th year of official organization, but it was also the centennial of missions literature and WMU's ministries with children. The Literature Department, established in Maryland in 1886, was officially transferred to WMU in 1906, and the first publication—*Our Mission Fields*—was issued that year. In 1986, WMU was producing 325 magazines, leaflets, and products. Then, in celebration of ministries with children, a Children's Centennial Pageant, written by Amelia Bishop of Texas and directed by WMU's June Whitlow, was performed by children from seven area churches in Atlanta.

Christine Gregory, past national president, spoke at this annual meeting, challenging the women to pray for the Convention as never before. She urged: "In order to bring a new day, let's govern our tongues this year, and whenever we are tempted to talk about someone else during the coming year, let's decide instead to talk about Jesus."

Additionally, delegates mourned the passing of Marie Mathis and paid tribute to her remarkable life of ministry. Mathis was called "without equal, not only as president of WMU, but in the entire world of Baptist leadership." This annual meeting was the last in which Dot Sample would preside. She had completed five years in office, and the audience honored her for the many ways she had contributed to the Union. In her closing address, Dr. Sample noted that Woman's Missionary Union is a never-ending story, and "we *yet* shall be women of vision, women of hope, and women of action." Delegates next elected Marjorie McCullough as national president, who had served as a missionary overseas. She had specialized in WMU work on two continents, in three countries—Nigeria, Ghana, and Brazil. She had also served as national director of Girls' Auxiliary and had written the new manual and handbook for Acteens. She came to the office with wide experience and expertise during a time when leadership would be a daily challenge.

AUXILIARY? AGENCY?

McCullough had her hands full from the very outset. There was never a time in the history of WMU when the question of "auxiliary vs. agency" was not looked upon, covertly or overtly, as an issue for WMU in relation to the SBC. When WMU was officially organized in 1888, it began as an *auxiliary* since the Convention did not look upon the Union as an integral part of the SBC. From the beginning, WMU's philosophy and intent regarding *auxiliary* remained consistent, regardless of the various arrows slung at the concept through the years following the official founding of the organization. WMU was an auxiliary to serve alongside the two mission boards, supporting and undergirding their program, not instigating separate agendas of its own.

During the 1970s and 1980s, more and more state WMU offices had to make a choice concerning another question: auxiliary or department? Many state WMU organizations were new, small in number, and without necessary funds, so there was no choice but to begin as a department and hope to be able to maintain a certain amount of autonomy in use of funds and in having a voice in decision-making. These were knotty issues in many states, given the ambiguous position of women's work throughout the Convention during this period. Several other state WMU organizations became departments due to lack of funding. Only a few states had a statewide missions offering for WMU work that allowed them to remain as auxiliaries as they served alongside their state Baptist office.

99 YEARS AND GOING STRONG

Regardless of developments in the Convention, WMU continued developing its own missions education programs and was deeply involved in preparing for the massive Centennial celebration scheduled for May 1988. The 1987 meeting in St. Louis was a prelude to the big year to come. Ninety-nine-year-old WMU was looking very spry and active, considering her venerable years. With the theme Celebrate, each session featured a sub-theme and a dramatic monologue by Laurita Mullins Miller. In these dramatic presentations, Miller portrayed Mary Magdalene of New Testament fame, WMU "founding mother"Ann Baker Graves, Annie Armstrong, Kathleen Mallory, and current missionary Martha Franks. Carolyn Weatherford set the tone for the meeting as she spoke of all the reasons WMU had to celebrate and concluded by saying, "We can hardly wait to finish celebrating the first century so we can get on with the second."

For the preceding three years, an incredible amount of effort had been going into preparations for the centennial celebration to take place in Richmond, Virginia, in May, exactly 100 years to the day from the official founding of Woman's Missionary Union. Word of the big celebration traveled around the world, and anticipation was high. Any self-respecting, red-blooded WMU woman who was mobile enough to make the trip and enterprising enough to figure out how to afford it made plans to be in Richmond, Virginia, on May 13-14, 1988.

CHAPTER

A Century to Celebrate: A Future to Fulfill

"People will not look forward to posterity who never look backward to their ancestors."

— Edmund Burke

RICHMOND, VIRGINIA — MAY 13, 1988

EXCITEMENT PERMEATED THE very air on May 13 as thousands of women gathered in Richmond, anticipating the significance of the coming day—Saturday—when Woman's Missionary Union would turn 100 years old. What a centenarian she was with blooming health, having fought off various life-threatening challenges over and over again throughout her lifetime. She always allowed those challenges to act as refiner's fire. Gathered now in Richmond were more than 11,000 women, the largest group of adult WMU members ever to assemble in one place. These twentieth-century women were remembering with pride and thankfulness those 32 brave delegates and the some 200 women who had met with them in Richmond's Broad Street Methodist Church basement on Monday morning, May 14, 1888. Those women were stepping out on faith—a giant move for sure in the 1800s culture of the South.

Past president Christian Gregory recalled the excitement of that 1888 gathering. She shared her amazement "that an organization could survive 100 years—still fueled by prayer, a shoestring budget, and singleness of purpose in carrying out the Great Commission."

The Richmond meeting was packed with women, many from countries far away, and there was an extraordinary sense of camaraderie. Overflow crowds from the Richmond Coliseum watched on closed circuit TV in the Grand Ballroom of the Richmond Centre. All the living general officers of WMU, SBC, were present as special guests, along with executive director emeritus Alma Hunt. With only one exception, the heads of all agencies and boards of the SBC were present. WMU felt especially honored that 203 home missionaries and 138 foreign missionaries attended, 166 of these being new appointees there to be commissioned. An astounding number of representatives from 23 countries also attended the festivities. Early attendees enjoyed visiting Lottie Moon's birthplace and Annie Armstrong's home in Baltimore.

Throughout Friday and Saturday, the most extensive exhibit of WMU history ever collected was open in Richmond Centre. Just by walking through Celebration Hall, you could follow the history of WMU from its forerunner Polly Webb in 1800 through countless historic personalities, as participants could view hundreds of displays illustrating WMU's rich history. Scattered throughout the hall, missionaries signed autographs and dramatists performed vignettes of WMU history.

UNDER THE BIG TENT

A picnic in Festival Park (the plaza surrounding the Coliseum) was billed as the "Celebration in the Park" and was the opening event. Thousands of the women attending wore historic dress and strolled the park area enjoying bands, choirs, soloists, puppets, bell ringers, and historical vignettes. A highly popular feature was the display of more than 225 centennial quilts. Ribbons were awarded to outstanding examples of WMU quilting skill. More than 13,000 onlookers experienced a memorable beginning to centennial festivities.

Delegates moved into the Coliseum for the opening session that Friday evening. Each of the four sessions had a Celebrate theme with this first one named "Celebrate God's Call." This session focused on WMU's summons to work. It began with a 20-minute parade of states, featuring a roll call of state WMU organizations in the order of their entry into the Union. It turned into a colorful and emotional event. Flags of the states were also part of the opening processional, along with costumed actors depicting the missionary themes of the Bible. A 15-minute drama presented a re-enactment of the 1888 founding meeting.

The biblical faith of WMU's early leaders was depicted in each session by Laurita Mullins Miller, who opened with her dramatic portrayal of Fannie Heck.

In the Saturday morning celebration, Miller portrayed Kathleen Mallory as the morning's theme focused on "Celebrate God's Creation." Each session featured a host of well-known WMU personalities, scores of home and foreign missionaries, and leaders from each SBC agency. Former national presidents Helen Fling and Christine Gregory both spoke, and Alma Hunt, executive director emeritus, reminisced with Frances Tyler, long-time national recording secretary. This session was viewed by more than 600 organized viewing audiences across the nation tuned via the Baptist Telecommunication Network and the American Christian TV System. This was a first for WMU.

The final two sessions focused on "Celebrate God's Community" and "Celebrate God's Commission." Miller dramatized the life of Ethlene Boone Cox, and both Annie Armstrong and Lottie Moon were featured in dramatic monologues. Saturday afternoon, Dr. Keith Parks, president of the FMB, made a surprise presentation to WMU—an 1845 portrait of Henrietta Hall Shuck, the first Southern woman to serve as a foreign missionary and the first American woman to go to China in 1836. The portrait now hangs in a place of honor in national WMU headquarters in Birmingham.

The closing session was highlighted by the commissioning service for 166 new home missionaries. Following flags of the nations and states, current missionaries and emeritus missionaries filed into the arena, and these in turn were followed by the missionaries to be commissioned. They were holding lighted candles, and the audience followed the example of the missionaries and spontaneously lighted the souvenir candle flashlights they had earlier been given. The audience was then directed to extinguish their candlelights and then slowly re-light them in sequence, as Dr. Bill O'Brien, executive vice-president of the FMB, sang "Send the Light." In a moving scene, twinkling lights slowly spread across the Coliseum. Dr. Larry Lewis, president of the Home Mission Board, delivered the charge to the missionaries, and O'Brien sang "Eternal Life." In good Baptist tradition, the celebration concluded with an invitation for commitment to missionary support and service, and 1,600 decisions were recorded that night. More than 1,700 people had been part of the programming for that remarkable centennial gathering.

"A FUTURE TO FULFILL" IN SAN ANTONIO

It had to have been somewhat anti-climactic to have the annual meeting just a month later in San Antonio. Certainly WMU could celebrate having brought off a memorable centennial. Now they were setting the stage for the coming 100 years, following the theme A Future to Fulfill. A video theme interpretation was prepared by the HMB and featured at each session, depicting trends that would affect missions in the future. Carolyn Weatherford reviewed WMU's great year of celebration and stated that it was now time to accept our heritage and move into our future, focusing on six elements. They revolved around the Union's magnificent obsession with the challenge of the Great Commission, even while acknowledging its role as a powerful minority. She emphasized the strength of the Union as part of its heritage, along with the spirit and attitude of sacrificial giving that had characterized WMU since its very beginning. Weatherford stressed the uniqueness of our heritage of missionary education, the spirit of innovation that had been evident since the earliest years. She joyfully reported the goal of paying for the new headquarters building by the time of the centennial had been met—WMU was free of debt.

Weatherford asked some key questions of those assembled in San Antonio: "What is the purpose of WMU? What fundamental truths define its borders today? To what will we give our support? What will WMU fight for, if necessary? It is not a struggle over rights of Southern Baptist women." Rather, Weatherford suggested, "it is the right and responsibility of every Southern Baptist woman to serve her Lord through the fundamentals of WMU." Weatherford praised WMU's historic auxiliary status that had "given WMU a firm base of operations, keeping us beyond Convention disagreements and politics." When she affirmed that WMU will remain "an auxiliary, helper alongside, voluntarily cooperative," she received a standing ovation. In a surprise move, Dr. Roy Honeycutt, president of Southern Baptist Theological Seminary, presented Weatherford with the prestigious E. Y. Mullins Denominational Service Award, the equivalent of an honorary doctorate and the seminary's highest honor.

The San Antonio gathering featured the premier of *Go Forward: The Story of WMU,* a documentary of the history of WMU. This was the year "Prayer Patterns," the monthly prayer feature in *Royal Service* that incorporated the missionary prayer calendar, was introduced. It has remained a significant and popular feature in the monthly magazine. In her address, Marjorie McCullough echoed the concerns that each delegate was sensing as she challenged the body: "We have celebrated our Centennial. Let's pull out of the past. Let's pull out of today's mistrust and confusion, and let's move on. . . . We need these things: commitment, imagination, risk-taking, relevance, and unity."

IN HIS NAME IN LAS VEGAS

As WMU moved toward the end of another decade, Carolyn Weatherford reported that membership was leveling out. The Annual Report showed that total membership stood at slightly more than 1,200,000. The women of WMU realized they faced a challenge in finding new ways to share the missions message as they approached a new decade. At the same time, they were highly encouraged with the steady growth of the Lottie Moon and Annie Armstrong offerings, which demonstrated an astounding ability to thrive.

Women assembled in Las Vegas on June 11, 1989, for the last annual meeting with Carolyn Weatherford as executive director. Marjorie McCullough called the women into session using the Luther Rice gavel, made from the original timbers of Pine Pleasant Baptist Church in Saluda, South Carolina, the site of his burial.

In bringing her final report, Weatherford "remembered 1974," when she first walked in the door of 600 North 20th Street, Birmingham, to become WMU's fifth executive director. She traced the intervening years since that moment, noting how WMU had enjoyed several highly productive years in that period when denominational cooperation was at a peak. She affirmed that those were fruitful years before the Convention was plunged into controversy. This was Weatherford's 16th time to address the annual meeting; she recalled the three significant reasons for being executive director that she gave in her acceptance speech those long years before: love for missions, love for WMU, and the assurance she had that the Lord had led her and the committee to that point.

Weatherford read from Numbers 13, relating how the spies brought reports of "giants in the land." She then pointed out some of WMU's "giants," like how to explain to a lost world that our Convention is not getting along. She challenged the women to face those giants unafraid as they depended on God's grace. She stated that August 11 would be her final day as director of WMU and expressed her deep gratitude for the opportunities afforded her for more than 15 years. Weatherford then announced that on August 19, she would gain the new name of Carolyn Weatherford Crumpler once she walked down the aisle to marry pastor Joe Crumpler.

This was also the year of the fourth Acteens National Convention, held in San Antonio and attended by 16,300 teenage girls.

A NEW DECADE — A NEW EXECUTIVE DIRECTOR

Just before the decade ended, WMU would gain a new executive director, its sixth in a line of highly gifted women. This leader would be a real departure from the leaders of previous years who had grown up in local WMU organizations, and had spent years involved in the organization and its ministries. This one indeed had a resume that resonated "missions," but from a different perspective. Dellanna West O'Brien and her husband, Bill, were appointed by the FMB in 1962 and served in Indonesia for 10 years. After Bill became vice-president of the FMB, Dellanna completed her doctorate and founded an International Family and Children's Educational Service. A true visionary, Dellanna brought to her new position a host of talents and skills. WMU's Executive Board, in a called meeting during WMU Week at Glorieta, elected Dellanna O'Brien as WMU's sixth executive director. She took office on September 1 and was "inaugurated" during Executive Board meetings in January 1990.

WMU began a new decade with a new leader; together they faced a veritable host of challenges. O'Brien knew when she began that she was not stepping into an easy situation, but she faced the issues with resolute determination, as did all of WMU leadership.

THE DAWNING OF A DECADE

The theme for the 1990 annual meeting in New Orleans—Hearts in One Accord—was an indication of the positive attitude to be found among WMU leadership in the face of all odds. Dr. O'Brien's inaugural report centered on Romans 15:5—being of one heart. She challenged the women to note endurance means "the act of suffering; a continuing or the power of continuing under pain or hardship without being overcome." WMU would continue, pain or hardship notwithstanding, and would not be overcome. She affirmed that not only were we to receive encouragement but also to be encouragers of others. The leadership of WMU, and women in local churches who were aware of conditions in their states and on a national level, were determined that their hearts would beat in one accord, remaining centered on their goal—to support world missions.

CHAPTER

These Are the Times

"These are the times that try men's souls"
—Thomas Paine, 1776

A DECADE OF CHALLENGES

TO PARAPHRASE THOMAS Paine: These are the times that try *women's* souls—and resolve, and determination, and patience. This was surely no time for the faint of heart. And thankfully, WMU possessed leaders with strong hearts and courageous resolve. The 1990s brought a new director and a new president, both of whom shared the determination of their predecessors to perpetuate the founders' goal of missions support. They also brought a new sense of vision as to how to *achieve* this goal.

Dellanna O'Brien became director of WMU at a critical juncture in its dealings with the SBC. O'Brien understood that through the years WMU had been an auxiliary in the highest sense of the term with only one purpose—to further the missions goal of the Convention itself. Additionally, she grasped the gravity of the situation. O'Brien and WMU's Executive Board met in special session in September 1990, following the meeting of the Convention in New Orleans that June. Years later, when asked about that June convention and the subsequent Executive Board meeting in September, O'Brien stated: "At that meeting it was very clear that the controversy was going full speed in our Convention. There seemed to be two alignments, those who wanted change and those who were satisfied with the Convention as it has been. It was a very hostile convention and . . . discouraging to those of us from WMU because we had hoped that we would avoid a cataclysmic conflict in the Convention. So this executive meeting was to define our position as WMU, and I think the comment that went out as a result of that meeting clearly explained that we were not going to be divisive within our group. The work we had to do was far more important, and we did say that we would work with any church regardless of their allegiance to one side or the other."

The September statement primarily restated WMU's basic purpose and goals, and called for prayer from women across the world. The report spoke to WMU's critics, stating: "We regret that our silence over the years might have been construed as consent or even support of the controversy. We further regret any suspicions that WMU might be politically involved in the denominational strife. We call upon you to work with us for the cause of missions."

On one hand, WMU celebrated a new decade, but at the same time, it was confronted with increased scrutiny and daily conflict. It was a time of contrasts. WMU stood steadfast in its focus on missions, but it also had to deal with new challenges.

WMU AND IMAGE

An image campaign for WMU had been discussed prior to the election of O'Brien. There were various misconceptions about

WMU and its purpose, even though it had been at work for more than a century. Leaders decided that an image campaign was needed to give Baptists and the general public a broader view of WMU. Advertisements were placed in several leading magazines and served as an introduction of WMU to a new audience, as well as giving longtime Union members a fresh look at what their organization was currently doing.

ATLANTA IN 1991

More than 4,000 women gathered in Atlanta at WMU's annual meeting in June, a meeting that showcased many aspects of missions. Marjorie McCullough presided for the last time, and handed the gavel of leadership to Carolyn Miller of Alabama. Miller and O'Brien would face a challenging new decade, and attitudes towards WMU did not improve.

The Atlanta meeting held many inspiring elements. A stirring moment was the testimony of foreign missionary Finlay Graham, who told of his experiences as a hostage at the US Embassy in Kuwait prior to the Persian Gulf War. Women at the meeting learned that the most tremendous growth in WMU work over the past several years was in new work areas. In the mainline states, there had been a minimal .8 percent growth, while in new work states, growth was a robust 9 percent. One reason for such growth was undoubtedly the cooperative effort of WMU and other boards in providing training through the Mega Focus Cities project. WMU designed a customized and workable program for churches in these vast cities.

The national staff of WMU now numbered approximately 170, and revenue was $13.3 million. The missionary housing office had completed its first year of operation with about 350 sponsors and nearly 400 homes for furloughing missionaries.

NEW PROJECTS, NEW IMAGE, NEW CHALLENGES

Although WMU had been talking about "image," a 15-month research project showed that it was not really image, but rather "awareness" at issue. Research done by a Birmingham advertising firm revealed that "WMU is . . . loved by some, distrusted by others, and either not known or misunderstood by just about everybody else." The research also indicated that WMU is most closely associated with Baptist women, and not as closely linked to the other age-level groups. Many did not understand that the age-level groups are also *part* of WMU. Nevertheless, the study clearly illustrated that the presence of WMU in a church is a healthy thing for that church. In general, WMU women are more involved and more faithful, give more to missions causes, *and* are more involved in witnessing of their faith. The research's bottom line revealed that WMU is often miscast, misunderstood, and underappreciated, mostly because people were not aware of what WMU actually did. Therefore, in April, in 15 states, a beautiful insert was placed in the regional editions of five magazines, inviting readers to contact a local SBC church for information about WMU. An underlying purpose was to give all Baptists a fresh look at WMU.

Age-level organizations received recognition in 1992 when Acteens Activators set a new record with 1,558 teenage girls and their leaders volunteering and working alongside home missionaries and other leaders in Bible schools and other special projects in over 30 states. Coed literature was released for the first time, including materials for youth groups as well as for adults in Baptist churches.

MEETING IN INDIANAPOLIS

Baptist women—some 4,000 strong—gathered in the city of Indianapolis in June 1992 and honored Dr. Keith Parks who was to retire in October as president of the FMB. Dellanna O'Brien told of her joy as she crossed the country in seeing women, children, and youth being points of light and beacons of hope for Christ from tiny towns to megacities. But much on the minds of everyone in this annual meeting was the Southern Baptist Convention meeting to begin just at the close of WMU's meeting, because yet again, the issue of "auxiliary" was to come up.

A motion had been made at the February SBC Executive Committee meeting to "invite WMU to initiate legal steps to become an agency of the SBC rather than remain as an auxiliary to the Convention." The motion was given to a subcommittee meeting in June in conjunction with the SBC, and at that meeting, the subcommittee recommended, and the Executive Committee approved, affirmation of WMU's historic relationship as an auxiliary.

A CALL FOR SPIRITUAL VISION

Southern Baptist leader Dr. Grady Cothen served as president of the Sunday School Board for 11 years and held numerous positions of leadership in Baptist life. In his first book chronicling the controversy in the SBC, he wrote of the remarkable missions contribution of WMU, stating: "Few SBC entities have had the profoundly positive effect on the missions enterprise that WMU has had. . . . if the support of WMU is lost for the mission boards, the work will suffer catastrophic results.

In the general session of the January 1992 Executive Board, Dellanna O'Brien declared that "in our 104 years in Woman's Missionary Union we have not walked this unfamiliar path before. There is no road map to give direction, no manual to dictate procedures. But spiritual vision is always better than physical sight. It's always frightening to walk along new paths, especially when you cannot see. But when there is someone who walks alongside guiding you . . . you are not alone . . . [and] when that 'someone' knows the path from beginning to end, you are not helpless." She concluded that: "One, we must not stop, but must keep marching forward. Two, we must not be consumed by the darkness of confusion. Three, we must trust our Guide and His promises. And four, we must always give Him the glory for His preservation."

At this same board meeting, president Carolyn Miller appointed 16 women to explore action plans and strategies that could lead the organization to meet missions challenges and seize the opportunities of the day. The group included seven state WMU presidents; three state WMU executive directors; four national WMU staff personnel; Martha Wennerberg, the national recording secretary; and Marjorie McCullough, immediate past president, to meet along with Miller. The group had no official name. It was simply "the Committee." They were charged with considering any and all directions, options, or scenarios as WMU planned for its future. They were to explore plans and strategies and bring back a report to the Executive Board, with an open time frame. The women met frequently throughout the year, gathered data, conducted interviews, and polled various audiences. It was a gravely challenging assignment and a massively busy year.

Keith Parks' Final Address to WMU

Dr. Keith Parks, as outgoing president of the Foreign Mission Board, spoke to WMU leadership during their annual Executive Board meeting, challenging WMU for the years to come and focusing on the five missions education challenges. He identified these as (1) dealing with a denomination full of "cut flowers," as the majority of Baptists have little biblical knowledge, denominational loyalty, and precious little missions education. He spoke of (2) overcoming a 90-second news bit mentality. Everyone wants to understand a world event in 90 seconds, so WMU must learn to grab attention and extend the attention span of Baptists. Parks stated we must (3) turn a "mirror" perspective into a "window" view. With mirrors, people see only themselves. The silver must be removed from behind the glass in order to see beyond to a needy world. (4) We need to change from "What's in it for me?" to "What would Christ have me do?" Parks concluded with the statement: (5) "Become more flexible in organizational matters—focus more on function rather than form, on ends rather than means." WMU leadership recognized that in the crucial year ahead, as they considered the future through the work of the Committee, these reminders from Dr. Parks would be of vital importance.

NEW BIRTH

The miracle of new life brings hope of posterity and the passing on of vision. This spirit of exhilaration came for WMU right in the midst of incredible stress and tension. At the annual meeting in Houston in June 1993, it was announced that the Executive Board had authorized the WMU Vision Fund to help finance operations at the national office and to fund missions activities not funded through other means. Additionally, an Office of Development (the forerunner of WMU Foundation) was established at national headquarters.

Another "birth"—a brainchild that grew out of deliberations from the Committee—was Project HELP. This project provided WMU with a way to target a specific national critical issue for concentrated study and action. Yet another "baby" of this time—the Mississippi River Ministry—had several parents. WMU partnered with the Home Mission Board and seven state conventions in developing the ministry. This project joins WMU volunteers with Baptists in those seven states in building bridges of hope by doing all sorts of things—from Bible clubs and repairing roofs to providing free health and dental care. The genius of this program is evidenced by its longevity; it continues to change lives. Volunteer Connection was an initiative "conceived" in January 1993 that came to fruition a few years later. Its function was to facilitate the consolidation of various volunteer missions efforts of WMU.

One more 1993 "conception" also came to maturity in the years to follow—Christian Women's Job Corps. This became one of the most successful initiatives ever conceived by WMU. In fall 1993, state and national WMU leaders toured the Appalachians and discovered crying needs among women and evidence of a possible way to help. They began right then to look to what God might do through a one-on-one program to help equip impoverished women to help themselves break out of the poverty cycle. Teaching them marketable skills, and introducing them to Christ as well, would prove invaluable to countless young women.

THE COMMITTEE

The women who made up the Committee met many times, deliberated, prayed, and agonized over what future direction to recommend. This was no hastily tossed together process; it was born from the crucible of concern for WMU and its future effectiveness. When the final proceedings and recommendations from the Committee were brought to the Executive Board, and each segment was reported and discussed individually over a period of several days, there was amazing unanimity of response, and the entire report was affirmed with no dissension. It was then presented at the annual meeting in Houston in June and passed there as well. Essentially, WMU's Vision Statement and Core Values made up the report.

Vision Statement: WMU exists to enable churches and believers to participate in introducing all persons in the world to Christ. Core Values: (1) We affirm and uphold the "priesthood of the believer." (2) We acknowledge God's call to every believer to carry the good news. (3) We recognize, emphasize, and affirm the giftedness of women and girls in Christian endeavors. (4) We acknowledge the biblical mandate to respond to social and moral issues with actions as modeled by Jesus Christ. (5) We acknowledge and accept the responsibility for developing missions leaders. (6) We covenant

to partner with Christians around the world.

HAIL TO THE CHIEF

There were numerous bright spots in a year fraught with change and confrontation, and none more encouraging than a surprise visit to national headquarters by former US President Jimmy Carter and his wife, Rosalynn. Dr. O'Brien received a phone call one morning in May 1993 saying that Carter and his wife were coming to Birmingham and wanted to stop by and see the WMU building. Excitement grew among employees as O'Brien wondered, "What in the world do you do to greet a President?" Carter greeted O'Brien with a big bear hug and said, "I've been wanting to meet you." Later speaking of the event, O'Brien explained that Carter "just wanted to express appreciation to WMU for what we had done and said that he really affirmed our actions about standing on our own two feet and not being swayed by the controversy." The Carter visit was a healthy helping of encouragement during tense times.

O'BRIEN'S MISSIONS CHALLENGE

O'Brien addressed the WMU Executive Board in January 1993 regarding the controversy in the Convention, pointing out that in spite of WMU's reluctance to be part of the conflict, there were times that the organization could not avoid being detracted from the main task. She acknowledged WMU's absolute commitment to remaining true to the missionaries, just as WMU has done from the very outset. "Missions is the song God has given us—not a new song, but a new rendition." WMU finished 1993 with many questions unanswered and with controversy inevitably swirling about them, but with faith undaunted. The organization focused on the challenges of new issues, new dangers, and new opportunities ahead.

CHAPTER

Reach Out

"WMU takes on the responsibility of finding new and innovative ways to make a difference in the lives of others for the cause of Christ."
—Dellanna O'Brien

"FROM CRISIS TO CRISIS"

A NUMBER OF years ago, an elderly missionary in Asia prayed every morning about the needs of his native America: "Dear Lord, just uphold our President as he goes from blunder to blunder." For the leaders of WMU, a daily prayer became "Lord, just uphold us as we go from crisis to crisis." Emergency situations seemed unending. Being proactive in the midst of such daily crises and threats to the organization's very existence as an entity was a constant challenge.

By this time, not only national and state leadership but also associational leaders and many women in local WMU organizations were aware of the issues facing WMU. Although many leaders in the Convention recognized the true value of WMU and its essential role in missions education, the majority of them were men no longer in positions of influence in Convention matters. One such man, Grady Cothen, made the forthright statement: "Few SBC entities have had the profoundly positive effect on the missions enterprise that WMU has had. Approximately one-half of budgets of the mission boards comes from the offerings originated and sponsored by WMU."

LOTTIE MOON AND THE FOREIGN MISSION BOARD

For the first time in a decade, the Executive Board was not hearing the report of the FMB from president Keith Parks. Dr. Parks had retired, and Jerry Rankin had been elected to the position. In January 1994, he gave his first report to WMU's annual Executive Board Meeting. Dellanna O'Brien introduced Rankin who had been a fellow missionary in Indonesia in the 1970s. Dr. Rankin brought the challenge that Southern Baptists may achieve their Bold Mission Thrust goals if they focus on what God is doing in the world rather than on their own strategies, methods, and plans.

Unknown to WMU at the time, the FMB had applied for a trademark on the name Lottie Moon Christmas Offering. Ten months later, WMU learned of this attempt. Upon being confronted, the FMB said they were trying to prevent churches from using the Lottie Moon Christmas Offering to raise funds for causes other than the FMB. When this action became public knowledge, the FMB received overwhelmingly negative response to what many Baptists viewed as a surreptitious action. The FMB subsequently dropped its efforts to trademark the name of the offering. However, wheels had already been set in motion, and consequently, WMU applied for legal trademarks on the Lottie Moon Christmas Offering and the Annie Armstrong Easter Offering, with the agreement of the two mission boards.

During these difficult months, Carolyn Miller, national WMU president, saw WMU's biggest challenge of the moment as keeping the organization focused on its central task in the midst of great conflict and uncertainly in the SBC. Dellanna O'Brien appealed to the WMU constituency: "WMU is committed to raising high the flag of missions." She urged that committed women and girls, as "laborers together with God, . . . continue to move forward with boldness and energy into our second century of missionary work."

GROWING IN LOVE

In 1995, WMU consolidated two adult missions organizations into one, combining Baptist Women and Baptist Young women into Women on Mission. They also decided to publish a new magazine, *Missions Mosaic,* to replace *Royal Service* and *Contempo.* Years later, Dellanna O'Brien reflected on these changes, saying that they were an effort to make the material in the women's magazines more up-to-date in makeup and more compelling in content.

Also this year, WMU began to offer coed missions opportunities through Adults on Mission; Youth on Mission; and Children in Action. Churches would have the option of traditional structure or coed approaches. In June 1994, more than 13,500 teenaged girls from across the nation gathered in Birmingham to celebrate their organization's 25th birthday at the National Acteens Convention.

INNOVATIONS AND UPDATES IN ATLANTA

The Vision Fund, established at the previous year's annual meeting, provided for two missions activities to be launched in 1994. It allowed WMU to provide each association with a kit to help leaders plan for the collection of 1 million cans of food on one February day in 1995. And, it allowed for the launch of the first national social issue—Project HELP: Hunger. A year later, the success of the campaign was celebrated. All states had participated and had contributed 1,239,019 cans of food, plus over $378,000 in donations to feed the hungry. At the 1995 annual meeting in Atlanta, WMU officially launched its national ministry project for 1995-96, Project HELP: AIDS, challenging women to lead their churches to become involved locally in AIDS ministries. The Atlanta meeting concluded with the commissioning of 39 new North American Mission Board (HMB) missionaries who would serve across the nation.

GA WORLD

The year 1995 also brought a significant change for Girls in Action with the release of a new magazine, *GA World,* for girls in grades 5 and 6. (*Discovery* continued as the magazine for younger GAs.) Another innovation was the National Leadership Consultants Training (NLCT) meeting in Birmingham and in Glorieta, New Mexico, where more than 450 women from all state conventions were trained in how to lead conferences in their own states. These women in turn trained more than 43,000 other women across the nation.

SHARING THE LEGACY, ENVISIONING THE FUTURE

Acknowledging the importance of passing on our legacy, WMU leadership envisioned a museum to house memorabilia relevant to nearly 200 years of missions endeavors by Baptist women. The museum was planned so significant artifacts and documents would be preserved and on display for the next generation to understand and enjoy. This vision became reality in January 1995, when several hundred guests gathered at WMU headquarters to dedicate the Alma Hunt Museum, named for the inimitable executive director of WMU who served from 1948 to 1974. It stands as a beacon to enhance the understanding and appreciation of all Baptists for the contribution WMU has made to the cause of missions. The treasures housed here speak to the stories and hearts of faithful women through the centuries who have been a vital part of missions thrust. Many of these documents, pictures, and pieces of missions history in this museum are considered priceless by women who value the message they encapsulate.

Nothing was more significant to the future of WMU during the tenure of Dellanna O'Brien than the WMU Foundation, which was officially established in January 1995. It had been an inner vision of Dr. O'Brien, and she had the joy of leading it to become a reality. Its primary purpose is to support national and international missions projects of WMU and provide contingency funds for its own operation and WMU work. In addition, it assures the financial security of WMU into the future. The Foundation was established as an independent corporation governed by its own board of trustees and headquartered in Birmingham. The Foundation organized with an initial nine trustees, and a president with WMU's executive director and national president serving as ex-officio members. Richard Carnes was named the first president in July of that year. Immediately upon beginning to function, the Foundation assumed oversight of the existing

Second Century Fund, the WMU Vision Fund, and a number of scholarships that were being administered by WMU.

THE SBC RESTRUCTURES

In 1993, the SBC set up a Program and Structure Study Committee (PSSC), with the purpose of evaluating the program statements of all SBC entities and the overall structure of the Convention. This committee, appointed by the SBC Executive Committee, in turn met with each of the various Convention agencies as part of their process. WMU was invited to meet with the PSSC committee, and during that meeting, the committee asked again if WMU wanted to become an agency. Dellanna O'Brien stated years later that WMU had discussed the possibility that this question would occur and had agreed that "becoming an agency" would not sit well with WMU membership. Therefore, WMU's response to the PSSC was "Thanks but no thanks," because the Union would lose too much. Auxiliary status had worked very well for over 100 years, and the relationship with the SBC had gone well most of that time. The Union's leaders were assured after the meeting that WMU would be left as it was, and the restructuring would just apply to the agencies. O'Brien found herself stunned when she and Carolyn Miller attended the February 1995 SBC Executive Committee meeting and discovered the committee's intent for the reorganization. Under the new structure, the FMB and NAMB would be given the responsibility of the missions offerings and of missions education for the whole church. When it was all sorted out, the committee's purpose appeared to be making WMU a mere footnote.

However, when the PSSC report was brought to the body of the Convention for a vote, a number of people there noted the omission of WMU. So the proposal was amended to affirm "the valued relationship with Woman's Missionary Union as an auxiliary to the Convention, and to welcome the continued voluntary contributions of WMU." On such reassurance, WMU continued to do its work as always, promoting missions giving and education.

LEARNING TO SUCCEED

Hearing a success story is always a heart lifter, and WMU stood in need of a lifted heart during this period of crises and confrontations. That is what they found in the birth of Christian Women's Job Corps. The seed of the idea originated in spring 1993, and by 1997 it had blossomed into official reality. The concept of providing a Christian context in which women in need could be equipped for employment and for life came through the efforts of women helping women.

In early 1993, several national WMU staff members visited a number of ministries in Chicago, including Uptown Baptist Church where they learned of a project that assisted women in developing job skills. They look at two specific target groups: women in poverty and women who needed a personal relationship with Jesus. Another trip to the Appalachians that fall revealed examples of programs where women were given help in changing their situations. By summer 1994, a strategic planning meeting was under way, with women from four state WMU organizations, the Texas River Ministry and national WMU participating. The issue before them: Should WMU develop a program to assist women in breaking out of the poverty cycle? Their conclusion? Definitely!

And thus did Christian Women's Job Corps begin to incubate, with pilot projects in San Antonio and several cities in South Carolina. Then NAMB personnel and volunteers joined in assisting in pilot projects in five other large cities scattered across the nation. CWJC was officially launched October 1, 1997, helping women through a team approach made up of individual women working one-on-one with participants, along with business people providing jobs and churches and Christian groups giving support. The way this new "child" blossomed in the following years amazed even those founding visionaries.

WMU at the Olympics

The women of WMU may not have entered Olympic competitions, but their presence certainly left an impression as 500 Acteens Activators and 37 teams of women attended the Olympics in Atlanta in July and August 1996. Among the Women on Mission Enterprisers team was a group of national WMU staffers who worked for a week at the ministry center in downtown Atlanta. Teams at the Olympics were involved in direct evangelism and a multitude of ministries, from interpreting for internationals to preparing and distributing gift bags, and even to helping clean public areas.

PROJECT HELP: AIDS

WMU's ministry project for the year brought an overwhelming outpouring of love and concern in an area where so many had preconceptions about such an affliction. Women were involved in projects of ministry to AIDS sufferers across the nation and in other countries as well. Many women overcame their fear of AIDS by participating in hands-on help offered to suffering people. Thousands were given to aid local ministries, and over $100,000 donated through the WMU Vision Fund for the House of Hope in Brazil.

A YEAR WITH NEW LEADERSHIP

It is rare in WMU leadership for there to be all new national leaders elected at one time. This happened in 1996 at the annual meeting in New Orleans, with the election of Wanda Lee, WMU state president from Georgia, as national president, and Janet Hoffman, Louisiana's state president, as WMU recording secretary. Both came with impeccable credentials and both served in their national offices during a time when strong leadership was critically needed. Not many weeks passed during their years in office that some new crisis or pressing need did not arise, demanding their wisdom and keen powers of perception. The two became a strong team.

CARVER AND CONTROVERSY

The Carver School of Missions and Social Work at Southern Seminary closed during this period, marking the end of a long chapter in WMU history. Carver was originally the WMU Training School (WMUTS), founded in 1907 in Louisville, Kentucky. WMUTS came about at the pleading of the FMB, which was appointing women for overseas mission service. However, these young women were ill-equipped through no fault of their own, because in 1907 only men were allowed to attend seminary. WMU, therefore, developed an educational plan for women. Thousands of Baptist women passed through its doors and emerged as strong, well-trained advocates of the gospel. (See earlier chapters that tell the story of WMUTS.) In 1952 and 1953, plans were set into motion for WMUTS to become Carver School of Missions and Social Work, offering graduate level degrees in social work and missionary training. A few years later, as women were allowed to attend seminary, it became financially difficult for WMU to operate Carver School. So in 1957, WMU leadership gave the school to the Southern Baptist Convention with the understanding that it would be continued for the purpose for which it was established.

Then in 1963, the SBC in its annual meeting voted that Carver School merge into Southern Seminary. With this merger, the seminary became the provisional beneficiary of several endowment funds related to Carver School. At this same time, WMU took action to make Southern Seminary the recipient of earnings from these funds, "provided that the seminary uses such income in conformity with the requirements of the trust agreement." In addition to these endowment funds, WMU also gave the seminary real estate valued at $800,000. However, the situation at Southern Seminary, in regard to Carver School, began to deteriorate in 1994. Due to changes in leadership and policy, the future of Carver's more than 100 students was suddenly in jeopardy.

For the students at Carver School, this was a time filled with uncertainty. Seminary president Al Mohler made the statement that theological education and social work were incongruent. A graduate who went through that experience related the daily tension of those final years. She persevered, graduated, and later became a leader of women in Southern Baptist ministry. In relating her feelings during those days, she remarked on the divisiveness of the time, characterized by conflict between faculty, staff, and students with scarcely a day going by without some type of conflict or discussion over the validity of the Carver School. She stated: "As a student who found herself defending her calling on a daily basis, I found myself intensely scrutinizing (Dr. Mohler's) statement so that any defense I gave was filled with integrity and scriptural direction. Reflecting on the time for me personally, I graduated from Southern with a certificate in theology and a master's degree in social work (MSW) with absolute certainty that the Bible teaches there can be no separation of the gospel message given in both word and *deed* . . . It was a time that led me to greater appreciation for WMU. I grew up in Mission Friends, GA, and Baptist Young Women. However, it was not until this time that I learned the stories of past WMU leaders who held to the same conviction, that missions is a dialogue between the spoken word and the deed, and thus created the school (WMUTS) for women. I learned of their courage and grace in the midst of conflict. . . Finding a heritage of women called to practice in both word and deed enabled me to stand taller."

The troubles at Carver School intensified, and in 1997, Southern closed it. The next year, they sold both the name and certain undisclosed assets to Campbellsville University, a Baptist liberal-arts school in Kentucky.

WMU entered into closed mediation with Southern Seminary in 1995. As a result of the mediation, the endowments and funds held in trust were returned to WMU.

The mid-1990s had held one crisis after another for women involved in missions education and leadership, but those times of crisis clearly served only to strengthen their inner core of determination and to encourage them to continue to follow Annie Armstrong's favorite admonition—Go *forward.*

CHAPTER

Work with Your Courage High

"Stars shall your brow adorn, your heart leap with the morn, and by His love upborne, hope and adore."
—Fannie Heck

MILLENNIUMS: ONE ENDS – ANOTHER BEGINS

NOT MANY PEOPLE actually have the opportunity of seeing an old millennium out and a new one in. The leaders of WMU were charged with envisioning plans to take the world's largest Protestant missions organization for women into a new era, while dealing with the uncertainties and issues resulting from changes within the SBC. Nonetheless, WMU developed new and inventive ways to tell the gospel story and creatively provide all ages with missions education.

In 1998, Dellanna O'Brien suffered a stroke, and WMU national president Wanda Lee assumed more responsibilities in order to assist O'Brien and WMU. After a period of recovery, O'Brien returned to work and continued her responsibilities until her retirement in 1999. Although facing uncertainty, WMU stood strong. The pace of work and rate of innovation did not diminish

Chapter 32

A NEW ADVENTURE: WORLDCRAFTS

WMU vision for missions developed into an adventure into new territory with the establishment of WorldCrafts, a sustainable, fair-trade business among impoverished people around the world. Ten years after the idea germinated in the minds of key leaders and missionaries overseas, Dellanna O'Brien told the story of WorldCrafts.

> *In Thailand, missionaries for a number of years had been meeting with women who were in poverty and having Bible study with them. Then they began to give the women patterns for making Christmas tree ornaments. They had done this for years. The women would take those home, put them together, come back the next week for Bible study and turn in the ornaments they had made. They were paid for the work, and the next week they'd do the same thing. This had gone on for a number of years, but nobody in the US had been marketing those things; they had someone in Europe, but not here. So we agreed to do that, and from this we thought of other products that might come from other countries. (It) would serve two purposes: one was to help the women in those areas and it was also a way of presenting the gospel to them; secondly it was to remind us here in the States to pray for those people.*
>
> *Whereas formerly we had been praying and giving, and now there was this intentional plan to become more involved in missions on a personal basis. Here was an opportunity to experience missions. It was a*

> *totally new approach. We had never done anything like this before. We felt like it would work, but it was a long time really getting started. You know, with international enterprise like that, we had a lot to learn. For a long time, it cost us money; some despaired of our ever breaking even, but others said to keep on.*

By 1996, WMU was giving crafters in various parts of the world a chance to make a living while also hearing the gospel. Other countries began to participate—Jordan, Mexico, Pakistan, and Tanzania. Additionally, WorldCrafts provided an opportunity for missionaries in these areas to relate redemptively to the artisans. This same year, WorldCrafts debuted its home party concept, with 12 parties held in the homes of WMU members. By 1997, with the support and publicity generated by Alabama WMU, nearly 100 parties were held. *Expansion* was the operative word for WorldCrafts, which now offered 86 unique items from 14 areas of the world. Another boost came when a Birmingham woman established, with WMU's new Foundation, an endowment fund for WorldCrafts. By the end of the decade (and the century!) the party concept had gone nationwide, greatly enhancing WorldCrafts' visibility. WorldCrafts offered more than 100 items from 16 different countries. Maybe the greatest benefit of all was seen in the lives of those who made the crafts. One missionary commented on how exciting it was to see when the "light" comes on as people learn about Christ's love for them. She noted that "when people are able to meet their own needs through working, it gives them such a greater sense of dignity and community."

Chapter 32

CHRISTIAN WOMEN'S JOB CORPS: NOW A HEALTHY TODDLER

WorldCrafts and Christian Women's Job Corps (CWJC) have a similar purpose—to help women learn to stand on their own, to go from poverty to self-sufficiency, and along the way learn the power of God's love in their lives. CWJC began as an experiment to help women meet their own needs through working. Mentors would come alongside the women, and by example and involvement, demonstrate the difference Christ makes. The five pilot projects began in 1996 had increased substantially by the end of the decade, with 140 sites in 26 states plus the District of Columbia. All the training in life skills and job readiness were provided in a Christian context. Each participant was involved in Bible study and had a mentor to encourage her. The mentor did not assume a "fixer" mentality, but invested herself in the woman she helped, walking beside her and modeling a Christian lifestyle while giving her encouragement to be her very best.

Local churches and community businesses joined forces to help change lives. By the end of the century, a special CWJC fund was opened with the WMU Foundation to endow the ministry. By 2000, the Foundation had awarded the first two grants, one in California and one in Mississippi! Training became a requirement for site coordinators, with more than one level of training, and systematic training developed into a vital element of the CWJC program. A surprising benefit developed, as a number of sites found that after they had helped women re-direct their lives and become self-sufficient, those women in turn wanted to give back, and a number became mentors themselves.

A FLOURISHING FOUNDATION

CWJC wasn't the only WMU "child" that was growing rapidly; WMU Foundation was a lively 5-year-old by the end of the twentieth century. Dellanna O'Brien, soon after assuming her work as executive director in 1989, had asked an outstanding Baptist leader (a family friend) if he thought WMU should start a foundation. After promising to think about it, he came back to O'Brien with the answer: "You should have done it years ago." And so it has proved to be, becoming a great asset to WMU by being a viable way to support the work of WMU through the making of charitable gifts. The Foundation has also proved successful at providing asset management to nonprofit Christian organizations, and this aspect has grown steadily. The last year of the century, WMU made a request to its members for direct support through a Vision Fund. That first year, 1999, gifts surpassed $265,000. These gifts plus others meant that for the first time, the Foundation surpassed $1 million. The Foundation also began sharing its story by publishing a newsletter titled "Legacy."

I'M A VOLUNTEER

More and more women were becoming volunteers, as WMU signed agreements with the two mission boards as recruiters of volunteers for specific projects, in response to specific needs. WMU hired its first volunteer coordinator, Delane Tew, in 1996, and placement of volunteers more than doubled by 1998. A most singular and satisfying project proved to be working with Habitat for Humanity. In 1998, the first WMU Habitat House was built in Birmingham, Alabama. Thanks to some 200 women (and a few good men) over a period of seven days, Birmingham resident Thelma Kirksey finally had a home. Kirksey beamed: "I've been in project housing for eight years, and I wanted a better life for my children. I thank God . . . I really appreciate everyone for coming together and doing this for me and my children. . . . They have shown love for us."

By 1999, WMU-Habitat had built seven houses in six cities. Accomplishing the task were 375 volunteers from 32 states, along with local volunteers who helped feed and house the workers. WMU also entered into a two-year partnership with WMU-Bosnia through which nearly 60 volunteers served in that Eastern European land so devastated by war. Volunteers worked rebuilding houses destroyed by war, and the medical personnel among the volunteers conducted medical clinics for people who had no medical services. When the two-year partnership concluded in 2000, more than 100 volunteers had made a difference in many lives in Bosnia, building homes, conducting medical clinics, and leading a Bible camp.

WMU's two-year projects drew thousands of volunteers. And Project:HELP continued three years, emphasizing hunger issues in 1995, AIDS awareness in 1996, and Child Advocacy in 1997. Women gave their time as advocates for children, with over 150,000 hours of volunteer service reported. WMU discovered that having a project for a two-year period was practical and workable. One year was just not enough time to both instigate *and* complete a project. By 1998, WMU was launching its fifth emphasis, this one addressing the challenges of violence and how to become peacemakers.

WMU also adopted "Pure Water, Pure Love" from Brotherhood in 1995 and had the joy of supplying Southern Baptist missionaries with high-tech water filtration units to guarantee pure water for those on the front lines.

LET'S INNOVATE

Innovation was the key word for WMU in 1997 when they decided to test new missions involvement ideas in three states, beginning in 1998. Three national staffers conducted the tests—Kathy Burns was deployed to Alabama, Sheryl Churchill to Virginia, and Sylvia DeLoach to Texas. Their roles were to test new approaches for missions activities and involvement in churches and associations. As a result, the following year, 40 people completed a week of Missions Innovators training, learning how to think outside the usual parameters and try new approaches to missions involvement.

COME TO THE FESTIVAL

Some lively "festivals grew out of Volunteer Connection. In 2000, WMU sponsored the first two MissionsFest events, both in beautiful Charleston, South Carolina. More than 430 women and teens were involved in two weeklong projects, working alongside local volunteers in a targeted effort to support ongoing missions projects. There were dozens of projects in North Charleston, with efforts in a plethora of activities, from teaching to construction to hosting block parties and building relationships. It was hard to know who gained the most—those in Charleston who were assisted or those who came to help and reaped the joy.

WORKING WITH A BLUEPRINT

WMU's Executive Board, national leaders, and state leaders, must have felt a bit like architects and engineers working with a blueprint. They pored over needs, plans, possibilities, and challenges, and then brought the Blueprint for the twenty-first Century to the annual Executive Board meeting in January 1999. Thousands of hours of research went into the recommendations for ethnic leadership development, international partnerships, intentional interim training, comprehensive marketing for WMU and New Hope products, new ways of measuring WMU involvement, and the establishment of a leadership center for women. The massive blueprint was overwhelming. However, it was all part of a bold plan to meet the needs of the new millennium rushing to meet them.

A NEW ACROSTIC: CWLC

Christian Women's Leadership Center (CWLC) was the result of WMU recognizing the need for a new way to provide the kind of training they had been famous for with the WMU Training School. In 1994, WMU recognized anew the critical need for leadership training for Baptist young women called of God to service in a new century. Upon the recommendation of the long-range planning committee, WMU's Executive Board voted to engage in dialogue with Samford University in Birmingham for the development of a women's institute for ministry that might be reproduced in other academic settings as well.

Then, a major contribution toward making this dream a reality came in August 1999 when Bob Terry, editor of the *Alabama Baptist,* made the lead gift in establishing the Dr. Eleanor F. Terry Chair for Christian Women's Leadership at Samford University in Birmingham. Samford and WMU became partners in training women in leadership. Dr. Carol Ann Vaughn became its first director in 2000, as the center began helping women prepare in a Christian context for leadership roles in the church as well as in government, the marketplace, and social institutions.

BNF, ACTEENS, GA, AND SUNBEAMS CONTINUE TO SHINE

In 1999, Baptist Nursing Fellowship (BNF) had a record number of new members, and the involvement of BNF members in meaningful ministry both across America and overseas was booming. Especially significant was the ministry in war-torn Bosnia and Kosovo. BNF ended the century with the largest ever national meeting in Jackson, Mississippi in 2000.

Age-level organizations were shining at the end of the century. WMU adopted Sunbeams (now called Mission Friends) in 1896 and celebrated 100 years in 1996. The children's organization continued to grow as youngsters learned how to "shine for Him each day." Girls in Action started a new approach to a familiar venture when their achievement plan, Mission Adventures (the successor to Forward Steps), became WorldVentures. And, their big sisters, the Acteens, turned out some 8,000 strong for the 1998 Acteens convention in Louisville, Kentucky, where girls donated more than 20,000 hours of community services and made nearly 1,000 quilts for ministries across the nation. Teenagers from 46 states had an impactful experience listening to the testimonies of nearly 60 missionaries.

New Hope Publishers was also keeping pace with WMU's efforts to reach out to an even larger constituency. In 2000 alone, New Hope released more than 20 new books aimed at meeting the needs and interests of a wide variety of readers, always providing quality missional and scriptural inspiration.

And, in another sign of keeping pace, in February 2000, WMU hosted four conferences to train leaders as the new century began, equipping 265 women representing 38 states to serve more effectively.

WHO ARE WE?

WMU's Marketing Services department literally asked this question in a hundred ways in 1999 as it researched "branding" for WMU. This "brand" was to be the essence of WMU's traditions and current efforts as it is perceived by the public. Research was conducted across the country, involving members, non-WMU Southern Baptist women, and pastors. As a result, WMU implemented branding techniques while firmly retaining its mission and integrity. WMU's look at its own branding was intentional, inclusive, declarative, and visionary; it examined all kinds of public relations.

THE DELLANNA O'BRIEN DECADE

In ways too many to enumerate, Dellanna O'Brien was the "face" of WMU in the final decade of the twentieth century. For 10 years, some of the hardest years WMU had ever encountered, O'Brien kept her mind and spirit intact in the midst of incredible challenges from those in the Convention. The attempt to make WMU an agency of the SBC was not successful, and one prime reason was the resolve and spiritual depth of Dellanna O'Brien and a remarkable staff who worked tirelessly with women of depth and character from each state that made up WMU's Executive Board. The successes of O'Brien's ten years are well documented, and they continue to live on. In her final address to

WMU's Executive Board, O'Brien declared: "God has protected us in the midst of criticism and directed us in times of confusion. Never have we been so aware of His guidance and love." Thanking the women of WMU at her final annual meeting, she once again encouraged them to move forward. "We are part of a seamless history in which we connect the stories of the past to write our own chapters in preparation for those who come after us."

An era had ended. Just ahead lay the unknown, not just a new decade but also a new century. Even more than a century—it was a new *millennium.* These were indeed "the times that try women's souls," but God had never failed them. Under His guidance, with His protection and direction, Woman's Missionary Union gladly and courageously awaited the new millennium.

CHAPTER

Ring in the New

"There is no end to sharing God's grace, only a succession of beginnings."
—STUART CALVERT

WANDA LEE HEADS WMU

THE LARGEST MISSIONARY organization for women in the world and the largest body of organized laity in the SBC are both answered by one entity: Woman's Missionary Union. And the women of this union began the twenty-first century and the new millennium with a new leader in place. Wanda Lee became WMU's seventh executive director in its more than 100-year history. Not only was she a seasoned veteran but she was one already tried in the crucible of a tenuous and contentious period in Southern Baptist life. This career nurse came with years of experience of compassionate ministry in her profession as well as having participated in every level of WMU leadership. Lee also came equipped with keen powers of observation and familiarity with every aspect of the Union she would be leading—small wonder she became a sterling and dynamic executive.

Lee, along with the approximately 1 million members who made up WMU, stepped into a new millennium with a renewed sense of dedication to their changeless commitment. She assumed leadership in March 2000 and was formally installed in June at WMU's annual meeting, in Orlando, Florida. At this same meeting, Janet Hoffman, national recording secretary, was elected as WMU's 20th national president. She and Lee had worked as a team for four years, and her election gave great continuity to the work of the Union as it began the new century. Hoffman, born in Oklahoma, grew up there and in neighboring Texas. She graduated from Baylor University and earned a degree from New Orleans Baptist Theological Seminary. Hoffman had been part of WMU since her Sunbeam days and held all sorts of leadership positions in addition to serving as a pastor's wife. She was now stepping into a new role in a new century, with major challenges ahead.

Wanda Lee brought her first report as executive director during the annual meeting in Orlando, stressing her belief that God is still calling women to be catalysts for missions. In the 2000 Annual Report, Lee reminded women: "WMU's commitment to the call is at the heart of our new tagline, "Discover the Joy of Missions."

Keynote speaker at the Orlando meeting was Dr. Emmanuel McCall, denominational leader and Georgia pastor. In his address, McCall emphasized the formula for growing a church: "If you really want to grow a strong, healthy, missions-minded church, you've got to have a WMU to do it!" He pictured WMU as musicians following the lead of the Conductor of the Ages who said to Woman's Missionary Union, "Don't stop. Keep playing!" McCall received a standing ovation. And so ended the 112th annual session of WMU, so different from that first 1888 meeting in Richmond but so alike in purpose and spirit.

Chapter 33

A PROJECT, A FOUNDATION, A CONNECTION

The new century began with Project HELP: Literacy. Women trained, prayed, and became involved in literacy ministries across the nation. They learned that one out of every five adults in the US cannot read at a functioning level; more than a half million international students with limited English language skills come to study in the States every year; and 600,000 legal immigrants have language challenges. In order to make literacy work lasting, an endowment was set up through the WMU Foundation. It was named for missionary Lillian Isaacs, whose many years of literacy work had inspired thousands. At the end of the two-year project, the first grant from the new endowment was awarded.

Just one year into the new millennium, WMU Foundation unanimously elected a new president, David George of Birmingham, a man whose background had uniquely fitted him for his new role. George was a former RA, one who had gone from carrying the scepter for a Girls' Auxiliary coronation service as a young RA to carrying the mantle of WMU Foundation leadership in the new century. George came with nearly two decades of experience in executive management, marketing, and team building, all skills he would put to full use with the Foundation. At the time George assumed leadership, the Foundation was only six years old and had funds of some $11 million that it managed. (It would grow exponentially under his leadership.)

In its turn, Volunteer Connection built on the fine work done in Charleston the previous year as it sponsored four MissionsFESTs and one FamilyFEST in 2001. It also placed over 700 Acteens in service across the country. FamilyFEST was a new idea, and one family participating in the Little Rock

Fest was national president Janet Hoffman. Her daughter, son, daughter-in-law, and granddaughter all joined her as they labeled and distributed thousands of canned goods to help feed hungry Americans. Hoffman spoke of the thrill of three generations of her family working side by side, calling it "fulfilling and bonding beyond description." MissionFESTs and FamilyFESTs continued to flourish in the following years. More than 700 volunteers from 24 states served in 2002, stretching from Baltimore to Seattle. In 2003, hundreds of volunteers were scattered across the country, and in 2004, more volunteers followed suit. The types of ministries varied with the local needs, anything from Bible clubs to construction and repairs. Several of these events included members of BNF, who conducted health fairs and helped meet medical needs. WMU women, youth, and entire families were putting feet to prayers.

WMU also knew how to train, and train they did, as two major events in 2001 gave leadership development to 450 women from 38 states, plus several foreign countries. A major feature of the training was introducing the new WMU "How-To" series. Those women in turn trained hundreds more in their home areas. Additionally, WMU embraced a fast-growing area of communications—the Internet. WMU resolved to use and develop Internet resources to help women train to become effective in their ministries. The Union was determined to stay ahead of the curve but recognized that many of their constituency did not use the Internet and were in fact intimidated by it. For WMU leadership, it became a question of being all things for all women, so we can—by any means—reach all. (To do a bit of paraphrasing!)

Chapter 33

BEYOND BELIEF: 2001

WMU's two-year theme for 2000-2002 could not have been more appropriately named. The miracles of God at work in the world was the underlying idea behind the choice of such a phrase, but who could have foretold what would happen in the United States on the morning of September 11, 2001. The terrorist action against the United States was indeed "beyond belief" and tended to overshadow anything that would occur in the many months to come. Never before had the urgency or the importance of the task facing WMU been more apparent: The world had a crying need for a Savior, and Baptist women had a new impetus to service. At WMU's annual meeting in New Orleans that June, Dellanna O'Brien, who had written the first volume of the theme book, *Beyond Belief,* and Barbara Joiner, author of the second volume of *Beyond Belief,* did the theme interpretation at each session, highlighting the amazing work of God through His servants around the world. The keynote message of the meeting was brought by Billy Kim, president of the BWA, who began by thanking WMU for its part in sending missionaries to Korea, where 100 years ago there was no Christian gospel message and where now there are more than 12 million Christians. He inspired and challenged the women by giving examples of the practice of prayer among Korean WMU women, emphasizing how prayer prepares a nation for revival. He stated that it takes women of courage to be determined to have revival in America, challenging them: "May God help WMU to see the horizon beyond the shore of the United States."

JOB CORPS, WMU STYLE

The new century got off to a great start in reaching out to women in need, helping to provide hope and a future for them one life at a time through Christian Women's Job Corps (CWJC). This program was a proven success. Nothing was more effective than the one-on-one mentoring system. By midway through the new decade, three CWJC-related funds were being managed by WMU Foundation, and in 2002, international partnerships began. A Central Mississippi site partnered with a CWJC group in Pretoria, South Africa; and South Carolina's York County CWJC initiated an agreement with a group in South Asia. CWJC had gone global!

More "new" developments were on the horizon. In 2004, WMU announced the very first Christian Men's Job Corps (CMJC) in San Angelo, Texas. Here men reached men with much-needed job skill training and the life-changing message of the gospel. This same year, four new CMJCs were in the beginning stages in Alabama. By 2005, the number of registered and certified CWJC/CMJC sites was up 30 percent, with a total of 127. Not only were women and men hearing the message of salvation and receiving job skills but CWJC was actually developing several micro-businesses to provide jobs!

IMPACTING THE NORTHEAST

A cooperative effort began as the new century kicked off, with partnerships being formed between five Northeast Conventions and six in the South. The idea was to help strengthen the efforts of Southern Baptists in this area of the greatest concentration of lostness in the nation. WMU leadership in those 11 states, along with national WMU staff, worked together in a variety of ways to impact that needy area. One illustrative project involved a small group of experienced WMU leaders from Alabama spending a week with the Baptist Convention of Pennsylvania-South Jersey to work with women and pastors who could envision what a missions organization in their churches could do to grow the work. From this one-week effort, 21 new missions organizations were born.

INTERNATIONAL INITIATIVES

The "Blueprint for the 21st Century" included a strategy for partnering with believing women abroad in meeting women's needs. Evelyn Tully, retired WMU director from Illionois, came back to WMU to help develop this strategy. International Initiatives resulted from this effort. By 2004, WMU had organized and led eight missions trips through International Initiatives, calling on the skills of 67 volunteers. Three teams ministered in Paris, sharing the gospel and life skills with scores of Muslim women, many of whom knew nothing of Jesus Christ and His gift of everlasting life. Three other teams ministered at the Olympics in its original site in Athens, Greece. Additionally, a medical team worked in Croatia to provide medical care in rural villages.

The number of volunteers in International Initiatives kept climbing, and in 2005 it was up 30 percent. As a result, Moldova had several strategic teams work in retreats, training social workers, and helping to establish GAs and Acteens in local churches.

GOD'S PLAN . . . MY PART

In 2002, when WMU gathered for its annual meeting in St. Louis, women focused on God's plan—for the world, the nation, the state, and the association. As Wanda Lee delivered her annual report, she challenged women to fit their part into God's redemptive plan. She illustrated the intertwining of the parts played by countless women who seek to contribute their part in God's plan, by telling about Debbie, a missionary recently appointed by the International Mission Board (IMB) to a Last Frontier country. Debbie then took the stage to thank all those who been used by God to groom her for service. The moment was electric as she first named her Sunbeam leader, then two GA leaders, a YWA director, and ultimately—her mother. Debbie asked all of these people to stand, and the house erupted in applause. Lee concluded: "It was applause for God's redemptive plan that had been caught, then taught, to a new generation."

A 90TH BIRTHDAY

GA and Acteens had a banner year in 2003. When Girls' Auxiliary first began, it was for girls ages 9 to 16. Years went by and Girls' Auxiliary became Girls in Action and included ages 6 to 15; a new organization called Acteens was created for girls ages 12 to17. In 2003, GA celebrated its 90th birthday with the adoption of new Scripture verses, a new motto, and a pledge to help members identify with the organization and its missions purpose. Additionally, the Dr. Martha Myers GA Alumnae of Distinction Award was established. This award was named for the renowned missionary doctor who was killed in Yemen in December 2002. Myers, who grew up in

GA, pushed back boundaries and offered the Yemeni people a better life through health care and a knowledge of God's redemptive plan.

In 2003, some 6,500 Acteens participated in the National Acteens Convention held in Nashville, Tennessee, where they demonstrated their love for Christ and for others as they gathered, focused on God's plan for their lives, and participated in ministry. Another notable event for Acteens in 2003 was the change in name for the magazine; *Accent* became *The Mag*.

WMU continued to do all those things they do so well, in the midst of the reality of Convention difficulties and the challenges that stared them in the face daily. WMU drew strength from its solidarity and from the inspiration of faithful leaders in each state and steadfast missionaries around the world. The Union garnered that strength to help them continue to hold the ropes of ministry as they looked to what might lie ahead.

Onward!—'Tis Our Lord's Command

"Missions is a long word. It reaches from creation to eternity."
—Ethlene Boone Cox

NEW CHALLENGES

NEW CHALLENGES EACH day were not surprising to WMU leadership. In fact, it had come to be somewhat of a normal thing. Devastation, both man-made (the attack on the World Trade Center) and naturally occurring (a giant tsunami in Indonesia and a horrendous hurricane in Louisiana) affected people around the world. And once again, WMU proved that truly, we do take seriously our role as our brothers' and sisters' keeper. Volunteers assembled in great numbers to meet the needs of the hurting world.

Other new challenges for WMU were not so glaringly apparent. The founders would surely look on with smiles as their descendants a century later showed that same determination to focus on missions.

Chapter 34

THE SHRINKING GLOBE AND TWO LEES

Two particular women's organizations on two continents are uniquely similar—in heart, in goals and purpose, in outreach, and in the name of their executive leader. The background story is a tale of two Lees. Both were nurses by profession; both became leaders of national WMU by call. The story of these two women is also the story of the women who influenced their lives. Korea's Sook Jae Lee's mentor in missions was Lucy Wagner, that plucky little lady from Missouri who answered God's call and went alone as a missionary to Korea, the Land of the Morning Calm. Wagner was only 11 years old when she lost her mother, and she lost her father while she was in high school. Wagner's aunt and uncle then cared for her.

In college, Wagner was active in WMU's Young Woman's Auxiliary (YWA). Her calling was to equip Korean women to become conduits of the gospel in their own right. She modeled her approach on the WMU she knew and loved in America but added a true Korean flavor. Then young nurse Sook Jae Lee learned at the feet of Lucy Wagner, and God then used *this* intrepid young woman in an unusual way. Lee calls Lucy Wagner her "American WMU mother." Lee felt her calling was to be a lifelong missionary nurse but learned that God had other plans. She bravely came alone to America to attend seminary and learn how to lead. Part of her preparation was an internship with Alabama WMU. Assuming her new duties in Korea, Sook Jae Lee followed in Wagner's footsteps and led in developing missions programs for Korean churches, building a home for retired pastors, and supporting the Korean missionaries being appointed from among their own churches. Here was Sook

Jae Lee, standing on the legacy of Lucy Wagner and passing on to a new generation a heritage of service and faith.

Sook Jae Lee and several of her leadership team members came to WMU headquarters in Alabama in 2003, and the two "leader Lees" had a wonderful time sharing ideas and inspirations as they discussed how to strengthen missions involvement around the world. The visionary Sook Jae Lee and her staff were preparing for their 50th anniversary the next year. America's Wanda Lee was a distinguished participant in that celebration in 2004. A highlight of the anniversary celebration was the presence of their beloved Lucy Wagner, who returned for the occasion. Wanda Lee took home her impressions of Korean women's anniversary celebrations and wore a beautiful Korean dress, a gift from Korea WMU, at WMU's 2005 annual meeting in Nashville, Tennessee.

In 2009, Wanda Lee returned to Korea to assist in leadership training. Sook Jae Lee continued in leadership in that country and also served as president of the Asian Baptist Women's Union of the Baptist World Alliance, which is made up of 19 countries and 35 member bodies. During this new millennium, Korean WMU and Kentucky WMU, under the leadership of Joy Bolton, enjoyed several fruitful years of partnership.

TSUNAMI!!

The day after Christmas, 2004, a giant tsunami hit Southeast Asia. The massive loss of life and the devastation was beyond imagination. When numbers were finally totaled many months later, nearly a quarter million people had lost their lives in Banda Aceh, Indonesia, Sri Lanka, Thailand, and other countries in the area.

WMU Foundation received inquiries and donations and was able to send emergency aid quickly. With safe drinking water an immediate need, WMU sent water filters and purification systems via Pure Water, Pure Love. WMU was able to do this quickly because women across the nation had been faithfully supporting Pure Water, Pure Love, so the funds were there.

Thousands of dollars in relief for Indonesia were provided through the Foundation's HEART Fund. A grant from another WMU fund helped with the travel expenses of Merlyn Kelley, a nurse and member of Baptist Nursing Fellowship. Kelley worked in an orphanage with children who had lost their parents. It didn't take her long to notice a cultural difference that affected the children. "Here, the children are made fun of if they do not have shoes or if they only have flip-flops," she explained. The HEART Fund provided shoes for the children in the orphanage, along with medicine, clothing, first-aid supplies, and the cost of digging a well. WMU had feet on the ground in an area of desperate need.

Sri Lanka was also hard hit, with some 50,000 deaths in that country alone. The gracious Indranie Premawardhana, a past officer in Asian Baptist Women's Union, helped with relief efforts there. She indicated: "Women are often neglected here. Often in Sri Lanka, women do not receive attention or aid. But your gifts to the Heart Fund are helping the Sri Lanka Baptist Women's League to buy medicine, clothing, food, and school supplies for women and children." She wrote: "A flood of compassion . . . has engulfed us . . . We thank God that we belong to a unique Baptist family, His family." The HEART Fund helped rebuild the tiny island of Gau Kahw Kaw, which had been completely destroyed by the tsunami. Dr. Harlan Willis, retired missionary and father of WMU's

Kaye Miller, along with his daughter Robin, were involved in the rebuilding efforts. The HEART Fund built five homes for islanders, and it was a way to *reach* hearts with the message of eternal life. Several in the area became believers, bringing hope out of devastation.

SISTERS WHO CARE

Meanwhile in the US, WMU was busy with work as usual while also focusing on new initiatives. Debra Berry, WMU's ministry consultant for women and co-ed audiences, was instrumental in the launching of a new venture, Sisters Who Care, in September 1999. The program is a way of letting African American audiences in the more than 3,000 African American churches in the SBC know that they can customize their Women on Mission groups to meet their particular needs.

In September 2003, more than 330 women from some 20 states gathered at Lifeway Ridgecrest Conference Center in North Carolina for the first ever national Sisters Who Care conference. It was a time of incredible unity and sisterhood; attendees were reminded that each one of them is a leader, as leadership is about influence. The sessions were jointly sponsored by WMU, NAMB, and LifeWay. Sisters Who Care followed with their next conference in Birmingham in February 2006.

DO YOU HAVE A VISION?

WMU does! Vision 2010 was first put forth in 2003, when WMU leadership began searching for a way to project long-range goals and a framework for how best to grow the kingdom. National WMU president Janet Hoffman identified a cross-section of state and national leaders to dream collectively God's dream for WMU's future. This select group spent more than a year "painting the broad strokes" of Vision 2010. Then in January 2005, the Executive Board approved the Vision 2010 recommendations as God's vision for WMU's future. One of the main ideas included involving families in missions and a focus on multicultural resources for new and expanding audiences. Over the whole plan, however, was the central purpose of WMU remaining focused on its goal: assisting all Southern Baptist churches in developing and implementing a total mission strategy. The approach would be two-pronged: church-based learning experiences alongside personal opportunities to serve in hands-on missions. A Vision 2010 Task Force remained busy with promotion of plans and their implementation.

THE BAPTIST WORLD ALLIANCE, THE SBC, AND WMU

The twenty-first century saw a seismic shift in the relationship between the SBC and the BWA. Such a shift meant that WMU had to determine the future of its relationship with the Women's Department of the BWA. This relationship was historic, dating back to the second-ever BWA meeting, when Edith Crane was selected as WMU's representative to the meeting. From that point on, WMU and the women of the BWA had worked in close and loving partnership. In fact, WMU had been a driving force in the formation of the Women's Department of BWA and instrumental in helping establish nearly all of the continental unions. (More than 40 nations have some form of WMU; these are our Baptist sisters and WMU sisters globally.)

SBC leaders were unhappy with some of BWA's decisions, so late in 2003, they announced the Executive Committee would meet in February 2004 to discuss the issue of withdrawing from the BWA, and then bring it to the floor at the 2004 Southern Baptist Convention. WMU realized that they would need to take some action on the issue before the February meeting. Therefore, in January, the national WMU Executive Board unanimously affirmed its historic relationship with the Women's Department of the BWA.

Janet Hoffman, WMU national president, was the only WMU representative on the SBC Executive Committee; so it was up to her to affirm WMU's view on the issue. At that crucial February meeting, and in spite of the negative tenor of the session, Hoffman rose, and with great poise and courage, reported that WMU stood "*unanimously* determined to affirm their relationship with the Women's Department of the BWA. It was as if they stood as one," she assured the Executive Committee. Hoffman further appealed to the committee that the Convention seek reconciliation with the BWA, not separation.

The records show that a handful of others among the more than 60 voting members, joined Hoffman in voting to retain ties with the BWA. WMU's status as an auxiliary had allowed it to take the action it felt essential in maintaining the historic relationship with Baptist women around the world. In later years, Janet Hoffman recalled that "the outpouring of joyous gratitude from our worldwide sisters began immediately and continues today . . . although tension was electric. On the evening I was privileged to share WMU's position regarding the Women's Department of BWA, I was not ostracized—perhaps because the Convention leaders finally began to hear the heart of WMU. In retrospect

I wonder: Could it be that the stance taken by WMU that day triggered the beginning of more cooperative relationships with Southern Baptist entities and leadership?"

A DISASTER NAMED KATRINA

On the morning of August 26, 2005, one of the deadliest hurricanes in US history struck the Gulf Coast, devastating Alabama, Mississippi, and Louisiana especially the historic city of New Orleans. Hurricane Katrina was a costly disaster, financially and emotionally. It resulted in more than $81 billion of property damages and more than 1,800 deaths. New Orleans would never be the same again. WMU immediately swung into action on all levels—local, state, and national. Disaster-relief teams went to work quickly, and state WMU organizations wasted no time in organizing relief efforts. National WMU served as a collection point for relief items that were donated. Churches and individuals across the nation contributed many thousands of dollars through the HEART Fund to alleviate desperate needs.

THE WORLD IN THEIR HEARTS — INTERNATIONAL INITIATIVES WOMEN

In 10 years, between 2001 and 2011, 715 volunteers had participated in International Initiatives, serving in countries across the globe. Each year, International Initiatives expanded, as volunteers discovered this terrific way to minister to women and children half a world away, some with desperate need and some with no previous access to the gospel. More than Gold is an organization that sends teams of volunteers to minister at Winter or Summer Olympics. Volunteers traveled to Turin, Italy, in 2006; Beijing, China, in 2008; Vancouver, Canada, in 2010; and London, England, in 2012. Trading pins, acts of service, balloon sculpting, and festival ministries provided avenues for sharing God's love.

HERE ARE THE KEYS!!

For more than 20 years, WMU has served as a liaison between missionaries on stateside assignment who need housing and people who have houses available. Churches, associations, even individuals, make a house available, and WMU informs missionaries of the availability. By 2012, WMU was helping coordinate over 700 houses in 31 states for missionaries needing a place to live. Hundreds of missionary families have found a welcome spot where they can relax, recoup, and involve themselves for a little while in life in America. Sometimes the houses are lifesavers for families in emergency circumstances. Such was the case for Mark and Jan Moses and their five children who served as missionaries in Iloilo City, Philippines. In 2004, aggressive cancer suddenly struck Jan. Then just a few months later, Mark was diagnosed with kidney cancer, and the family was stunned. WMU partnered with wonderful Baptist friends and churches in the Dallas / Ft. Worth area to provide a safe haven for the Moses. The parents were relieved that they did not have to spend energy and time on worrying about finding a home where they could lay their heads.

PROJECT HELP – CONFRONTED WITH MASSIVE NEEDS

In 2004, WMU's Project HELP extended from a two-year focus to a six-year focus on the critical issue of poverty.

Women decided that poverty, being a common factor in scores of social and moral issues, needed more than two years to address. There are many countries on various continents known to have pervasive poverty, but many well-meaning people still seem surprised to learn how much poverty there is in the United States. In 2006 alone, there were 37 million Americans living in poverty. That's over 12 percent of our population. Nearly 35 percent of those are children.

WMU targeted poverty both here and abroad. International Initiatives and WorldCrafts were two WMU programs that reached out to poverty-stricken women and children in countries around the world during this focus. The organization provided ideas, resources, and flexible plans to help churches, groups, and individuals approach the issues of poverty. Having four or five years to focus on ministries gave participants a chance to get more deeply involved. New Hope joined the focus by publishing Jimmy Dorrell's *Trolls and Truth: 14 Realities About Today's Church That We Don't Want to See*, a book that made a real impact in the area of poverty.

Beginning in 2010, Project HELP shifted to a closely related issue profoundly affected by poverty—human exploitation. This focus addressed the unethical, selfish use of human beings for the satisfaction of personal desires and/or profit. Human exploitation takes many forms: sex trafficking, labor trafficking, pornography, bullying, exploiting natural resources for personal gain, and media exploitation of women and children. WMU provided resources to challenge participants of all age levels to not just become aware but to take action and get involved.

In the first decade of the new millennium, national WMU staff had been reduced by about half the number employed in the 1970s. However, the amount of work each staff member was assigned had grown exponentially, for the same basic needs of consultation and materials remained. WMU fought an honorable battle as a history-making economic downturn affected the entire nation. WMU worked at "keeping up with the times" and entering the age of technology on the cutting edge. Leadership and employees alike retrenched, tightened their metaphorical belt, and kept functioning at full capacity. Funds were tighter but the needs were just as great; so was the faith and courage of national and state WMU staffs.

Change a Life

"Tomorrow's dreams require today's courage."
—KAYE MILLER, 2009

CHRIST FOLLOWERS – PASS ON THE PASSION

THE NEW MILLENNIUM was in full swing, and WMU found that the twenty-first century was no less filled with challenges than had been the twentieth! After all, human nature is consistent, so issues had a way of shifting with the times but never failing to present a fresh challenge. *Issues* was a popular word in the decade, often replacing *problems*. By whatever name or label, WMU had them every day. Some issues came from overseas, others from within the Convention. And before the decade ended, the economy had presented WMU with one of its most daunting challenges.

The two-year theme for 2004-2006 was Christ Followers. As women gathered in Indianapolis in 2004, they were urged to carry His message forward to a waiting world. Kathy Hillman of Texas was elected national recording secretary, and Janet Hoffman began her final year as president. In 2005 in Nashville, Christ Followers were challenged to Pass On the Passion. Kaye Miller of Arkansas was elected national president, the first time an MK (missionary kid) had ever held that position. Miller grew up in Thailand with her medical missionary parents and brought a new perspective and infectious enthusiasm with her to the office of president.

LIFE-GIVING WATER

The Pure Water, Pure Love (PWPL) ministry was a tangible, physical expression of the living water provided for mankind by God Himself. It was a way to supply safe water for places where there was none. Pure Water, Pure Love was expanding every year, reaching out to new countries and new projects, ministering both spiritually and tangibly from India to Nicaragua, from Sudan to Laos. Thousands of caring people in America, not just women but men and children as well, gave several hundred thousands of dollars to fund this vital outreach.

A missionary in North Africa wrote: "The PWPL project has given us a great deal of credibility in the whole region and gives us a great platform from which to preach the gospel. . . . Believers [in this area] are under a lot of persecution, and this project helped to enhance the reputation of believers." The missionary concluded: "These villages will never be the same again thanks to you and so many wonderful PWPL donors."

PWPL was on the ground working in Haiti soon after a catastrophic earthquake hit in 2010. Within a matter of weeks, PWPL had sent $10,000 through Mission Waco for a massive well project there. PWPL has been a boon to a vital outreach in many areas of the world.

Chapter 35

CRAFTING CHANGE — PERSON BY PERSON

WorldCrafts, begun in 1996, is a vital part of 2010–2014 Project HELP: Human Exploitation. In 2009, WorldCrafts launched the Set1Free campaign to highlight artisan groups working with women escaping sexual exploitation and and those particularly vulnerable to human trafficking. The campaign has been highly visible in WMU materials, on the Web, and in media outlets. By 2011, there were 15 WorldCrafts artisan groups involved.

WorldCrafts offers all sorts of party ideas to help Baptist women plan and bring off successful WorldCraft parties, many of them geared to involving entire churches in this ministry. Always the artisans are paid for their products when they are completed; they don't have to wait until their crafts reach America and are sold. Well-designed catalogs and a Web site make it easy for individuals to purchase items and support the ministry, even without going to a party.

LIFE-CHANGING FESTS

WMU has become expert at enlisting and utilizing volunteers, who in turn make a difference in the lives of people with needs. These volunteers at the same time experience personal change and enrichment through helping others. All sorts of volunteer opportunities are part of MissionsFEST/FamilyFEST—depending upon the part of the country and the needs of the local communities. Volunteers might conduct a sports camp, have a VBS, do a block party, conduct a health clinic, or tutor children. Some do light construction and repairs, and others work in homeless shelters. In the first 12 years, WMU sponsored 24 MissionsFESTS and

22 FamilyFESTS involving more than 6,200 volunteers—a veritable army! Kristy Carr, WMU's MissionsFEST coordinator, noted that the real heart of the program is all of us being laborers together with God. "People want your time; this is a ministry of presence," she explained. "Relationships are more important than the tasks."

WMU's annual Missions Celebration in 2007 in San Antonio featured a dramatic example of the life-changing impact of MissionsFESTs. Dwight Simpson is an associational missions director in California, near the border next to Tijuana, Mexico's fourth-largest city. His association had only small churches with bivocational pastors. They wanted to help in that vast area of need but felt hopelessly understaffed. Then Simpson heard about MissionsFEST and wrote a letter to national WMU, not really expecting an answer. But WMU quickly responded and used MissionsFEST to transform the outreach in that association. The Gonzalez family from North Carolina took part in the FEST and could scarcely believe their eyes as they saw children eating trash from the dumpster. Nurse Maria Gonzalez and her husband, Juvenal, could not forget their experience, and on faith, they moved to that area to continue serving. In the two years following the arrival of the Gonzalez family, there have been 4 new church starts and 20 congregations affiliating with work in the association.

ALONG THE RIVER

More than 20 years after its inception, the Mississippi River Ministry (MRM) continues to depend heavily on volunteers for the effectiveness of its work. In 2009 alone, more than 10,000 volunteers had taken part in meeting needs. With 196 counties in 8 states along the great river, the needs are nearly overwhelming. Poverty is apparent on every hand. America's highest infant mortality rate is found here, as well as the lowest ratio of doctors and nurses per population. Many along the river are completely unreached by the gospel.

Early in 2011, George and Cathy Chinn, both retired from their professions and having spent some 10 years as Missions Service Corps workers, were named coordinators of MRM and led outreach projects all along the Mississippi. In 2012, the Chinns led more than 200 volunteers in effective ministry through a FamilyFEST held in Memphis, Tennessee.

HEAR — UNDERSTAND — EMBRACE — LIVE THE CALL

WMU departed a bit from its "normal" form of Annual Meeting in 2006. In June, they held the annual Missions Celebration in Greensboro, North Carolina, just prior to the SBC, and then held their Annual Meeting at Ridgecrest in September. Wanda Lee's focus book *Live the Call* became the theme of the Greensboro celebration. Lee, President Kaye Miller, and Rosalie Hunt focused on "The Call—Yesterday and Today," as Hunt depicted in monologues the lives of Fannie Heck, Annie Armstrong, Lottie Moon, and Ann Judson. Greensboro was also the place where, again, the age-old issue of WMU: Auxiliary vs. Agency, once more entered the limelight. At the SBC in Nashville the previous year, one motion asked the SBC to "extend an invitation" to WMU to become an entity of the SBC." That motion was referred to the SBC Executive Committee and thus became a live issue yet again. Such a change in status would have meant that WMU would no longer be governed by an Executive Board of elected and employed leaders from state WMU organizations but instead would have their board of trustees selected by the SBC. Immediately, WMU leaders went into discussions with the SBC Executive Committee, and discussions continued through the course of 2005 until shortly prior to the Greensboro meeting. WMU leadership went to Greensboro, confident that they had been "heard" and that WMU would hear affirmation of its auxiliary status.

On Monday afternoon prior to the Convention on Tuesday, the SBC Executive Committee voted to bring to the floor of the SBC a recommendation to invite WMU to become an agency. When WMU learned of this proposal, members of WMU's Executive Board and state leaders met to pray for God's guidance and wisdom. WMU's Executive Board—polled later that same night—gave unanimous support to declining the invitation of the SBC Executive Committee.

Realizing that these were perilous days for the Union, the 97-year-old Alma Hunt, WMU's beloved former executive director, had made the trip to Greensboro for the annual meeting. As WMU met to pray, Hunt continued to pray, asking for divine intervention. That Tuesday, the SBC Executive Committee indeed brought to the floor of the Convention their WMU proposal. Wanda Lee and Kaye Miller asked to speak to the motion. Miller and Lee succinctly explained to the Convention WMU's grassroots trustee process and singular focus on missions and requested the motion be defeated. Joy Bolton, executive director of Kentucky WMU, and David Waltz, executive director of Pennsylvania-South Jersey Convention, also called for a defeat of the proposal. SBC messengers then overwhelmingly defeated the motion and thus affirmed once more WMU's historic auxiliary status. The overwhelming emotion in the hearts of WMU women everywhere, as well as their faithful partners in missions, was gratitude for God's guidance and intervention.

FUNDING CHANGES LOOM

Since 1888, WMU had been promoting missions giving. That first year they began special giving to foreign and home missions. These became the Lottie Moon Christmas Offering and the Annie Armstrong Easter Offering. Throughout the years, all the money raised has gone to the mission boards for support—none was ever retained by WMU for their own use. Nor has Cooperative Program money ever been allocated to national WMU. For many years, however, IMB and NAMB had reimbursed WMU for direct expenses the Union incurred in promoting these two offerings. Then in October 2006, WMU received a letter from IMB, announcing that budget constraints were causing them to eliminate their annual gift to WMU. For the year of 2006, the IMB would give $250,000 to WMU for the offering promotion expenses. This amount would be reduced each year, and by 2009, eliminated. Although this was only a small percent of WMU's annual budget, the organization had already been forced to operate at a deficit for the past decade. Yet again, WMU took a deep breath, remembered the courage and fortitude of its pioneer forerunners, and found a way to continue to operate effectively with reduced means.

CHANGE A LIFE – CHANGE THE WORLD

A new tagline had been born for WMU, one that reminded members that God was using them, one on one, to make an eternal difference. First coined in 2007, it became official the following year. In 2007, WMU held its Annual Meeting and Missions Celebration, Called!, in San Antonio, Texas. At that meeting, Debby Akerman, longtime GA leader and past president of New England WMU, received the Dellanna West O'Brien Award for Leadership Development. (This name would soon become a familiar one to women around the nation!) In October, a conference titled "Live the Joy of Missions" was held in Little Rock, Arkansas, providing additional leadership training.

The following year, 2008, WMU's Missions Celebration was held in Indianapolis with the theme "For God So Loved . . ." Along with the many meetings, conferences, workshops, and missions functions conducted during the year was the notable passing of two remarkable women. In all of WMU's history from the very beginning until the latter part of the first decade of the new millennium, only seven women had served as executive director. How singular, that in just one year, two of those women went to their heavenly reward. For many years, the name Alma Hunt had been synonymous with Woman's Missionary Union. She had served as executive director for 26 years, and then continued in ministry around the world. She was a living legacy. In June 2008, Alma Hunt died at age 98, in Roanoke, Virginia, the place of her birth. Less than three months later, Dellanna O'Brien, WMU's sixth executive director, died in Texas at age 75. This woman of vision had made an impact that left a lasting missions legacy. The lives of these two women epitomized all that was beautiful and lasting in Woman's Missionary Union service. They had truly served by example, and the women of the Union took courage from their lives, moving forward into the next millennium determined to continue the legacy for yet another generation.

CHAPTER

Change the World

"Lord, we would endure, O sift us clear of weakness, make us strong."

—Amy Wilson Carmichael,
Edges of His Ways

FIFTY YEARS LATER – LOUISVILLE AGAIN

IT HAD BEEN 50 years since WMU had met in annual session in Louisville, and a large crowd gathered at St. Matthews Baptist Church in 2009 as they celebrated the theme Change a Life—Change the World. It was the last year for Kaye Miller to serve as national president. Rosalie Hunt of Alabama, a retired missionary, was elected secretary. This was the first time in WMU's history that both the national president and national recording secretary were missionary kids (MKs). Miller grew up in Thailand, Hunt grew up in China. Another first in Louisville was the performance in the afternoon session of the choir of the Karen (Burmese) congregation of Crescent Hills Baptist Church in Louisville. These refugees consider themselves spiritual descendants of Baptists' first missionaries, Ann and Adoniram Judson.

NEW HOPE GROWS

WMU's imprint, New Hope Publishers, entered into a partnership with Riggins International in 2008, making it possible for New Hope books to be published in any language throughout the world. In just four months of this new agreement, New Hope books were available in 17 languages. In 2010, New Hope launched its first fiction series; an "Extreme Devotion" series engaged readers in stories of romance and intrigue, aimed toward transforming the lives of readers and encouraging them to live radically for God's mission. Within a year, author Kathi Macias's third book, *Red Ink,* was named the 2011 Golden Scroll Book Awards Novel of the Year. Technical innovations marked the year as New Hope books became available in electronic format. NewHopeDigital.com was launched in 2011 as a pioneering Web venture, each month featuring a new theme.

New Hope's best-selling *Live a Praying Life,* and other related titles by Jennifer Kennedy Dean, reveals New Hope's heart for offering intimate fellowship with the Father. Another leading seller was Henry and Norman Blackaby's *Called and Accountable.* This popular volume is representative of New Hope's commitment to encouraging Christian growth in every setting. New Hope also has a line of Impact books that guide readers to be on mission with Christ through loving those He loves. Tony Merido and Rick Morton's *Orphanology* is just such an Impact book, as are the novels of Kathi Macias.

Chapter 36

GIVE US THE CHILDREN OF TODAY FOR MISSIONS

A different area of WMU's endeavors presented an extraordinary event through GA and Children in Action in 2007. International Initiatives ministry promoted Project MOST, inviting people to make donations to buy goats and other animals for struggling families in war-torn Croatia. This would provide a way for Croatian families to farm and raise livestock. The donations were to go through WMU Foundation, and the initial goal was $5,000. But when the project for Croatia was featured in the February GA and Children in Action magazines, the giving took off! Children learned in a big way that they could make a real difference. Before the year was over, donations totaled more than $350,000. For sure, there were goats for Croatia! And the children were just getting warmed up.

The next year, they celebrated the first-ever Children's Ministry Day. The theme for the first year was Hope for the Hungry, and an estimated 15,000 children actively served in their communities for a one-day concerted effort to minister. This was the beginning of an annual event, now held each February, to meet a targeted local need in the children's own community. The first ten years of the new century also saw the redesign of all children and youth curriculum, including magazines, and leaders' resources.

From 1972 until 2007, National Acteens Conference (NAC) was held every four to five years. Then in 2007, NAC was renamed BLUME, and more than 3,000 teenage girls met in Kansas City to share their excitement and commitment to a missions lifestyle. Four years later, in 2011, BLUME gathered in Orlando at Disney's Coronado Springs Resort. Then more than 2,300 girls focused on "living a legacy" and learned how to be part of the war on human trafficking. They were astounded to learn that human trafficking is a $32 billion industry in America. Actually, they were so moved that they chose to support the Beginning of Life Foundation in Moldova, whose purpose is preventing exploitation of children and teens. At the Orlando BLUME gathering, Acteens gave more than $20,000 to support the foundation. And, a private foundation in California matched that offering. The result was a total of $50,000!

In September 2012, WMU began generating RA (Royal Ambassadors) and Challengers curriculum for boys again. WMU began Royal Ambassadors in 1908, but the administration of the boys' program was later transferred to the Brotherhood in 1957. WMU began working with North American Mission Board in 2010 to transition the program back to WMU. RA and GA materials now cover the same general themes, with each being prepared with the special interests of either girls or boys in mind. Response from Baptist churches across the nation was overwhelmingly supportive of the move. Typical of reaction from constituents was a letter to WMU from a former RA who was preparing for the ministry: "It's been at least 18 years since I set foot in an RA classroom, but, as my wife can testify, I can still nail the pledge! Thank you so much for the work that you all do! It has a ripple effect through eternity that you may never see." Sunbeams had begun in Virginia in 1886, and WMU was asked to lead them in 1896. However, the very first children's group specifically founded by WMU was Royal Ambassadors—and now they were back!

CWJC COMES OF AGE

Another Woman's Missionary Union initiative was gaining strength—Christian Women's Job Corps (CWJC). Each year, from its beginnings in the mid-1990s, there have been national certification training sessions offered in multiple states. In 2011, there were over 16,000 volunteers and mentors at work in 187 sites in America and overseas. In 2011 alone, there were more than 2,500 participants registered at certified sites across the nation.

The individual stories of the women and men who go through the program strike a chord in every heart. Of course, every site has some dropouts; however, many times "dropouts" return at a later time and finish their programs, going on to become successful and productive members of the community. A lot of those also become active in local churches.

Veronica was an early participant at a new CWJC site, coming out of the depths of drug addiction and looking a dozen years older than her actual age. The life of an addict was miserable, demeaning, and aging. Veronica was trying to cling on to a touch of hope, and CWJC gave her the ability, not only through preparing her to face the world and be productive, but also by introducing her to Christ as the answer to her deepest need. Veronica became a certified dental hygienist, moved to another state, secured a lucrative position, and didn't forget what God had done for her. She now volunteers through a state agency to rehabilitate drug addicts, going into homes, schools, and prisons to do direct drug intervention. Veronica is a walking example of the change God can make in a life.

More recently, Lacy faced a similar crisis in her life. She grew up in an average family, with no major problems but with a strange sense of insecurity. She longed for approval from her peers and decided she could get it through being "cool" and doing drugs and alcohol. When Lacy was high, she felt approval.

In her teen years, while still just a child herself, Lacy had a baby. For the first couple of years of her little girl's life, Lacy stayed clean; she even got married. But that empty hole in her heart was still there. Again she turned to drugs, ended up in an abusive relationship, and then became pregnant again. Within a year, she was on meth and was a full-blown addict, causing her to lose her children, her marriage, and even her freedom.

After serving time in jail, Lacy was invited to church by the police officer who had arrested her. She began attending the church's drug recovery sessions, and then someone told her about CWJC. Lacy found real hope and learned all sorts of skills—from cooking to proper hygiene to parenting and relationships. And she found Christ, and she finally knew she was truly accepted without reservation. Of CWJC, Lacy beamed as she said: "This is God's story. He used the people at CWJC to give me what this world never could. They gave me a Savior!" Lacy is now working and in college; not only involved in her church, but also actively serving as a mentor herself for a young girl in the local CWJC.

The CWJC located in Philadelphia, Mississippi, is in an area with great economic needs and with many young women needing a hand up. This spot is a glowing example of crossing ethnic and economic barriers and ministering to the whole community, and doing so in a way that actually helps draw the community together. Sandi Lewis is site coordinator, and her prayer coordinator is a Choctaw Native American. Sandra Nash (Mississippi CWJC coordinator) says of her visits to Philadelphia: "When I attend these celebrations, there are usually at least three different ethnic groups involved in this outreach in a town of less than 9,000. Always at their celebrations, there is a prayer offered in

Choctaw; many barriers in this community are being broken down through this wonderful ministry."

2010 — WMU RETURNS TO ORLANDO

Unhindered was the basic two-year theme for WMU, beginning in 2010. New Hope author Jennifer Kennedy Dean wrote the 2010 focus book, *Life Unhindered,* and was keynote speaker for the Annual Meeting in Orlando. At the sessions, Wanda Lee was recognized and honored upon her 10th anniversary as executive director and was surprised with the news that the WMU Foundation's Joy Fund had been renamed The Wanda Lee Joy Fund. The offering taken during this Annual Meeting was then designated to this newly named fund. This was also the final meeting for Kaye Miller to serve as president. By a unanimous vote, Debby Akerman of South Carolina was named the new national president of WMU. Appropriately, it had just been three years since she had received the Dellanna West O'Brien Leadership Award.

PROCLAIM IN PHOENIX

Proclaim was the theme for WMU's Annual Meeting in June 2011. Dr. Jeff Iorg, president of Golden Gate Baptist Theological Seminary, was the keynote speaker, focusing on "Live Like a Missionary," which was the title of his New Hope book released this same month. National president Debby Akerman traveled to Burkina Faso in August, leading out in training women from six African nations on how to start and maintain age-level missions organizations. These were patterned on the long-standing work of Nigeria's WMU, where they have missions programs for all ages of girls. Then at the end of January, national WMU hosted more than 50 missions leaders from 13 states for an Ethnic Leadership Summit. Representatives from 11 cultures were eager to increase missions involvement through WMU.

THE STORY LIVES ON IN NEW ORLEANS

As WMU made plans to celebrate 125 years of organized missions endeavors, the Executive Board selected as their two-year theme The Story Lives On.

Wanda Lee wrote the focus book for 2012: *The Story Lives On: God's Power Throughout Generations.* This Annual Meeting, held in New Orleans, was year number 124 of an official WMU organization. The New Orleans meeting featured accounts of WMU women and youth from across the nation who had pitched in to help when Katrina hit the city with such devastation. David Crosby, pastor of New Orleans First Baptist Church, gave an amazing account of God at work in the midst of the chaos that was Katrina. Monday's first session looked at the way WMU and Baptists have been involved in prison ministry, focusing on the prison education ministry of New Orleans seminary, the Acteens of South Carolina ministering in the juvenile justice system, and the riveting account of the ministry of Stacey Smith, NAMB missionary to prisoners in Arkansas. Smith explained that she had been an inmate there for 12 years and that God used this to prepare her for service in that very place.

This was also the year Woman's Missionary Union developed a new "brand" to better articulate the goal and aims of WMU. This new presentation of WMU's "brand" incorporated a new graphic, which began to appear on WMU materials this year. The year 2012 also saw the introduction of a new Internet resource for young women ages 18–34.

Missions Interchange and myMissionFulfilled joined forces to become myMission. The Web site was up and running by February.

Once again, WMU had a presence at the Olympics. WMU sent two dozen volunteers to London, England, in July 2012 to minister through servant evangelism, hospitality, and pin trading. Blatant evangelism or literature distribution was not allowed, but nothing prevented the volunteers from talking to people. These volunteers came from 11 states and ranged in age from 24 to 84! WMU plans to have volunteers at the 2014 Winter Olympics in Sochi, Russia, and at many Olympic events in many years to come.

"Brands" may look different, magazines may have new titles, advances in technology may change an approach or add a new dimension, but one thing remains unchanged back to the very first year of WMU's official organization, and actually, many years before that: WMU's purpose always has been and always will be missions. Fannie E. S. Heck is the sterling illustration of the visionary long ago who looked far into the future and saw the heart of WMU in the years yet unborn. Baptist women in the twenty-first century have the privilege of looking back on what God has done and then looking forward to see what He is going to do next! There is more to come.

CHAPTER

Grace, Grit and Gumption: The Women of WMU

"The future is as bright as the promises of God."
—ADONIRAM JUDSON

ONCE UPON A TIME – NOW TIME

THINK OF 1800 and Polly Webb. Think of 1888 and 32 brave women meeting in a basement, making history. Think of horses and buggies, clipper ships, telegraphs, and the Pony Express. Now think of email, I-phones, Internet, conference calls, Skype, jets, and Amtrak. So much has changed, but so much more has not. Once upon a time there were Polly Webb, Henrietta Hall Shuck, Annie Armstrong, Fannie Heck, and Lottie Moon. Then there were Kathleen Mallory, Alma Hunt, Carolyn Weatherford, Dellanna O'Brien, Helen Fling, and Juliette Mather. And now there are Wanda Lee, Janet Hoffman, Kaye Miller, June Whitlow, Evelyn Blount, and Reva Salter. Although more than two centuries separate the oldest from the youngest, these remarkable women are more alike than different. Consider some characteristics and personality traits that are very apparent: intrepid, steadfast, dauntless, adventurous, resolute, diligent, committed, focused, dedicated, unwavering, dynamic. The list could be endless for these women of faith, courage, and commitment to Christ's commission.

ANNIE AND ALMA

Reflecting on the personalities of a few of WMU's most noted leaders reveals some fascinating differences, as well as striking similarities. Two unforgettable executive directors, Annie Armstrong and Alma Hunt, were dynamic leaders. One led WMU from its first tentative beginnings; the other led during WMU's heyday. Annie Armstrong was an introvert and somewhat solitary; conversely, Alma Hunt was an extrovert, gregarious, and involved with every age group. Armstrong occasionally had difficulties working with people who did not view solutions from her personal perspective. Hunt, however, was adept at not treading on egos. Armstrong was more a homebody, whose only real pleasure in traveling was visiting the Indian reservations in Oklahoma. Hunt was literally a globetrotter. She loved travel and meeting new people and confronting new challenges. However, similarities were far more numerous and the hand of God at work in both was very evident. Annie Armstrong created a missions consciousness among Baptist women. Alma Hunt built upon that consciousness. These two built consensus with and between denominational leaders. Both Armstrong and Hunt worked well with men. What an admirable skill for women whose Convention involvement was almost solely with male leadership! Just a few of the characteristics the two shared include tenacity, efficiency, and loyalty. In her era, Annie

Armstrong was the face of WMU. In her time, Alma Hunt was the voice.

KATHLEEN AND WANDA

One was petite and graceful; the other is tall and graceful. Both were daughters of Alabama, and both were an honor to their home state. Kathleen Mallory and Wanda Lee were, and are, very much a part of their eras, and both were consumed with a passion for missions and sharing the good news. Both were noted for power in prayer and for compassion in caring. Kathleen Mallory lost her fiancée to tuberculosis and never married; Wanda Lee was very much a pastor's wife and a hands-on mother. Mallory never drove a car; Lee has driven thousands of miles in her service as executive director. Mallory was quite young when coming to the office; Wanda was more mature and experienced. Both were very much hands-on directors, who were cognizant of every facet of the work conducted at national headquarters. Both loved to travel, and both declared that one of the most life-changing experiences of their lives had been a trip to China to view our missions legacy there. Mallory not only kept WMU afloat during the Great Depression, but also led WMU to be the means of saving both the Foreign Mission Board and the Home Mission Board from literal bankruptcy. Wanda Lee served during the radical economic recession that struck in 2008 and made the necessary but difficult decisions to pare back on salaries and spending in order to save jobs and maintain the essential work of the national WMU office. Neither women had trained as a financier; both became one. And, both incredible women helped define the identity of Woman's Missionary Union for their era.

Chapter 37

STUDIES IN CHARACTER

Hundreds of thousands of women have been part of WMU's past; many thousands are presently at work in the Master's service; multitudes more will follow in the years and decades yet to come. The face of WMU is multifaceted. It might be very quiet and behind the scenes, working unnoticed and unheralded. It might be taking a public stand, reaching out, and taking a risk.

WMU has been blessed with so many remarkable leaders in its 125 years of organization (plus the amazing pioneer women who led up to 1888) that it makes a compelling study to just think of one of the early heroes, then consider a more modern leader who embodies some striking similarities. Take Fannie E. S. Heck—that fascinating woman who was such a visionary—rather like a prophet pointing the way to thousands of women who would follow. Her modern counterpart was surely Dellanna O'Brien, a woman used of God to envision and then instigate far-reaching programs that would take WMU into a new millennium. Note Helen Fling: speaker, writer, and organizer, who became national recording secretary and then national president, leaving her stamp on her generation. Then move to Janet Hoffman, also a pastor's wife, also a writer, also first the national secretary and then the national president, also leading with ease and charm as did her predecessor, Helen Fling. So much concerning their paths of service was similar as was their grace under pressure. When a difficult and controversial issue arose, each took courageous stands, even in the face of opposition.

Focus on national president Marjorie McCullough, bringing to that office her years of experience as a missionary, lending an authenticity to all her appeals for mission service.

Then look to Kaye Miller, who in her turn brought the same personal involvement in hands-on missions from her years growing up in Thailand and her deep love and passion for that nation. That love translated into a zeal for missions that caught fire with Baptist women working alongside her in the new century.

FOCUS AND THE FUTURE

An old adage says: "If you chase two rabbits, both will escape." WMU has never chased two rabbits—for 125 years, it has maintained a single focus: missions. That focus is singularly simple: to equip little ones, children, youth, adults—to understand and find their unique place in missions involvement. WMU considers it a privilege to rally support for Southern Baptist missionaries. They do not take this privilege lightly. The same vision that stirred the heart of Polly Webb in 1800 likewise stirs the hearts of hundreds or thousands of Baptist women in this millennium. They keep the vision burning in hearts as they teach, pray, give sacrificially, and go. Ann Baker Graves, Annie Armstrong, Mattie McIntosh, Fannie Heck—they too were surrounded by challenges. Much has changed—much hasn't! Human nature is certainly the same. So is the passion for passing on the missions vision that motivated those pioneer women. With so much anxiety in a nation dealing with economic instability, in a denomination facing uncertainty and divisiveness, WMU leaders are frequently asked how they view the future of Woman's Missionary Union. Their answer echoes the affirmation made nearly 200 years ago by America's first missionary—that man who had endured nearly two years of prison and had lived through at least six life-threatening illnesses for the cause of Christ.

Adoniram Judson never wavered in his confidence because it was rooted in the One he served. His declaration—"the future is as bright as the promises of God"—has become the declaration of Woman's Missionary Union.

WE'VE A STORY TO TELL

Considering all that faces our world, nation, and denomination today, what is the future of Woman's Missionary Union? A concern for that future is woven into the very fabric of WMU. Its teaching materials, publications, program, and ministries are all aimed at fulfilling Christ's commission to go into all the world. The women of WMU intend to outlive themselves. Their aim? To leave a living legacy. No one person can illustrate this purpose more heroically than does the life of Ann Judson, our first woman missionary. Ann lived and worked in Burma just 14 years, but she changed that nation and influenced the missions conscience of her own land through her legacy of faith and courage.

Throughout the years following Ann's death in South Burma in 1826, accounts of her heroic life and ministry continued to surface. In the late 1880s, more than 50 years after Ann had died, an elderly missionary in South Burma, the widowed Murilla Ingalls, was on a jungle trip to a nearly inaccessible area. On this particular day, Ingalls was telling of Creator God and His love for all. An elderly man in the crowd begged her to come to his remote village and tell his neighbors this wonderful story too. Ingalls asked, "Where do you live?" He told her the location of his village, and she explained that her present itinerary was headed in the other direction, but she promised, "I will surely come and visit you."

And visit she did. The villagers welcomed her gladly that day, and she was given a seat on a veranda from which to tell the gospel story. The crowd grew and grew, and as she was telling of Christ's coming and of His sacrifice, she suddenly heard a voice coming from the far end of the veranda, "That's the rest of it! That's the rest of it!" Ingalls looked toward the elderly woman who had stood up and spoken so eagerly. The frail old woman pushed her way through the crowd and drew near to Mrs. Ingalls.

"Long, long ago," she explained in excitement, "when I was young, I lived in Ava; my husband was one of the king's courtiers. During a part of the time, there was a white foreigner, a lady who was destitute and in great anxiety about her husband. He was lying in chains in the death prison," the venerable old lady recalled. "I pitied her and used to carry her rice and eggs, and she would talk to me about her God, and how He had provided a way of salvation from our sins. . . . But later," she continued, "my husband fell under the king's displeasure, and we fled to the river, and taking a little boat, we hastened down the Irrawaddy. After many days, we dared to land and hide away in this jungle. But," she fervently declared, "I never forgot the white lady and what she said about the one true God who created all things; but I could not remember just how we could get rid of our sins. Now you have told the part that I had forgotten—and that is the 'rest' of it!"

Murilla Ingalls heard the story in amazement. The elderly man who had invited her to this village was the son of this very woman. The Lord had remembered this lady's kindness to Ann Judson and had permitted her to hear the rest of the story. She believed, as did her son, and they were joyfully baptized. And, shortly thereafter, she joined Ann in glory.

Long after the Baptist women of the early twenty-first century have left for their eternal rewards, the legacy of their faithful praying, going, ministering, and teaching will continue to change lives. And, because of their faithfulness, a new generation will realize that they too, have a story to tell, a song to be sung, a message to give, and a Savior to show. The immediacy of our Great Commission remains unchanged as we capture a fresh vision of the task lying before us. God—find us faithful.

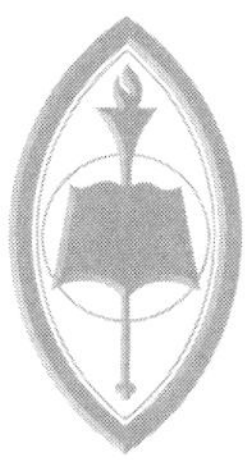

Profiles of Missions Pioneers

Polly (Mary) Webb — 1778–1861

SHE COULD NOT walk, but she blazed a missions trail that women have followed into the twenty-first century. Born in Boston in 1779, POLLY (MARY) WEBB suffered a devastating fever at age five and was paralyzed from the waist down. Her father Samuel made her a little carriage with a green cover, and people all around Boston knew the intrepid little Polly. Her pastor, Dr. Thomas Baldwin, of the influential Second Baptist Church, was a leader in the dawning missions consciousness among Baptists in America. When Dr. Baldwin preached a powerful missions sermon in 1800, Polly's heart was stirred to missions action that in turn spread to her neighborhood, and within a few years, across America.

Polly Webb could not go but she could inspire; crippled legs did not slow her down, and she first brought together women in her home as the Boston Female Society for Missionary Purposes. The group began as Baptist and Congregational and later became two groups. Polly led that Baptist group for the rest of her long and remarkable life, dying at age 82 of cancer, but not before igniting the hearts of Baptist women to reach out to a world in need of Christ. When Polly and her society learned of the sailing of America's first missionaries, Ann and Adoniram Judson, their excitement was contagious. Polly not only led, she wrote letters, and women in state after state learned what women could do in missions. Thanks to Polly, by the time the Triennial Convention met in 1814 there were 17 known women's societies; they grew exponentially in the following years. Because of Polly Webb, the seeds of a missions organization for Baptist women had been planted and within the century would come to beautiful bloom.

(From Albert Vail, *Mary Webb and the Morning Hour of American Baptist Missions*. Philadelphia: American Baptist Publication Society, 1907.)

Hephzibah Jenkins Townsend—1780–1847

On March 19, 1780, the dying HEPHZIBAH JENKINS in Charleston gave birth to a tiny namesake. America was at war, and Captain Jenkins, the baby's father, was in a British prison. Trusted family servants spirited baby Hephzibah away to safety on Edisto Island with the Townsend family. Young Hephzibah married a captain of her own when not yet 16. Captain Daniel Townsend, according to law, gained control of her fortune upon their marriage. Hephzibah was baptized by Richard Furman in 1807 and was committed to Christ and sharing His message for the rest of her life. Described as beautiful, gifted, brilliant, and strong-willed, Hephzibah learned from Furman about Polly Webb and her mission society. She immediately devised a plan, but Daniel was not willing to release money for people half a world away. Undaunted, Hephzibah and her friend and trusted servant Belle began baking gingerbread. The revenue became her missions giving. Hephzibah enlisted friends, and together they formed the first women's mission society in the south, the Wadamalaw and Edisto Female Mite Society. The mother of 15 children, Hephzibah raised her kids even as she raised the missions consciousness of women of the South. One of the first offerings to support the Judsons came from those Edisto women. The influence of that extraordinary woman still resonates two centuries later.

(Catherine Allen, *A Century to Celebrate.*
Birmingham: Woman's Missionary Union, 1986,
and Nell S. Craydon, *Tales of Edisto.*
Orangeburg: Sandlapper Publishing Company, 2000.)

Richard Furman — 1755–1825

RICHARD FURMAN—patriot, educator, pastor, statesman, and friend of women with missions hearts, was born in New York (his parents moved to Charleston, South Carolina, shortly after his birth) in 1755 and lived to lead a denomination in order to fulfill the Great Commission. His remarkable mind could read something and quickly memorize it. Converted at 16, Richard was preaching with power within a year and was an outspoken patriot with a price on his head during the Revolutionary War. As pastor of the powerful First Baptist Church of Charleston, Richard had a vision for missions that became a spark to set aflame the missions spirit of Baptists. Leading in the organizational meeting of the Triennial Convention of Baptists, he was elected president and set the tone for the years ahead. He and Luther Rice and their common vision guided the missions vision of nineteenth-century Baptists. Ever a friend of women in missions and committed to teaching children of Christ's command, Richard Furman left twenty-first-century Baptists a priceless legacy.

(James A. Rogers, *Richard Furman: Life and Legacy*. Macon: Mercer University Press, 2001.)

Luther Rice—1783–1836

LUTHER RICE had a weakness—he was excessively hopeful! Rice the dreamer, the visionary, could well be the "father" of WMU, for he was ever the champion of women's missions societies. A dynamic speaker—Rice could hold an audience spellbound. Born in Massachusetts in 1783, young seminarian Rice joined several other students at Andover Seminary in considering overseas missions. He was appointed for foreign missions, and his fiancée refused to go. Optimistic, Rice never gave up trying to change Rebecca's mind; he died single. He became a Baptist by conviction upon reaching the Far East, and ill health sent him home; he simply went to work to organize Baptists to support the Judsons, their first missionaries. Arriving back in America in late 1813, he traveled from Maine to South Carolina, urging Baptists to organize to support missions. It became reality in 1814 with the Triennial Convention. And Luther kept traveling, helping encourage women's groups to organize for missions; persuasion was perhaps his greatest gift. In September 1836, he grew ill while traveling in South Carolina; less than four weeks later he was gone. There in Pine Pleasant churchyard lies the body of one of Baptists' great heroes—the man, more than any other, responsible for organizing Baptists for missions. The convention is this dreamer's lasting memorial.

(Evelyn Thompson, *Luther Rice, Believer in Tomorrow.* Nashville: Broadman Press, 1982.)

Henrietta Hall Shuck—1817–1844

Born in Kilmarnock, Virginia, in 1817, HENRIETTA HALL was the apple of her father's eye. The child displayed an immense intellect, and when she was just 13, her teacher posed a question that changed the course of her life: "Where shall I be a hundred years hence?" That summer, Henrietta accepted Christ and was baptized by the renowned Dr. J. B. Jeter (who later wrote her biography). At age 17, she married young minister Lewis Shuck, who was studying at Virginia Baptist Seminary. That same month they sailed for China, where no American woman had ever gone as a missionary. Henrietta refused to believe the "rumors" that women couldn't learn the Chinese language, and she learned with remarkable speed. The young couple began language study in Singapore and then sailed for Macau, which was as close as they could get to mainland China, where Americans were not welcome.

By 1837, Henrietta had two sons, had helped organize a church, and had started a school. To make her even busier, many of the students boarded with the Shucks; at times she was preparing food for 30 people. To encourage education for girls, she only accepted a boy in the class if a girl came also.

Much of that time she was deathly ill. Henrietta had a real sense that her days might be numbered. She managed to write many letters to family and friends, pleading the cause of missions and encouraging folk at home to pray, to give, and to come help. Her little girl, Henrietta, was born in 1841. The fragile young mother only weighed about 85 pounds.

China became a reality in 1842, and she had the joy of helping organize the first Chinese church there, and of course, a school. Baby number four was born in 1842, and her last child in November 1844. Knowing she didn't have long to live, Henrietta's last letter to her beloved father ended: "Do what you can for China."

To this day in Hong Kong, "Mama Shuck" is honored; the Henrietta Hall Shuck High School is large and thriving. The life of Henrietta still challenges the women of WMU to "do what you can for China."

(Jeremiah B. Jeter, *A Memoir of Mrs. Henrietta Hall Shuck: the First American Female Missionary to China*, Gould, Kendall, and Lincoln, 1850.)

Lottie Moon—1840–1912

Born in 1840, the fun-loving CHARLOTTE ("LOTTIE") MOON accepted Christ while in college, and her life took on great purpose. The fact that she was a woman did not make her think God could not call her and use her. She arrived in China in 1873 and adopted that country as her own, learning the language with the determination she put to every task and also adopting Chinese dress.

She braved wars, disease, indifference, scorn, and loneliness to fulfill Christ's mission for her, and her influence on women's societies in American can never be over-emphasized. She saw women's societies were supporting Methodist missions. Surely Baptists could do the same! The power of her pen opened the hearts of American women, and her life of service and sacrifice inspired a denomination both in her own era and the ones that followed. Lottie Moon, more than any other one person, is responsible for the beginning of an annual Christmas offering for missions. She *wrote* it into being, as she placed before women the crying needs of her beloved China. There is no clear answer to what happened to her those last years; possibly, she had a tumor on her brain. She grew increasingly despondent and frail and seemed to suffer confusion. Lottie's mission family insisted on getting her to America in an attempt to save her life, but she died on board ship in the harbor of Kobe, Japan, on Christmas Eve 1912. The legacy of a small woman who devoted herself completely to her calling lives on across her own nation and in the land that became her heart home.

(Catherine Allen, *The New Lottie Moon Story.* Nashville: Broadman Press, 1980.)

Eliza Broadus – 1851–1931

Daughter of famous Baptist theologian John Broadus, ELIZA was born in Virginia and spent most of her adult life in Kentucky, where her father taught at Southern Seminary. Her mother died when Eliza was only 6. John Broadus remarried, and the family moved to Greenville, South Carolina, where he became one of the first teachers at the newly organized Southern Seminary. Not only was he Eliza's father, he was also her teacher and mentor. During the Civil War, John was often away; teenager Eliza maintained his correspondence and developed keen administrative skills in the process. In 1877, the family moved with the seminary to Louisville, Kentucky, and Walnut St. Baptist Church became Eliza's church for the remainder of her life. She was an early member of the woman's missionary society, and it helped define her life and ministry.

Eliza Broadus was asked to be one of the founding members of Kentucky's WMU Central Committee. She served on the committee for an astounding 50 years, 32 of them as chair. She was most instrumental in the statewide organizing of WMU, and one of her pet projects was the Woman's Missionary Union Training School. Eliza lived to see hundreds of young women come for training and move out across the world. For her 80th birthday, the training school gave her a beautiful surprise party. Only a week later, the profoundly deaf Eliza was struck by a speeding truck and killed. She left behind the imprint of her character and heart on the thousands whose lives she touched.

(Mrs. O. B. Mylum, *Biographical Sketch of Eliza S. Broadus*. Louisville: Kentucky WMU.)

Maud Reynolds McLure—1863–1938

MAUD REYNOLDS could have stepped out of the pages of *Gone with the Wind*. Born on an Alabama plantation in 1863, she studied at Judson College and later attended finishing school. Maud and young attorney Tom McLure's wedding was a grand occasion. Just three years later, Tom tragically died. Maud had a rich voice and became a college instructor. In 1907, she came to the attention of WMU, when the Woman's Training School asked her to become the first principal. Maud set the standard high as she gave the school an ambience that enriched the life of each young woman. It became a place of training but also a source of spiritual and cultural development. Maud lay the foundations of what made the school unique, shaping its ideals and determining its methods. She led in the development of a curriculum and practicum for social work, through the Good Will Center in Louisville. Another of her innovations was VBS, a novel idea in that day. Maud personally taught the course called Practical Work; to her, social work and soul-winning went hand in hand. Her life was an illustration to the students, and she left behind the imprint of her character.

(T. Laine Scales, *All That Fits a Woman*. Macon: Mercer University Press, 2000.)

Nannie Helen Burroughs — 1879–1968

In her long and remarkable life, Nannie Helen Burroughs sought to change the little word "no" to "yes!" Slavery had recently been abolished when she was born in Virginia in 1879. Jennie Burroughs knew education was key to her daughter's success and moved to Washington so she could be well-educated. The brilliant child absorbed knowledge like a sponge, and her faith ran deep and true.

Upon graduation, Nannie sought a job, but it was her age and likely the color of her skin that kept her from getting one right away. Her writing skills eventually got her a job as an assistant editor and brought her to the attention of the National Baptist Convention. She addressed the Convention's 1900 meeting, and from this speech and her contacts with Annie Armstrong, Nannie was able to organize the woman's missions auxiliary for the NBC. Armstrong and Burroughs bonded and held deep mutual respect and admiration for each other. Nannie later electrified the audience of the BWA in London in 1904 and grew in influence in subsequent years.

Nannie Burroughs headed the National Baptist Convention Women's Auxiliary for an amazing 61 years and achieved her dream of establishing a school for African American girls. Giving up was never an option for Nannie, and as a result, she inspired thousands.

The school for African American girls opened in Washington in 1909; she called it the School of the "Three Bs—The Bible, The Bath, and The Broom." Six years after Nannie's death at age 82, the school was renamed the Nannie Helen Burroughs School. This extraordinary woman was sometimes called the Booker T. Washington of her generation. All Baptist women of America owe a debt of gratitude to this servant of God who let "no" inspire her. She remains a model for what leaving a legacy is all about.

(Sondra Washington, *The Story of Nannie Helen Burroughs.* Birmingham: Woman's Missionary Union, 2006.)

Juliette Mather—1896–1983

A direct descendant of the famous colonial Mathers, JULIETTE looked more like a sprite than a brilliant woman of multiple talents. She grew up in Chicago surrounded by equally bright siblings and parents of deep faith. When Juliette entered Woman's Training School in 1919, she was told by a Foreign Mission Board official that she was "too scrawny and would never make it." But she certainly did make it! In 1921, at the Woman's Missionary Union Training School, Maud McLure told Juliette that national WMU wanted her for a new position, one that didn't have a job description. She would actually need to create it! Juliette loved challenges and took on the challenge of becoming the first young people's secretary. She carved her niche in WMU history with her pioneering spirit and remarkable capacity to inspire young people. In her position, Juliette developed programs for all age groups and staged the first-ever youth camp at Ridgecrest in 1924.

Juliette was youth leader for 27 years and spent 9 more years as editorial secretary, producing missions material for all ages of youth, from *World Comrades* to *Sunbeam Activities.* She also developed the successful Forward Steps for GAs and then edited *Royal Service.* But during all of this, she never forgot her missions call. Juliette retired at 60 to fulfill her dream of missions. She taught in Japan, in Taiwan, and in Hong Kong and left a bright trail of faith and enthusiasm in her wake. Even after her death at age 87, she continues to witness, as the Juliette Mather Fund of the WMU Foundation gives scholarships to young people who are even now preparing to follow God's call.

(WMU archives.)

PROFILES OF WMU PRESIDENTS

Martha McIntosh—1888–1892

Born to privilege in South Carolina in 1848, MARTHA ("MATTIE") MCINTOSH was surprisingly unspoiled. Active in the strong Welsh Neck Church, she was nurtured on missions and longed to become a missionary to China. Civil War devastated the South but did not touch Mattie's missions zeal. When contacted to head the formation of a Central Committee in South Carolina, she was hesitant to be a leader. Conscience prompted her acceptance, and the committee's work was stellar. Her fund-raising was so successful that Foreign Mission Board secretary Tupper said: "You are a wonderfully wise little woman. If you were not such a humble soul, you would be very proud!"

Annie Armstrong and Mattie McIntosh in 1887 skillfully led women toward organizing. In Richmond the next year, women perceived the depth of the quiet but keen McIntosh and unanimously chose her as WMU's first president. She served superbly until 1892, helping form and shape a strong Union. One leader remarked that her "gentle, refined ways often masked unsuspected force and executive ability."

After her years of service, she surprised everyone when at 47 she married T. P. Bell, the recently widowed head of the Sunday School Board, and became mother to his two daughters. And her dream of China came true, when at age 70 she joined her missionary stepdaughter Ada in China. Ada summed up the remarkable Mattie: "I know of no one else who explains the word *service* in all situations of life. So very rare, a consistent Christian all day, every day."

(Catherine Allen, *Laborers Together with God*. Birmingham: Woman's Missionary Union, 1987.)

Fannie Exile Scudder Heck—1892–1894, 1895–1899, 1906–1915

Was there ever such a leader? FANNIE HECK was the amazing visionary who left a trail of "firsts" in WMU, including first magazine, first WMU history, and WMU's first hymn. Raised in Raleigh, North Carolina, in a wealthy home, she early on felt concern for the lost and needy around her. Fannie's mother, Mattie, had a missions passion that passed directly to her daughter. Fannie was a young and fascinated observer of that organizational 1888 meeting. Tall, graceful, with speaking dark eyes and prematurely graying hair, she was strikingly beautiful. However, it was the inner beauty that glowed undiminished over three decades as she continued to deepen spiritually. When McIntosh declined nomination in 1892, delegates immediately turned to Fannie Heck. She became national president at age 29.

Both Fannie Heck and Annie Armstrong were brilliant, with strong personalities and often conflicting views. For the sake of the Union, Fannie declined re-election in 1899. However, in 1906, she returned to office, and her contributions were incalculable.

Fannie was the guiding light in the organizations for children and youth in missions: RAs, GAs, and YWAs. Mission study was another innovation that was part of her creative leadership, and personal service (the forerunner of mission action) was one of Fannie's passions. Fannie touched every aspect of WMU's formative years and enriched them all. Her platform leadership was quite remarkable. Fannie's major address at the BWA Congress women's meeting in 1911 was memorable. Not only Fannie's full, resonant, persuasive voice, but her very message, was compelling. Struck with cancer in 1914, she suffered intense pain and died at 53. Praise was global and her impact continued throughout the century and into the next. Fannie Heck put the stamp of her spiritual depth and gifts on an organization that shared her passion for a lost world.

(Minnie Kennedy James, *Fannie E. S. Heck: A Study of the Hidden Springs in a Rarely Useful and Victorious Llife.* Nashville: Broadman Press, 1949)

Abby Manly Gwathmey—1894–1895

Alabama born ABBY had a Baptist "pedigree." Her father, Basil Manly, Sr., was a renowned pastor and educator, as were most

of her brothers. She was in the first college class of Richmond Female Institute when she met one of the school's founders, wealthy bachelor Dr. William Gwathmey, who promptly fell in love with the charming student. Just before turning 19, she became Abby Gawthmey. They survived the Civil War, but their fortune did not. Abby spent a lifetime loving missions and helping WMU lay a strong foundation. William died, leaving Abby with nine children and little money. Abby got a job related to her life's love for missions; she became bookkeeper for the *Foreign Mission Journal,* thus becoming the first-ever WMU officer to hold an official job.

Abby was involved in every level of WMU, and when Heck was unable to serve another year in 1894, she was the choice to replace her. Because of demands of family and job she could only serve one year, but in that year the Week of Prayer for Home Missions was born. Until her death at 78, she remained highly active in Virginia WMU. One secular reporter noted: "Truly hers was a beautiful life with a beautiful close."

(Catherine Allen, *Laborers Together with God*. Birmingham: Woman's Missionary Union, 1987.)

Sarah Jessie Davis Stakely – 1899–1903

JESSIE STAKELY has a distinction held by no other WMU president; she was the only one to have a baby while in office.

Born in January 1961, just as the Civil War was breaking out, Jessie's gifts and service consistently impacted the early years of a new organization. Shortly after their marriage, her husband Charles was called to the influential First Baptist Church of Washington, D.C. Due greatly to Jessie's influence, the women of D.C. soon became part of the Union.

Jessie Stakely was unanimously elected national WMU president in 1899, and shortly thereafter, the Stakely's moved to First Baptist Church of Montgomery, Alabama. Jessie effectively served WMU for four years, and two weeks prior to the 1903 meeting, she informed Annie Armstrong that she could not attend; on the eve of the meeting, 41-year-old Jessie Stakely gave birth to her fifth child. In years to come, Jessie continued to be heavily involved in WMU, serving as Alabama state president for 13 years. She lived by her precept that no woman and no church had the scriptural right to exist apart from the Great Commission.

(Catherine Allen, *Laborers Together with God.* Birmingham: Woman's Missionary Union, 1987.)

Lillie Easterby Barker—1903–1906

Born in South Carolina the year the Civil War ended, LILLIE EASTERBY moved to Virginia with her parents and married one of her professors, John Barker. Within three months they sailed to Brazil as missionaries, but in less than a year Lillie came close to death with the disease beriberi. There was no choice but to return to the US. Lillie poured herself into missions endeavors and became a mainstay of Virginia WMU. By 1903 she was elected to national leadership. Always a scholar, Lillie Barker especially loved mission study and pushed WMU in the direction of systematic study.

During Lillie's tenure, WMU was deep in the controversy over a woman's training school, and Lillie remained supportive of Annie Armstrong's position, thinking a united front was important. When Armstrong resigned, Lillie submitted her own resignation as well. By no means did her mission service end, though. She remained extremely active and was mission study superintendent for Virginia. Later, she became a college dean. Lillie died at age 60 but used her years to touch many lives with her commitment and spiritual depth.

(Catherine Allen, *Laborers Together with God.* Birmingham: Woman's Missionary Union, 1987.)

Minnie Kennedy James – 1916–1925

Texas-born MINNIE KENNEDY was a young Episcopalian teacher who married her superintendent, William Carey (W. C.) James. (A stellar Baptist name!) Shortly after their 1894 wedding, W. C. felt called to the ministry; Minnie at once offered to become a Baptist. He turned her down, declaring he wanted no "Baptist by convenience" in the congregation. Minnie began a careful study of Scripture, and four years later, she became a "Baptist by conviction." Soon they moved, with their only child, Margaret, to Louisville for doctoral study and then to a Richmond pastorate. Brilliant, blue-eyed Minnie had a keen intellect and was gifted in relationships; she soon became a committed WMU leader, both locally and in the state. Thus began a rich career of missions ministry; she was Fannie Heck's protégée and a quick learner. It would have been difficult for anyone to follow Fannie Heck but Minnie James did so with great grace and an intuitive perceptiveness that brought out the best in others.

She and Mallory were the first WMU leaders to sit at a conference table for business with the men of the SBC. Her reputation for sound thinking grew quickly, and she was known as the woman "who had the mind of a man and the emotions of a woman." Minnie had a large hand in developing the Cooperative Program. She always looked on this as her strongest accomplishment in office. Even after nine years as president, she served in many capacities and wrote regularly for *Royal Service.*

In her last message as president she challenged women: "I know of but one thing that can cause us to fail and that is to lose the vision of the Saviour." Minnie lived to be 89. On the tombstone of Minnie and W. C. these fitting words are carved: Laborers Together with God.

(Catherine Allen, *Laborers Together with God.* Birmingham: Woman's Missionary Union, 1987.)

Ethlene Boone Cox—1935–1952

She was one more remarkable woman; you could use all the superlatives to describe her. A direct descendant of Daniel Boone, ETHLENE BOONE was born in Tennessee in 1890. In early school years, an elocution teacher discovered Ethlene's unusual voice and speaking ability and spent extra hours training such talent. Young Methodist Ethlene fell in love with Baptist deacon Wiley Cox in Memphis, and they married at First Baptist Church. She became a staunch Baptist and active in her missionary society. Within months, Ethlene's speaking skill had drawn attention. After speaking at Tennessee WMU's annual meeting, she was instantly catapulted into leadership as state president. The talents with which she had been blessed became a blessing to thousands. Her gift of speech was such that her beautiful carrying voice made deep and lasting impressions.

In 1925, Minnie James announced she would no longer serve as president, and within days, Ethlene Cox was elected. Women quickly discovered she not only could charm with speech but also lead with keen skill. Cox and Mallory led in helping the Cooperative Program develop a sound footing, and they helped keep WMU solvent through the Depression.

In 1929, Ethlene became the first woman to make a key address to the Convention. Women were not surprised at the power of her message, but countless men were in awe at what they heard and learned. George W. Truett, president of the BWA and considered his day's greatest orator, was one of Ethlene's biggest fans. Ethlene served with consummate skill until 1933, when Wiley developed serious heart problems. She resigned in order to care for him, but her talents and wisdom were not lost, for she became WMU's first full-time treasurer. Thus WMU continued to be blessed with her continued contributions, not only with finances but as trusted advisor for Mallory and national presidents. Ethlene helped steer WMU through several changes in offices. The sagacity of this unusual woman permeated throughout the organization to which she had devoted her life. Ethlene Cox lovingly described WMU's chief aims by declaring: "Stand afar off and you can catch the superb sweep of the Union's missionary skyline." In August 1965, Ethlene Boone Cox , the "servant heart with the golden voice," arrived at her eternal home.

(Catherine Allen, *Laborers Together with God*. Birmingham: Woman's Missionary Union, 1987.)

Laura Malotte Armstrong—1933–1945

"Laura D," as her father called her, was born in Missouri in 1886, her pastor father's pride and joy. She fulfilled his dreams, this woman who led Baptist women across the nation through 12 perilous years of financial depression and war. Teacher Laura Malotte married young attorney Frank Armstrong and gained valuable experience as a clerk in his probate judge office. Passionate about YWAs, Laura soon became influential in Missouri women's work, leading them from a committee to a state WMU plan. She became Missouri's first WMU president in 1923 and quickly took on leadership roles in the Southwide organization.

In 1927, SBC broke long tradition and selected two women as members of the influential Executive Committee. One was Laura Armstrong. She served until her death 17 years later. Elected national president in 1933, Laura brought sound leadership experience to the office, becoming the first president from west of the Mississippi. It can't have been easy following Ethlene Boone Cox, the "woman with the golden voice." Although Laura's voice was melodious, her speech was somewhat halting, but that did not distract from her leadership gifts.

The Depression and war brought out the steel in Laura. She had an understanding of human nature that put the many women with whom she worked at ease. Laura valued the opinions of others and encouraged their expertise. In 1945, her blood pressure became dangerously high, and she let it be known that she intended to retire from her position. On Mother's Day that year, Laura Armstrong died of a cerebral hemorrhage at age 59. A great tribute came in a statement from the Foreign Mission Board: "She counted not her life dear unto herself."

(Catherine Allen, *Laborers Together with God.* Birmingham: Woman's Missionary Union, 1987.)

Olive Brinson Martin—1945–1956

She was called the "ultimate strategist." OLIVE BRINSON was born in 1893. At 19, she married George Martin. By the time she was 22, this energetic organizer was local WMU president, and in short order, associational director. Whatever she touched prospered. Not surprisingly, she became Virginia WMU president, and for many years she was Virginia's vice-president on the national board. Olive's heart embraced the world, and she was way ahead of her time in race relations.

Olive, a master of money-raising, became Southwide stewardship chairman and was a natural at getting others committed and involved. War prevented the annual meeting in 1945. WMU national president Laura Armstrong had just died, and WMU needed a president. In emergency action, the Executive Committee pondered, prayed, and selected Olive Martin. Then at the 1946 meeting, she was voted on by the delegates, going on to serve 11 years.

Many of Olive's assets predicated her success as a leader. In addition to phenomenal skill in organizing, she had an astounding memory and a rich, vibrant voice. Her speaking skills grew over the years and her guiding hand was felt in all areas of leadership. She presided over vast changes in WMU, and she worked with two executive directors during those years. Many of the changes were accompanied by some angst and differing opinions, and Olive experienced some difficulties with SBC leadership. The election of someone else to the presidency was not easy for her to handle; it took time, but she mellowed through the years. Olive's leadership in BWA continued without a pause. This monumental strategist was remembered with affection and admiration for her countless contributions to WMU and to worldwide ministry. More than anything else, Martin was known as the molder of magnificent organizations.

(Catherine Allen, *Laborers Together with God.* Birmingham: Woman's Missionary Union, 1987.)

Marie Wiley Mathis—1956–1963, 1969–1975

Only Fannie Heck served longer than Marie Mathis. Marie's own charismatic personality has been etched into WMU's history. Born in Texas in 1903, Marie Wiley married young

banker Robert Mathis, and they had one daughter. A beautiful young woman, Marie had a smile that would light up a room. Upon gaining a vision of world needs, the young socialite redirected her life's energies. Marie became youth secretary for Texas Baptists and played a major role in the growth of that area. In fact, Texas youth led the nation in size at the time. Then tragedy stuck and Robert died in 1946, when Marie was just 43. In 1949 she was elected president of Texas WMU, and in 1952 began serving as social director at Baylor University where she employed her diverse skills in dramas, pageants, and innovative student programs.

As state WMU president, Marie Mathis began promoting the Lottie Moon offering for all church members. Soon, Texas led the nation in giving. It followed naturally that this remarkable woman was chosen national WMU president. Marie was elected in 1956 and served until 1963. She was a consummate communicator whose power as a leader emanated from her personal magnetism and obvious spiritual depth; she would frequently stop a proceeding and take the women to prayer. In 1963, Alma Hunt realized her need for Marie Mathis in the national office as Promotion Division director; she was the perfect representative of WMU with Convention boards and agencies. In 1969, Marie agreed to return to the presidency, leading through a time when women's roles were changing rapidly. Marie's calm good sense and flair for the unusual helped provide steady leadership during denominational instability. She was also elected president of BWA Women's Department in 1970. Always active, always charming, Marie never admitted to being ill, appearing to ignore the cancer draining her life away. Marie Mathis died in 1985 and was mourned throughout the Union, and literally around the world.

(Catherine Allen, *Laborers Together with God*. Birmingham: Woman's Missionary Union, 1987.)

Helen Long Fling—1963–1969

Talented, articulate, gifted with a pen, passionate about missions—each describes Helen Long, born in Oklahoma in 1914 to a pioneer frontier Baptist pastor. Helen early learned from her parents that missions was the responsibility of every believer. Their example taught that "Blessings are for service, not for self." The college beauty captured the heart of young evangelist Robert Fling who preached in their church, and they married when Helen was 19. The young couple committed themselves to God's call; Robert became pastor in Oklahoma and Texas churches, and Helen was an important part of WMU in each place. Helen never felt capable but never failed to give her best effort.

Helen's number one cheerleader was Robert. Marie Mathis quickly got Helen involved in Texas WMU leadership; here, the bud began to bloom. She excelled in teaching mission studies and was soon in demand as speaker, teacher, and writer. Then came 1957, and Helen was asked to be national recording secretary. Her eloquent pen graced the position, and six years later, she was asked to be president. Helen immediately replied that she was not capable. Leadership did not believe that, and she was unanimously elected; for six years this was her life. What a decade—one challenge after another, from the tense racial issue to the massive upheavals whirling in Southern Baptist church programming It was a daily challenge, and Helen displayed ever-growing spirituality, someone able to find opportunity in obstacle.

Then the Flings moved to New York to do pioneer missions and after one year, Helen realized there were not enough hours in the day and was forced to resign as president to give full time to home missions. Not surprisingly, WMU work began to flourish in that state. The Flings also pastored in Germany for a year. Bob Fling died in 1982, and Helen continued traveling and strengthening WMU work. One of her most vital ministries was her daily prayer for hundreds of missionaries. She reached the world through her prayers; even in her nineties, her concern for the lost never wavered. Helen Fling died in 2012, loved and honored by all who knew her and who gave thanks for the glowing example of what God can do with a woman who places herself under His leadership.

(Catherine Allen, *Laborers Together with God*. Birmingham: Woman's Missionary Union, 1987.)

Christine Gregory—1975–1981

Born in South Carolina and later becoming a Virginian, Christine Burton Gregory has been claimed many times by both states. GAs were a big part of her early years. Christine became BSU president at Winthrop College and thrived on speaking and debating. In 1948, 27-year-old Christine married the love of her life, A. Harrison Gregory, and the couple lived in Danville, Virginia. Christine became WMU president in her local church. Her interests and innovative projects then led her into leadership with Virginia WMU. Christine honestly believed that leadership meant servanthood. She led out in thinking, planning, praying, even taking risks when necessary.

Christine Gregory was shocked when asked to be national president in 1975, insisting she didn't fit the mold. She spoke frankly when accepting the position: "I'm a plain woman." If plain meant strong, deep, straightforward, and solid, then yes, she was. Christine thrived on programs with strong content, and she looked at issues from various viewpoints. These were not easy days in the SBC as controversy abounded. Yet Christine handled issues with grace and never pushed her own opinions or only her personal agenda. Repeatedly she made a stance: "My subject is missions." Along the way, she met oppositions with determination and a smile. When Convention tensions were high in 1975, she was selected as one of only two women on the Peace Committee. She often commented that some considered her a liberal because, "I don't tell other people what God is saying to them." She was also vice-president of the BWA from 1985 to 1990 and her influence stretched across many nations. Throughout life this remarkable servant remained true to her principles of soul competency and Christ's call. She died in 2011 at 89, leaving behind a rich heritage of "plain," solid, and inspiring leadership.

(Catherine Allen, *Laborers Together with God*. Birmingham: Woman's Missionary Union, 1987. Other sources: Associated Baptist Press and personal interview.)

Dorothy Sample – 1981–1986

Dorothy (Dot) Sample is a prime example of WMU's knack for selecting uniquely gifted presidents whose talents so fit the needs of a particular time. Born Dorothy Elliott in a tiny mining town in Alabama in 1938, Dot graduated from college as valedictorian. There she met her husband, Richard Sample, the salutatorian! Both obtained doctorates in theology, and

Dot became a mother during the process. As a result, she demonstrated her special gift of balancing three or four major tasks simultaneously.

The Samples became Baptists, and Richard was bi-vocational pastor of several small churches in Michigan, where Southern Baptist work was just beginning. Dot developed a rare form of a blood disorder which prevented their appointment as foreign missionaries, so they poured their missions passion into new work in Michigan. Dot was wife, mother, teacher, and part-time psychologist when she also became involved in WMU. By 1979, she was active on the state level and was exhibiting those skills that helped the work to flourish.

In 1981, the girl from a tiny mining town became the first president from outside the southern states. She was the youngest president in 56 years and the first in 82 years to have young children at home. Juggling a dozen jobs was never easy, but Dot became an inspiration to thousands of working women who also felt called of God. She was uniquely fitted to counsel and encourage others. Dot traveled a prodigious number of miles in her five years as president, and during her tenure, WMU completed and moved into its new headquarters. Dot also managed to travel to 34 countries. Those were difficult years in the SBC, and Dot joined Carolyn Weatherford in leading meetings that emphasized love, unity, and a spirit of hope. Dot loved to challenge women: "Be eagle women. . . . Fly into the storm and soar above it, as the eagle does." And surely, her own life demonstrated this precept.

(Catherine Allen, *Laborers Together with God*. Birmingham: Woman's Missionary Union, 1987.)

Marjorie McCullough—1986–1991

MARJORIE JONES was born in Louisiana in 1924 and grew up in GAs, where she felt God's call to missions. After college, she attended seminary on a WMU scholarship and was a state WMU staffer, first in Kentucky and then in Louisiana. In 1953, a trip overseas rekindled her early call, and in 1955 she was appointed to Nigeria. Marjorie the teacher also became an understudy to Neale Young, the WMU secretary in Nigeria. She felt right at home but soon was asked to move to Ghana to pioneer WMU work. It meant learning another language, as she led WMU there for eight years.

While she was on furlough in 1964, executive director Alma Hunt asked her to become the first general director of Girls' Auxiliary. Thus Marjorie became part of the most profound changes WMU had ever encountered. She helped design the WMU of the future, rewriting GA materials and building on a strong foundation. Then Brazil's WMU invited her to speak, and the call once more ignited; this time she served in Brazil and learned yet *another* language.

On furlough in 1972, Marjorie met an old friend, Glendon McCullough, director of Brotherhood Commission, who was widowed with four children. When Marjorie returned to

Brazil, she took with her a marriage proposal from Glendon. In 1974, Marjorie Jones married and became the instant mother of four. In a shockingly brief time, Glendon was killed by a drunk driver. Marjorie then adopted those four children and raised them herself.

In 1980, Tennessee WMU asked Marjorie to be president, and by 1986, she was elected as national president, bringing to the job a wealth of experience. Marjorie presided with skill and grace during chaotic years in the SBC. She died in 2006 after a prolonged illness, but the GA endowment at WMU Foundation, named for her, keeps the legacy of this remarkable woman burning brightly.

(Catherine Allen, *Laborers Together with God.* Birmingham: Woman's Missionary Union, 1987. Other sources: *Royal Service,* January, 1987.)

Carolyn Downes Miller—1991–1996

CAROLYN tried using a spoon to dig a hole to China to help the children there learn about Jesus. She couldn't dig enough, but she learned to "hold the ropes" at home in prayer and missions support. Carolyn Downes was born in Alabama in 1937 and adored GAs. God was uniquely preparing her for His future plans as she taught school, married a NASA executive, and at one time or another, filled nearly every local WMU office, then associational leadership, before becoming state president two times. Carolyn had served eight strategic years on the SBC Executive Committee, where she gained terrific experience for when she later represented WMU on this same committee.

Carolyn Miller viewed WMU as a main connecting fiber of the entire missions effort of SBC. She took office by stating emphatically that speaking was not her gift—then proceeded to speak literally hundreds of times. Carolyn had the gift of administration, combined with a personality that loved people and didn't hold grudges. She was not one to be intimated and could clearly articulate the position of WMU and its goals, a crucial skill during those tense five years in the SBC. Carolyn worked continuously at finding ways to involve women who worked outside the home in missions. Following her tenure, she still "holds the ropes," passionate about ensuring the future of WMU through the WMU Foundation. Carolyn Miller remains a blessing to countless people in her own nation and around the world.

(Sources: *Royal Service,* February, 1992; personal interview; and other sources.)

Wanda Seay Lee—1996–2000

See profile under WMU executive directors.

Janet Hoffman—2000–2005

The deceptively delicate appearance of quiet, poised Janet Hoffman cloaks a strong core, lined with the steel of faith and fired by a missions passion.

Born in Oklahoma in 1935, Janet became a Sunbeam at age 3 and a Sunbeam leader by 14. Graduating from Baylor, young teacher Janet Thompson married Harvey Hoffman and became a pastor's wife. She neglected no part of her busy life—loving mother, teacher, WMU leader, pastor's wife. Influencing others to seek and find God's call was her mission. Janet's WMU leadership encompassed nearly every aspect of the organization, and eventually, at all levels.

Elected Louisiana WMU president in 1991, Janet couldn't know it was just the beginning of many years of state and national leadership. She became national recording secretary in 1996 and president in 2000. In those troubled years in Baptist life, Janet Hoffman never failed to lead with a gracious spirit. That calm demeanor cloaked an astute and incisive intellect which analyzed and interpreted situations with keen skill, bathing every decision in prayer. Weekly, she confronted situations that demanded insight, perceptiveness, and courage—she possessed all three. Janet often declared to convention leadership: "Missions. Our middle name is missions." Her courageous stand for Baptist women around the world in the face of Convention opposition will long be remembered.

Janet invested her diverse talents in helping WMU plot its course for the future as they worked through Vision 2010.

Always serving, always involved, Janet wrote curriculum for WMU for more than 20 years, in addition to authoring several books. This woman left a legacy that will resonate long after her generation. "Her children rise up and call her blessed." So do the women of WMU.

(*Missions Mosaic,* October 1996, November 2000, June 2005; and other sources.)

Kaye Willis Miller—2010–2015

KAYE WILLIS MILLER was the first MK (missionary kid) to serve as national leader. Born in Illinois; her parents went as medical missionaries to Thailand when she was 5. Thailand became her heart home, and Thai was her heart language. When hearing her doctor father witness to a leper, she felt her own need of the Savior. This MK/GA, who became a Queen Regent in Service, went to college in a land foreign to her—America. Studying nursing at Baylor, Kaye was taken to the hearts of WMU women who nurtured her through all the "newness." She met Mark Miller on a blind date while working in Baylor University Medical Center's ICU, and a year later they married.

Busy nurse, wife, and mother of four, Kaye was deeply involved with WMU. Early WMU leaders were heroes to her, and she would have done them proud, leading GAs and Acteens and soon being elected Arkansas state president. National WMU had observed her qualities of leadership and innovation, and in 2005, she became president. One daughter spoke of her mother's intense focus, while another stressed her tremendous strength and courage. Husband Mark noted her "unique ability to bring people together." Kaye brought these gifts in abundance to leadership during a period of convention tension and change. Her goal: guiding state and national leaders to work together as a family, setting the example by her own consistent involvement and using her gifts of focus and "people diplomacy" to bring about consensus. Kaye viewed "relationships" as her great challenge and worked tirelessly strengthening the Union's ties with the SBC. She relished meeting with grassroots women everywhere and sharing her missions passion. And it was her fervent hope that WMU would be in the DNA of each church so that future generations would continue the legacy. Kaye Miller left the imprint of her heart on the office she graced and continues to minister daily wherever God places her.

(Rosalie Hunt, *The Story of WMU*. Birmingham: Woman's Missionary Union, 2006. Other sources: *Missions Mosaic,* October, 2005; and personal interview)

Debby MacNevin Akerman—2010–present

A diminutive dynamo became WMU's 22nd president in 2010. Born and raised in New England, Debby MacNevin became a transplanted South Carolinian in 1998. Compassionate by nature, Debby chose nursing and worked in that profession more than 30 years. She met Brad Akerman when a nursing student, and they married while he was in the US

Navy. The Akermans had one daughter, Kim, who became the influence that first led Debby to WMU. At Screven Baptist Church in Portsmouth, New Hampshire, Kim became a GA. When Kim's leader could no longer teach, Debby decided to work with the GAs. Her missions passion was instantly captured—she loved everything about them. She reflects that no one organization did more to shape her life than did WMU. It was a natural fit for her missions heart.

Debby Akerman was soon deeply involved in area and state WMU and became state president, which in New England means six states. In 1998, the Akermans moved to South Carolina, and Debby became very active locally and statewide in GAs and WMU. She was the recipient of the Dellanna O'Brien Leadership Award in 2007. In 2010, WMU tapped into Debby's missions passion by electing her national president. Despite her delicate frame, Debby is a pint-sized powerhouse. When she opens her mouth to speak, a strong and resonant voice emerges, accompanied by a seemingly unflagging energy. Debby brought to her office skill and confidence, a sense of energy she may have picked up from her beloved GAs, and a singular commitment to fulfilling Christ's commission.

(From *Missions Mosaic,* September, 2010; personal interviews; WMU archives.)

WMU EXECUTIVE DIRECTORS

Annie Armstrong—1888–1906

ANNIE ARMSTRONG was surely the creator of a Baptist information highway 100 years before telecommunications shrank the globe. She literally created a network between the various boards; her name is synonymous with missions giving. Annie was born into a prominent Baltimore family in 1850 but lost her father when she was only 2. Her valiant mother of deep faith raised an exceptional family alone.

Annie went through the Civil War before accepting Christ at age 20. From that moment on, service was the focus of her life. She coined for WMU the wonderful phrase: "Go Forward!" By the time WMU officially organized in 1888, Armstrong had six years of experience as president of Maryland Baptist Women's Society. She became involved in helping the mission to Indians in Oklahoma, and that was a lifelong love of hers. Annie was a driving force behind missions information and publishing.

Annie's sister, Alice, used her gifted pen to help tell the missions story and pave the way for national organization. Annie would have made a fine executive in any company;

one of her true gifts was building consensus between denominational leaders by using them as sounding boards and confidants. She was a master at finding innovative ways to promote missions.

Annie was also an inveterate letter writer—in one year alone she wrote more than 10,000 letters seeking missions support. Tall, regal, efficient, she didn't suffer fools gladly but was quick to give honor where honor was due. Inevitably, she had differences with some officers of WMU but handled them in such a way as to not hurt the organization.

Retiring in 1906, Annie continued the rest of her life active in multiple missions ministries. Alma Hunt summed it up beautifully: "Her strengths, both as a person and as a leader, are like golden threads woven into the fabric of her loved Union—threads which will endure into eternity."

(Alma Hunt, *History of Woman's Missionary Union.* Nashville: Convention Press, 1964.)

Edith Campbell Crane – 1907–1912

Like her predecessor as corresponding secretary, EDITH CRANE was born in Baltimore and was baptized at Annie Armstrong's church. Both were capable businesswomen, but Annie was hands-on in approach while Edith was more contemplative and philosophical. Just 31 when assuming office, Edith already had a wealth of experience with young people in YWCA work. She was not physically strong but her schedule was grueling; in office less than five years, she traveled over 50,000 miles and gave hundreds of speeches. Every area of WMU received her keen attention.

Then in 1911, the pressures began to mount on the introspective and frail Edith. Her doctor advised complete rest, and she reluctantly resigned from the job she loved in January 1912. Before the end of the year, she married Samuel Lanham, a young lawyer. They had two daughters, and Edith was very active in her church, beloved to all who knew her. She died at 57. At her memorial service, her minister paid tribute to Edith as he declared, "She has been my pastor."

(Catherine Allen, *Laborers Together with God*. Birmingham: Woman's Missionary Union, 1987.)

Kathleen Mallory—1912–1948

She was unparalleled in WMU history—the slender, delicate, lovely woman with the silvery hair. You picture her as the epitome of Southern grace. Yes, and she led WMU with calm effectiveness and incisive skill through the Great Depression, World War I, and World War II, to say nothing of denominational debts that would have daunted a lesser figure. Kathleen Mallory of Selma, Alabama, was a lawyer's daughter with every privilege yet amazingly unspoiled or self-centered. During her senior year at Woman's College of Baltimore (now Goucher College) in Baltimore, she met the young doctor who became the love of her life. Then tuberculosis took his life, and she never opened her heart to another. Within a year, God had redirected her path through the reading of a letter from a missionary to China. Kathleen became involved in Alabama WMU and was soon made state director. The frail appearance of the beautiful blue-eyed lady was deceptive. As several leaders noted, her seeming fragility disguised "a fine little business woman." She quickly caught the eye of national WMU, and in 1912, the 33-year-old Kathleen became the new leader of WMU.

That began an amazing 36 years of sterling leadership. At her retirement in 1948, annual contributions were 2,817 percent greater than 1912. Kathleen Mallory became one of the most beloved leaders of Baptists. Her self-discipline was awesome; though raised in luxury, she lived frugally. She never owned a car, always lived in a tiny apartment, and somehow found the energy to maintain a grueling schedule. Kathleen traveled widely and wrote prolifically. She was unbending in her convictions but democratic in practice, always throwing the full weight of her effort behind the majority opinion. This was the strength of her leadership, and her prayer life was a potent force in all she did. By retirement time at 69, Kathleen had led WMU to a position of strength and respect. She lived just six more years but continued to shed joy on all privileged to pass her way. Thousands never forgot the little woman who knelt in prayer, talking to the Lord as child to father. One who paid tribute to her declared: "May the mantle of her beautiful, useful life fall tenderly upon all who follow her Lord."

(Annie Wright Ussery, *The Story of Kathleen Mallory*, Literary Licensing, LLC, 2012; and other sources.)

Alma Hunt – 1948–1974

ALMA HUNT was the "face" of WMU for more than two decades, as well as its "voice." She was born in Roanoke, Virginia, in 1909, and her grandmother noted her personality very early, commenting, "Alma will talk herself to death!" Alma initially balked at considering the job of executive director because she was convinced she was no speaker. Her career marked her as one of the most dynamic speakers Southern Baptists have even known. From inventive Sunbeam to outstanding YWA, she always shone brightly. A school teacher, Alma spent long hours in YWA ministry, especially summer camps, and WMU leadership early noted her vivacity and skill. Ethlene Boone Cox liked to call her "Dear Winsome Elf," and Juliette Mather became her mentor. Her clear talents in leadership soon led to her becoming dean of women at William Jewell College.

WMU likewise noted exceptional ability and chose her to succeed the remarkable Mallory. Alma Hunt, too, became a legend in her time as she focused her gifts and energy on leading WMU during times of tremendous advance and change. During her 26 years, WMU's growth was significant. Denominational change was so intense it threatened to overwhelm the Union. Somehow Alma found opportunities in the midst of obstacles and reached new heights even when faced with challenges that appeared potentially devastating. Men would comment on her acumen, declaring she had "the mind of a man." Women countered: "She has the mind of a good woman." Alma Hunt was authentically herself and made a point to be feminine and fashionable. To those who looked with question at her polished red nails she asserted: "Make yourself as put-together as you can, everything in place. Then appear in public and never give it another thought."

Alma Hunt consistently kept WMU on the cutting edge of missions advance, with her special knack of working with leaders and not treading on egos; thus she led WMU into closer harmony with the SBC, in 1955 becoming president of the SBC Inter-Agency Council. The most massive overhauls in organizations and publications in WMU took place during her years. To racial tensions, she lent a progressive voice, and she firmly held WMU to its purpose. Alma Hunt retired after 26 years but never really retired, continuing to travel, lead, and enrich the lives of many. The essential Alma never changed—fun-loving, active, vivacious, a keen observer of human nature. Ethlene Cox liked to say of her: "You have a way of lingering in the hearts of those who have known you." Alma Hunt lived to be nearly 99 and indeed lingers in the hearts of the thousands who have been blessed by her ministry and honored to call her friend.

(Catherine Allen, *Laborers Together with God.* Birmingham: Woman's Missionary Union, 1987.)

Carolyn Weatherford – 1974–1989

Growing up in Florida, Mississippi-born CAROLYN WEATHERFORD had the good fortune of a small but missions-minded church where God spoke to her heart early on. Carolyn was a GA leader at 14; a wise WMU leader saw tremendous potential and made it possible for her to attend Ridgecrest. There, at 16, Carolyn committed herself to God's service. Graduating with a library science degree, she worked in a high school and was constantly involved in church leadership; however, she never forgot that commitment. Deciding to attend New Orleans Seminary, Carolyn continued in library work and church ministries. So capable was she that professors encouraged her to consider professional WMU work. Carolyn was prevented from foreign missions appointment because of a medical condition, but God led her into WMU work. Her service on WMU staffs in

Alabama and Florida made it clear her appreciation for WMU had grown into devotion.

National leadership recognized that combination of talents and sunshiny personality, and when Alma Hunt retired, Carolyn was chosen as her successor. Her leadership style fit her personality. She was a master delegator and was blessed with an outstanding staff. The majority of her time was spent speaking, writing, and promoting WMU. Carolyn developed excellent relationships with SBC leaders during a difficult time in the denomination. Controversy swirled, and Carolyn's stance was: "Do not get involved in squabbles." WMU's beautiful new building was built during her tenure—and paid for as well.

One of Carolyn's favorite lines in speaking was: "I'm not married—yet!" And sure enough, shortly after she retired, she became Carolyn Crumpler (Mrs. Joe), a pastor's wife. But that call of God to a 16-year-old girl continued to be lived out in a woman who remained "on mission."

(Catherine Allen, *Laborers Together with God.* Birmingham: Woman's Missionary Union, 1987.)

Dellanna West O'Brien – 1989–1999

A perfect one-word description of DELLANNA O'BRIEN would be *visionary.* Her gift in that area enriched the organization she led for a decade. Dellanna West was born in Texas in 1933. She met Bill O'Brien at Hardin-Simmons, and they married in 1952. After a decade of teaching and pastoring, the O'Briens were appointed to Indonesia. Following 10 years of service, they returned to the US, and both worked on graduate degrees. Dellanna used her doctorate in education to found a nonprofit organization aiding children living overseas. However, when WMU was searching for a new leader, they were led to a *first*—the first-ever foreign missionary to hold the position. The response of most WMU women when they heard the name was, "Who?" They quickly learned, and came to give thanks for this unique woman with singular skills that guided WMU through a turbulent decade for Southern Baptists.

In the midst of deep denominational divide, Dellanna's gifts and determination guided WMU in remaining on task. She early determined that the conflict seething around WMU would *not* be divisive internally; it took constant diligence and spiritual depth to achieve this goal. Even in the midst of denominational fragmentation, the visionary O'Brien launched numerous successful initiatives including Volunteer Connection, Christian Women's Job Corps, and WorldCrafts. Nothing could be more important, though, than Dellanna's vision for a WMU Foundation to ensure WMU's future. Founded in 1995, the Foundation yearly advances as it undergirds the operations of WMU and supports worldwide ministries.

Dellanna suffered a stroke in 1998 but managed to weather the blow with valor. Retiring in 1999, she continued to serve, both in America and abroad. In September 2008, she died of stroke complications. At her memorial service, Bill called Dellanna "a woman with a steel fist in a velvet glove . . . she was a woman of grace and grit." And the women of WMU remember one of her favorite maxims: "God isn't finished with us yet." Those words continue to challenge.

(Sources: personal interviews; *Royal Service,* January, 1990; and *Florida Baptist Witness,* September 16, 2008.)

Wanda Seay Lee; President—1996–2000; Executive Director 2000–present

WANDA LEE has filled a tall order in her many careers, several of them simultaneously: wife, mother, nurse, missionary, national leader. Born Wanda Seay in Alabama and living in Michigan, Wanda and her family later moved to the warmth of Florida. Wanda lost her mother to cancer all too early, but those teen years developed the compassionate heart of the daughter who became a nurse; her faith was tried in the crucible of grief. Wanda traces four marked calls in her life: call to faith, call to nursing ministry, call to missions, and, ultimately, the call to become executive director of WMU.

Five fine women in her church played cupid for Wanda and ministerial student Larry Lee. Two years later they married. The traits that made her a skilled nurse, wife, and mother were the ones that molded her into a dynamic leader of women. Always orderly and organized, Wanda has the ability to process information and utilize the skills of others. She was a productive nurse for 30 years, as well as an effective pastor's wife, devoted mother, proficient missionary, and outstanding administrator. She was part of everything WMU for many years, including 25 years as an Acteens leader.

Wanda became Georgia state president in 1992 and national president in 1996, being thrust immediately into the political situation facing Southern Baptists. It was a sensitive and demanding time in Baptist life with daily challenges. Then executive director Dellanna O'Brien suffered a stroke, and Wanda needed to step in and assume even more responsibilities. She walked through the maze of ticklish issues with the aplomb of a diplomat. Upon O'Brien's retirement, Wanda was tapped to succeed her, a huge challenge indeed. This leader is determined to remain on the cutting edge of technology, guiding WMU in sharing the old, old story in a new and innovative way. The financial crisis of 2008 demanded new skills and wisdom, and she employed both to keep the national staff intact. She has been a significant reason that WMU has been able to maintain its identity in the swirling waters of denominational change. Facing daily challenges has become the norm for Wanda Lee. She is leaving her stamp on a generation of women, providing an authentic example of living the call to go into the world. (WMU Archives.)

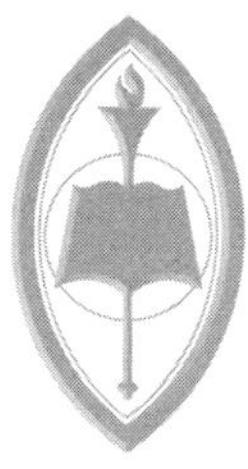

Bibliography

THIS VOLUME HAS been extensively researched. While endnotes have been omitted for ease of reading, a documentation of the volume is on file with the national WMU Library and Archives. If you have questions or need verification of any of the information contained herein, contact WMUArchives@wmu.com.

BOOKS

Allen, Catherine, *A Century to Celebrate*. Birmingham, AL: Woman's Missionary Union (WMU), 1987.

Allen, Catherine, *Laborers Together with God*. Birmingham, AL: Woman's Missionary Union, 1987.

Allen, Catherine, *The New Lottie Moon Story.* Nashville, TN: Broadman Press, 1980.

Allred, Dorothy, *And So Much More: Living Legacies of North Carolina Women on Mission*. Brentwood, TN: Baptist History and Heritage Society, 2002.

Baker, Robert A., and Paul J. Craven, *History of the First Baptist Church of Charleston, South Carolina, 1682-2007*. Asheville, NC: Revival Literature, 2007.

Boyd, Jesse L. *A History of Baptists in America Prior to 1845*. New York: American Press, 1957.

Brame, Mrs. Webb, et al. *Hearts the Lord Opened: The History of Mississippi Woman's Missionary Union*. Jackson: Woman's Missionary Union of Mississippi, 1954.

Carpenter, Kathryn E. *Across the Years in Louisiana Baptist Woman's Missionary Union*. Alexandria, LA: Louisiana Woman's Missionary Union, 1988.

Cothen, Grady C. *What Happened to the Southern Baptist Convention?* Macon, GA: Smyth and Helwys, 1993.

Cox, Ethlene Boone. *Following in His Train*. Nashville, TN: Broadman Press, 1938.

Dunaway, Thomas S. *Pioneering for Jesus: The Story of Henrietta Hall Shuck*. Nashville, TN: Sunday School Board of the Southern Baptist Convention, 1930.

Duncan, Robert Samuel. *A History of the Baptists in Missouri: Embracing an Account of the Organization and Growth of Baptist Churches in Missouri*. Google E-books. Saint Louis: Scammell and Co, 1882.

Evans, Elizabeth Marshall. *Annie Armstrong*. Birmingham, AL: Woman's Missionary Union, 1963.

Enstam, Elizabeth York. *Women and the Creation of Urban Life of Dallas, Texas, 1843-1920*. College Station, TX: Texas A&M University Press, 1998.

Farmer, Foy Johnson. *Hitherto: History of North Carolina Woman's Missionary Union*. Raleigh: Woman's Missionary Union of North Carolina, 1952.

Flynt, J. Wayne and Gerald W. Berkley. *Taking Christianity to China: Alabama Missionaries in the Middle Kingdom, 1850-1950*. Tuscaloosa: University of Alabama Press, 1997

Foster, Mary B. *We the Women, Telling His Story: the Story of South Carolina WMU*. Columbia, SC: Woman's Missionary Union of South Carolina, 2003.

Graydon, Nell S. *Tales of Edisto*. Orangeburg, SC: Sandlapper Publishing Co. 1955.

Greene, Kathryn A. *The Eternal Now: A History of Woman's Missionary Union Auxiliary to South Carolina Baptist Convention*. Columbia: South Carolina Woman's Missionary Union, 1980.

Harper, Keith, ed. *Rescue the Perishing: Selected Correspondence of Annie W. Armstrong*. Macon, GA: Mercer University Press, 2004.

Harper, Keith, ed. *Send the Light: Lottie Moon*'s Letters and Other Writings. Macon, GA: Mercer University Press, 2002.

Heck, Fannie Exile Scudder, *In Royal Service*. Richmond, VA: Foreign Mission Board, SBC, 1913.

Hill, James Langdon. *The Immortal Seven: Judson and his associates, Dr. and Mrs. Adoniram Judson, Samuel Newell, Harriet Newell, Gordon Hall, Samuel Nott, Luther Rice*. Google E-book. Philadelphia: American Baptist Publication Society, 1913.

Hunt, Alma. *History of Woman's Missionary Union*. Nashville, TN: Convention Press, 1964.

Hunt, Rosalie Hall. *Bless God and Take Courage*. Valley Forge, PA: Judson Press, 2005.

Hunt, Rosalie Hall. *The Story of WMU*. Birmingham, AL: Woman's Missionary Union, 2006.

Jackson, Hermoine and Mary Essie Stephens. *Women of Vision: History of Woman's Missionary Union of Alabama*. Montgomery, AL: Woman's Missionary Union of Alabama, 1988.

James, Minnie K. *Fannie E. S. Heck: A Study of the Hidden Springs in a Rarely Useful and Victorious Life*. Nashville, TN: Broadman Press, 1949.

Jeter, Jeremiah Bell. *A Memoir of Mrs Henrietta Shuck, the First American Female Missionary to China*. Google E-book. Boston, Gould, Kendall, and Lincoln, 1846.

Leonard, Bill J. *Baptist Ways: A History*. Valley Forge, PA: Judson Press, 2003.

Martin, Joyce S. *Links to the Past, Designs for the Future: A Short History of Woman's Missionary Union in New England*. Northboro, MA: New England WMU, 1988.

Mather, Juliette. *Light Three Candles: History of Woman's Missionary Union of Virginia 1874-1973*. Richmond: Woman's Missionary Union of Virginia.

McWilliams, Cora Frances Cowgill. *Women and Missions in Missouri, 1876-1951*. Jefferson City, MO: Missouri Woman's Missionary Union, 1951.

Mylum, Dixie Bale. *Proclaiming Christ: History of Woman's Missionary Union of Kentucky, 1878-1978*. Louisville, KY: Woman's Missionary Union of Kentucky, 1978.

Mason, Laura. *Ye Are the Branches: A History of Missiouri Baptist Woman's Missionary Organizations*. Jefferson City, MO: Missouri Woman's Missionary Union, 1987.

Neel, Isa-Beall. *His Story in Georgia WMU History.* Atlanta, GA: Woman's Missionary Union, Auxiliary to the Southern Baptist Convention, 1939.

Owens, Loulie Latimer. *Banners in the Wind: The Story of South Carolina Baptist Women in Missions*. Columbia, SC: Woman's Missionary Union of South Carolina, 1950.

Pate, Anna Thurmond. *The Incense Road: A History of Louisiana Woman's Missionary Union*. New Orleans: New Orleans Bible Institute Press, 1939.

Patterson, Marjean. *Covered Foundations*. Jackson: Mississippi Woman's Missionary Union, 1978.

Patterson, Roberta Turner. *Candle By Night: A History of Woman's Missionary Union Auxiliary to The Baptist General Convention of Texas, 1800-1955*. Dallas: Woman's Missionary Union of Texas, 1955.

Phelps, Rosalie Garret. *Give Me a Mountain: The Centennial History of Tennessee Woman's Missionary Union, 1888-1988*. Nashville, TN: Woman's Missionary Union of Tennessee, 1988.

Poe, Mrs. E. D. *From Strength to Strength: History of the Woman's Missionary Union of Virginia, 1874-1949*. Richmond: Woman's Missionary Union of Virginia, 1949.

Putnam, Robert D., and David E. Campbell, *American Grace: How Religion Divides and Unites Us*. New York: Simon and Schuster, 2010.

Pye, Lila Westbrook. *The Yield of the Golden Years: A History of the Baptist Woman's Missionary Union of Arkansas, written to commemorate the Golden Jubilee*. Privately published, 1938.

Roberts, Cokie. *We Are Our Mothers' Daughters*. New York: Harper Perennial, 2010.

Sorrill, Bobbie. *Annie Armstrong: Dreamer in Action*. Nashville, TN: Broadman Press, 1984.

Thompson, Evelyn Wingo. *Luther Rice: Believer in Tomorrow.* Nashville, TN: Broadman, 1961.

Tucker, Ruth A. *Guardians of the Great Commission: The Story of Women in Modern Missions*. Grand Rapids, MI: Zondervan, 1994.

Trotter, Martha Pope. *Faithful Servants: the Story of Florida Woman's Missionary Union*. Jacksonville: Florida Woman's Missionary Union: 1994.

Ussery, Annie Wright. *The Story of Kathleen Mallory*. Nashville, TN: Broadman Press,1956.

Vail, Albert. *Mary Webb and the Mother Society*. Philadelphia: American Baptist Publication Society, 1914.

Vail, Albert. *The Morning Hour of American Baptist Missions*. Philadelphia: American Baptist Publication Society, 1907.

Washington, Sondra. *The Story of Nannie Helen Burroughs*. Birmingham, AL: Woman's Missionary Union, 2006.

Watson, Jane B. *Labourers Together . . . A History of Arkansas Woman's Missionary Union*, Little Rock: Arkansas Woman's Missionary Union, 1987.

White, Blanche Sydnor. *Our Heritage: History of Woman's Missionary Union, Auxiliary to the Maryland Baptist Union Association, 1742-1958*. Baltimore: Woman's Missionary Union of Maryland, 1954.

Williams, Mrs. W. L. *Golden Years: An Autobiography of Mrs. W. L. Williams.*, Dallas: Baptist Standard Publishing Co., 1921.

ARTICLES

Florida Baptist Witness, September 16, 2008.

"Missionary Intelligence: Communication from the Rev Luther Rice to the Corresponding Secretary of the Baptist Board of Foreign Missions for the United States."Google E-book. *American Baptist Missionary Magazine and Missionary Intelligencer* 1 (November 1817): 216.

Missions Mosaic: October 1996; November 2000; June 2005; October 2005; September 2010. Birmingham, AL: Woman's Missionary Union.

Royal Service: January, 1987; January, 1990; February, 1992. Birmingham, AL: Woman's Missionary Union.

PERSONAL INTERVIEWS

Akerman, Debby, president, national WMU, 2010–

Miller, Carolyn, president, national WMU, 1991–1996.

Miller, Kaye, president, national WMU, 20052010.

Phillips, Candy, executive director, Tennessee WMU, 2011.

OTHER SOURCES

"A Continuing Light." Richmond, VA: The Woman's Missionary Society, First Baptist Church, 1963.

American Baptist Historical Society, Mercer University Campus, Vertical File.

Butler, Cathy, *Project HELP: Literacy Kit.* Birmingham, AL: Woman's Missionary Union, 2000.

Falls, Helen E., *The Sisters May Pray On*, Richmond, Virginia, First Baptist Church, 1813-1990, 1992.

Florida Baptist Historical Society's Gallery of Historic Baptist Leaders, www.floridabaptisthistory.org.

Minutes of the Foreign Mission Board, Richmond, Virginia, April 3; July 1; and October 7, 1872.

Furman University Archives, Records of Woman's Missionary Societies Organized Prior to 1842, p. 372.

Religious Herald, Richmond, Virginia.

Whitsitt, William Heth, "Historical Discourse on the Fiftieth Anniversary of the Southern Baptist Convention, *Southern Baptist Convention Annual, 1895.*

Woman's Missionary Union Annual Reports, 1888-2012. Birmingham:, AL WMU Library and Archives.

PHOTO CREDITS

Photo of Eliza Broadus courtesy of Southern Baptist Historical Library and Archives, Nashville, Tennessee.

Photo of Richard Furman courtesy of Southern Baptist Historical Library and Archives, Nashville, Tennessee.

Photos of Eliza Broadus and Richard Furman courtesy of Southern Baptist Historical Library and Archives, Nashville, Tennessee.